RUGBY
NOMADS

RUGBY NOMADS

Bob Howitt and Dianne Haworth

Harper*Sports*
An imprint of HarperCollins*Publishers*

National Library of New Zealand Cataloguing-in-Publication Data

Howitt, Bob, 1941-
Rugby nomads / Bob Howitt and Dianne Haworth.
ISBN 1-86950-447-X
1. Rugby football players—New Zealand. 2. Rugby football coaches—
New Zealand. 3. Rugby Union football. I. Haworth, Dianne. II. Title.
796.333092—dc 21

Harper*Sports*
An imprint of HarperCollins*Publishers*

First published 2002
HarperCollins*Publishers (New Zealand) Limited*
P.O. Box 1, Auckland

ISBN 1 86950 447 X

Designed and typeset by Chris O'Brien/PLP
Printed by Griffin Press, Australia

Contents

Introduction

They don't feature in the New Zealand Government's balance of payments portfolio. Maybe they should, for they are among the country's most significant exports. They are the Rugby Nomads: itinerant rugby individuals, ranging from celebrated All Blacks and famous coaches through to humble club players, who have chosen to take their talents offshore.

At the beginning of the 2002 season, no fewer than 650 New Zealanders were registered as playing overseas, most of them in the United Kingdom, France and Japan. The exodus, which began as a trickle in rugby's innocent amateur days, has exploded into a near mass migration.

Initially, players ventured overseas almost exclusively to have their OE. The more mercenary among them discovered that, in France and Italy particularly, well-heeled clubs were prepared to fund their stay, and once that was known, more players followed. It's doubtful many of them ever returned to New Zealand with their bank balances enhanced, but they were unquestionably richer for the experience. They usually had their accommodation and a car provided, and were paid a modest wage for an even more modest amount of toil.

New Zealand's administrators were hugely suspicious of those early Rugby Nomads; the game was so unashamedly amateur that any individual found to be benefiting tangibly from clubs or unions was instantly expelled from the code. If you wanted to play football for reward, you switched to league. You played rugby for the sheer exhilaration of the game.

All that changed, virtually overnight, in 1995. The IRB — under threat from WRC (the Australia-based rebel organisation that sought to take control of the game and introduce a professional international competition) and league, which was tempting amateur players with huge contracts — went pro.

The UK clubs were largely taken over by entrepreneurial businessmen, who, with millions to spend, began scouring the globe for quality footballers and coaches. Naturally, they found New Zealand a rich source of talent. As did the incredibly wealthy Japanese clubs, most of whom are directly linked to internationally renowned corporate firms. Today, the best contract a New Zealand-based player who is not an All Black can hope to negotiate is around $80,000, perhaps a little more. The same individual might sign with a UK club for three times that. And similar mouth-watering packages are available in Japan. So it isn't surprising that vast numbers of New Zealand rugby personalities have been leaving their homeland for exotic destinations.

And it's the exotic nature of those faraway places that provided the inspiration for *Rugby Nomads*.

The trigger for the book was a Bledisloe Cup lunch organised by the Condors Club at which the guest speaker, former All Black prop Graham Purvis, recalled highlights of his fascinating rugby career, delighting the crowd with anecdotes from the six seasons he spent living and playing in France.

That sparkling, witty address, which the audience lapped up, left a deep impression on one individual present, experienced journalist-author Dianne Haworth. Why not capture some of those stories in a rugby book with a difference, she reasoned, a concept she had no difficulty selling to colleague Bob Howitt, author of 13 books on rugby, with whom she had worked on *Rugby News* for almost a decade.

The fact there were 650 registered New Zealanders playing and coaching overseas, among whom were such celebrated personalities as Laurie Mains, Graham Henry, Alex Wyllie, Warren Gatland and Brad Johnstone (not to mention the entire All Black coaching panel of 2001), along with many other distinguished provincial players and coaches, meant there would be no shortage of subjects available. As well, there were scores of players and coaches who, having completed their OE, had returned to New Zealand.

How to bring coherence and appropriate variety to such a work presented an initial challenge to the authors, who decided to divide the book into countries. Readers would soon tire of half a dozen variations of life in Japan, so it was decided no more than three people would feature for each rugby destination (although it was stretched to four for South Africa).

Predictably, there were outbursts of criticism from those who believe that no New Zealander should be permitted to leave these shores mid-career in case his country needs him. That's a no-brainer, according to former All Black and Crusaders midfielder Tabai Matson, one of the book's subjects, who emphasises the many personal benefits that accrue from widening one's horizons.

Rugby Nomads started out as an innocuous book in which the subjects innocently told their stories. But the tenor of the book altered dramatically as the authors found their subjects eager to divulge controversial, dramatic and startling incidents about their careers. Many of them have used the book to get previously undisclosed incidents off their chest. Some of the revelations are truly sensational.

Not all the Nomads are Kiwis who have headed off-shore. Several, like England captain Martin Johnson, Wallaby hooker Jeremy Paul, French prop Christian Califano, Blues halfback Steve Devine and former Springbok front rower Balie Swart, are overseas celebrities who have brought their talents to New Zealand.

Others, like Brad Meurant and Ross Cooper, had brief coaching sojourns in two of the game's true outposts, Georgia and Romania, and their reminiscences are absolutely fascinating. None of their stories, though, quite matches the experience of Brian Steele of Waikato, who in the early 1950s was transferred by his New Zealand employer to Karachi, the capital of Pakistan, where he joined the Gymkhana Club, one of the city's two rugby clubs. In 1953, Steele went on to represent All-Pakistan (whose emblem, not unexpectedly, is a dromedary), an experience unlike anything he had known before.

One of rugby's more exotic line-ups, the All-Pakistan team of 1953. That's New Zealander Brian Steele on the extreme left of the back row.

There was no training, the ground was marked out with a stick before games and there were no after-match functions as the players' first priority at the final whistle was to sprint home as fast as possible to catch a shower before the water ran out. Karachi's rugby ground was a flat, grassless tidal plain, with the tide determining the start of play, unless a stickler for the rules insisted the game start on time, when the entire match could be played under a couple of inches of water.

Steele didn't quite qualify for an entire chapter in *Rugby Nomads*, but it's events and experiences like his that together make *Rugby Nomads* one of the more enchanting, entertaining and enlightening rugby books to be published.

AUSTRALIA

No nation has benefited more from rugby's rapid transformation into a professional sport than Australia. For many years previously the code had been pillaged by league scouts, tempting gifted players with fat chequebooks. Now the reverse is happening and the 2002 Wallaby team includes celebrated league converts Wendell Sailor and Matt Rogers. Until the Canberra-based ACT Brumbies emerged following the formation of the Super 12 championship in 1996, rugby in Australia was almost exclusively confined to Sydney and Brisbane. Until the 1970s, the Wallabies were generally regarded as international easy-beats, but regular competition across the Tasman dramatically improved standards to a level which allowed Australia to win the 1991 and 1999 Rugby World Cups.

Founded
1949
IRB
1949
Clubs
413
Players
135,950 men, 1866 women
Rugby Nomads
Jeremy Paul, Grant Holms, Paul Koteka

Jeremy Paul

You wouldn't have to probe far among the Australian rugby team to identify an individual who grew up in a league environment and who played league before 'discovering' rugby. But only one of them would have entertained himself by jumping off the Ngaruawahia Railway Bridge as a 6-year-old. His name is Jeremy Paul.

Paul, one of the exciting modern breed of highly mobile hookers, who distinguished himself by winning selection in the Australian squad before he'd played for the Brumbies, is a dinkum Kiwi-bred lad who, through his exceptional achievements in Super 12 and for the Wallabies, has finally convinced his father that there is another worthwhile winter code besides league.

Jeremy Paul's dad, Dave, one of a family of 14, did more than just play league for Ngaruawahia. He and Jeremy's mother, Carol, served variously as secretary, treasurer and committee members of the club and were as engrossed in the code as it's possible to get.

Young Jeremy, who used to indulge in the favourite local pastime of diving off the railway bridge, naturally absorbed this passion for the 13-man code and launched into his footballing career with the Ngaruawahia league club.

That lasted until the family moved to Paeroa, where there was no league. So while Paul senior followed the fortunes of the Ngaruawahia league side from afar, Jeremy tried his luck at rugby, with instant success. In a flash, he was in the Thames Valley primary-school representative team as a tearaway loose forward. And as captain, what's more. The team that he led to the 1979 Roller Mills tournament included a rangy lock named Keith Robinson. They would oppose each other in the Brumbies versus Chiefs Super 12 contest at Rotorua in 2002.

It was a memorable tournament in 1979 because, for the first time in 37 years, Thames Valley triumphed. But Jeremy, who, as a youngster, was possessed of enormous enthusiasm

Jeremy Paul . . . the Wallaby hooker who hails from Ngaruawahia.

12

and energy for sport, wouldn't contribute further to Thames Valley rugby because, the following year, he followed his brothers, Chris and Clifford, as a boarder to St Stephen's College in south Auckland. But his stay would be brief — just one year — because the Paul family was on the move again, this time to Brisbane. Jeremy was given the option to remain at St Stephen's, but Australia beckoned.

'I was excited about the opportunity to continue my education in Australia,' he says. 'Clifford remained behind to complete his seventh-form studies, but I was off on a great new adventure.' Jeremy found himself enrolled at a school called Capalaba in Brisbane's southern suburbs. One thing it didn't feature was rugby. That was a disappointment for Jeremy. But as a consolation, it had girls. It was a co-ed school and, after St Stephen's College, Jeremy found that extremely appealing!

So it was back to a diet of league for the youngest Paul because that's all that was played at Capalaba High School. And that, very possibly, would have been the code that ensnared him, had it not been for a passionate rugby coach called Gary Jessiman. Jeremy got to know Jessiman through Jessiman's younger brother, Dave, whom he befriended at college.

'The rugby ground was about 20 kilometres from where I lived,' says Paul. 'There's no way I would have been involved without Gary Jessiman, who enthusiastically drove a group of us to and from trainings and matches every week. I wouldn't have got there otherwise. My father was still wanting me to play league.'

Jessiman would have a major influence on young Paul's career; indeed, Australian rugby owes him a huge debt of gratitude. Without his dedication and obvious coaching talents, it's unlikely Paul would have pursued the game.

'He made it all happen,' says Paul, who for a while was playing league for his school on Saturdays and rugby for the Capalaba club on Sundays. Paul was enormously encouraged by the fact that in the first outing for his new team they won 100–nil, with Paul, starring as a breakaway, scoring three tries. 'I guess if we'd lost by a huge margin, things might have been different, but I was hooked straightaway. I liked the game, the coach and our team's attitude.'

That attitude would see Capalaba go through to win the Queensland under-16 championship, with Paul contributing heaps from the side of the scrum.

When the next season rolled around, it was time, Jessiman decided, for a major change. Oh yes, he was still coaching the Capalaba youngsters, and still providing his chauffeur service three times a week for a cluster of boys living varying distances from the club. The change was to do with Jeremy Paul.

'He told me I was at an important stage in my rugby career,' says Paul, 'and there were two ways I could go. I could either get myself superbly fit and become a back rower, but to succeed there I really needed to grow to about 6 ft 4 in [1.93 m], or I could switch to hooker and play like a back rower.

'It was obvious I was never going to make it to 6 ft 4 in, so a hooker I became. It was an easy choice, really, because I've never been the greatest trainer, and not having to get myself superbly fit appealed to me!'

Paul had won schoolboy representative honours in league since arriving in Brisbane, which left his father more perplexed than ever as to why he should prefer the rival code. 'I enjoyed rugby more, that's why,' he says.

The energetic Paul prospered in his new role as a hooker and in his first season wearing the No 2 jersey he forced his way into the Queensland schools team, 'forced' being the operative word because the prospects of him winning recognition from a state school were almost nil when the season started. Indeed, of the 42 players who participated in the final trial, only two, Paul and a gangly lock named Nathan Ross, who'd grown to 2.03 m by the age of 17, were state schoolboys.

'The other 40 were all from private schools,' recalls Paul. 'The private schools played amongst themselves and were always in the limelight whereas I had to come through three different tournaments to make the final trial.'

From an unfashionable school he may have been, but Paul impressed officials sufficiently to claim a place in the shadow squad for the Australian schoolboys tour of the UK and also to win a scholarship to the Queensland Academy of Sport, which he attended throughout the summer of 1994–95.

At the Academy, he put muscle on his not-so-robust frame and, through the input of highly qualified coaches and Wallabies called in to assist, he developed the skills relevant to his specialised role of hooker. Ironically, one of the special advisors was Michael Foley. Paul laughs about it now. 'I guess no one suspected that within three years

I would be his main rival for the Wallaby hooking job!'

Paul perfectly fitted the mould of the modern hooker. He could throw accurately to the lineout, was extremely mobile and possessed a loose forward's pace. And what he lacked in bulk in the scrum he compensated for in technique.

In rapid succession he progressed from the Queensland Under 19s to the Australian Under 19s and in 1997, while only 19, became the hooker for the national Under 21 team which took out the southern-hemisphere colts tournament in Sydney.

Assisting with the preparation of the colts was Andrew Blades, who, as a prop, would make more than 30 test appearances for Australia and in 2002 became technical adviser to the Brumbies. Blades remembers Paul as a player with 'a great deal of self-confidence, with an air about him'. Blades compares him to Phil Kearns at the comparable stage of his career — 'a positive, almost cocky, individual who knew where he was headed'.

Also in 1997 Paul won a share of the Brisbane senior club championship with Easts, a team coached by two New Zealanders, former All Black winger Grant Batty and ex-Waikato forward Mike Thomas. Oddly, it was Batty who provided the most valuable assistance for Paul regarding his lineout duties. That's because Batty played his rugby (in the 1970s) in an era when wingers threw the ball into the lineout. 'Bats reckons he had 35 different calls for lineout throws,' says Paul, 'including one where he baulked his throw four times. These days, you're penalised if you baulk once.'

Late in the 1997 season Paul fielded a call from Canberra from Eddie Jones, coach of the Brumbies, whose development squad was off on an eight-match tour of England and Scotland. Jones said if Paul wanted to relocate himself in Canberra, he could be part of the tour.

Paul jumped at the chance and loved every minute of touring the UK. 'We were just a bunch of kids,' he recalls. 'The tour benefited us all hugely. It's unfortunate that such tours seem to have fallen by the wayside.'

If 1997 had seen Paul's career prosper, it was nothing compared to 1998. First, he was contracted to the Brumbies as the understudy hooker to Marco Caputo, which put him on the bench for the entire 11-match Super 12 campaign, in which, it has to be said, the Brumbies failed miserably, winning just three games.

Paul took the field on seven occasions as a reserve, playing about 80 minutes of rugby all up, including 40 minutes against the Blues. He had celebrated his 21st birthday in March, and anticipated he would serve a two-season apprenticeship behind Caputo before, with luck, and if Caputo didn't possess the resilience of hookers like Sean Fitzpatrick, easing into the Brumbies front row.

He certainly hadn't set his sights any higher, so he was gobsmacked when, at the conclusion of the Super 12, and having yet to parade himself in the Brumbies No 2 jersey, he was named in the Australian test squad.

'I went from the Brumbies bench to the Wallabies bench — it was amazing,' says Paul. 'My goal had been to become the Brumbies first-choice hooker by 2000. Suddenly, not halfway through 1998, I was in the test squad.'

Rod Macqueen, the Australian coach, told Paul he had been introduced as an investment for the World Cup the following year.

'Here I was alongside Phil Kearns, John Eales, Tim Horan, Jason Little and others I regarded as my heroes,' says Paul. 'It all seemed rather surreal at the time.'

Paul didn't have to wait long to register his maiden test appearance. He got some late action against Scotland at the Sydney Football Stadium a week after the Aussies had smashed England 76–nil in Brisbane. He also made cameo appearances against the All Blacks at Melbourne, the Springboks at Perth and Fiji in the first of the World Cup qualifying fixtures, before being selected to wear the No 2 jersey against Tonga in front of his home crowd in Canberra. On the eve of his first run-on game, he dined alongside Jason Little.

'Will you be nervous when you take the field tomorrow?' asked Little.

'I'd been hellishly nervous all week,' says Paul, but, trying to act tough, he assured Jason he was feeling just fine.

'Well, *I'll* be nervous,' Little replied.

Paul says at that moment he felt terrible, wishing the floor would open up and swallow him.

'Then about 30 seconds later, Jason burst out laughing, and I realised he'd been having me on. He says someone did the same to him before his test debut in France many years earlier. I later pulled it on Jim Williams before he made his Wallaby debut.'

Against Fiji, in his brief time on the field, Paul had scored a try and he managed another against Tonga.

He taunted fellow front rower Dan Crowley about that. 'I was two tries ahead of him already, and he'd played 35 tests. He hated that!' Paul was overlooked for the Wallabies' end-of-year tour to the UK, but as the 1999 season unfolded, it became apparent that, at the age of 22, he had acquired the status of Australia's leading hooker. He first displaced Caputo from the Brumbies scrum, wearing the No 2 jersey in all 11 matches, and then, unexpectedly, was preferred to Michael Foley and the old warhorse Kearns for Australia's opening five internationals. But the crushing 34–15 loss to the All Blacks at Eden Park when Andrew Mehrtens kicked nine penalty goals — a 'blackout', as Paul describes it — saw him dropped to the reserves' bench for the balance of the Tri-Nations fixtures. He would remain a reserves'-bench regular throughout the World Cup later in the year.

Because of concerns over Kearns's fitness, Australia took three hookers to the World Cup, which was as well because Kearns's career came to an abrupt end when he broke down during the pool game against Ireland, allowing Paul to play 70 minutes at Lansdowne Road. Without once being on the field for the opening whistle, Paul got to appear in five matches at the World Cup, including the quarterfinal against Wales, the semifinal against South Africa and the grand final against France, substituting for Foley on those three big occasions. Far from being disappointed at never getting a start, Paul admits to being 'enthralled' at being part of rugby's greatest showcase, made the more memorable by being a member of the team which claimed the Webb Ellis Trophy at the Millennium Stadium.

Since then, although Foley, 10 years his senior, has been Australia's preferred hooker, Paul has remained an integral part of the Wallaby squad.

One of the more memorable encounters in which he featured as a replacement was the dramatic Bledisloe Cup/Tri-Nations match in Wellington in 2000, when, with 30 seconds on the clock and the score 23–21 to the All Blacks, the Wallabies were awarded a penalty.

John Eales, the Australian captain, having indicated to the referee that his team would kick for goal, prepared to hand the ball to his trusty goalkicker Stirling Mortlock. Where was Mortlock? Unbeknown to Eales, the winger had left the field minutes earlier with bad cramp.

It was Paul who, as Peter FitzSimons describes it so aptly in Eales's biography, 'articulated the obvious: "Stirling's off, John. You're up!"' It's history now that Eales slotted the challenging, wide-angle goal to secure his team a famous victory and all the silverware.

Paul has gone on to register 48 consecutive Super 12 appearances, which was briefly a Brumbies record until George Gregan surpassed it while Paul was sidelined, missing the game against the Hurricanes in 2002 with an ankle injury.

In addition to being an uncommonly talented footballer, Paul has stamped himself as one of the rich personalities of the Brumbies and Wallabies teams.

From an earnest viewpoint, Andrew Blades says it was obvious from an early age that Paul was a 'fantastic' footballer who only needed to work on his technique in the set pieces to go right to the top.

'When he first joined the Australian squad, he roomed with Phil Kearns. We gave Kearnsey heaps about them being the past and present. Some felt Jeremy was a young upstart because he was so confident and cheeky, but he and Kearnsey got on famously.

'He's a naturally confident guy who backs himself in any situation, and that's important in top-level rugby. Before a test against the All Blacks we were talking about attitude and he said he believed it was better to regret something you'd done than something you hadn't done. To me, that typifies great players; they're willing to back themselves. When George Gregan runs laterally from breakdowns, when he sights a forward out wide, often he won't pass, but he'll always give the ball to Jeremy, because he knows he can run and pass like a back.'

On the lighter side, Paul consistently amuses his team-mates with his misuse of colloquialisms, which has led to him acquiring the nickname Rainman, taken from the movie starring Dustin Hoffman.

Paul himself admits he is much sharper mathematically than with words. When he was interviewed about his damaged ankle during 2002 and asked what his chances of playing a particular game were, he replied, 'Oh, about 60-50.'

During an inhouse Brumbies session of *The Weakest Link*, he identified a basset hound as a cat. And when perusing the account at a restaurant where the Brumbies had eaten, he asked what this word 'gravity' was doing on the bill. It was explained that the word was actually 'gratuity'.

His more common nickname is Ming, which refers to the oriental appearance he conveys through his habit of squinting. In the heat of battle, when one of his team-mates urgently wants his attention, Ming is the name hollered out.

Despite his New Zealand roots, Paul regards himself now as a true Australian. 'My brothers still class themselves as Kiwis, but having lived as long in Australia as I did in New Zealand, I regard myself as a full-blooded Australian.'

He retains his New Zealand links, though. His grandparents still live on the outskirts of Hamilton and whenever his rugby travels take him to Blues or Chiefs territory, or to Eden Park on test-match duty, he makes the effort to call on them.

For the record

Player
- ACT Brumbies, 1998–2002 (56 games)
- Australia, 1998–2002 (29 tests)

Grant Holms

In 1929 Grant Holms played as a wing forward for his province, Bush (later amalgamated into Wairarapa-Bush). His captain was Winston McCarthy (of 'Wait for it . . . wait for it . . . it's a goal!' broadcasting fame), the scrums packed down in 2-3-2 formation, the forwards were strapping country lads and the Great Depression had just begun.

Seventy years on, at the age of 88, Holms decided to hang up his boots and officially retire as the world's second-oldest rugby player.

The 91-year-old patron of Queensland's Hervey Bay Rugby Football Club says he is humbled that the club has chosen to name a grandstand at the ground in his honour. His adopted country has done him proud.

The former Auckland primary-school principal and his wife, Pam, left New Zealand for health reasons in 1989 to retire to Queensland. On arrival, Holms responded to Hervey Bay's call for players to join its newly formed Golden Oldies team and for the next decade he would don the Golden Oldies purple shorts (signalling to opposition teams that these players met the 'no tackle' age criterion) and run out onto the field of play with his team-mates, some of whom were 50 years his junior.

Holms said he played with vigour — 'no mucking around' — until the late 1990s, when stiffness in the back, old bruises and arthritis took their toll.

'In an interview at the time I was asked why I was retiring when there was a Japanese player a year older than me who was still playing. "How can he play at his age, and you're stepping down?" I was asked. I replied that the Japanese gentleman had probably drunk more water throughout his life than me!'

These days Holms, who is also a Life Member of Queensland's Wide Bay Union and recipient of an Australian Citizens' Sports Award, confines his rugby activities to kicking off at the start of each season's play.

For the record

Player
- Bush, 1929–1930 (5 games)
- Fighting Whitings Golden Oldies, Hervey Bay RFU, 1989–1999

Paul Koteka

On a dank, chill winter night in 1978 the coach of the All Blacks, Peter Burke, and Waikato's coach, George Simpkin, stood on the sidelines watching a training session at the Old Boys Rugby Club in Tokoroa. They had come to the south Waikato mill town on Simpkin's recommendation that there was a brawny local lad, close to Waikato provincial selection, who might just fit the ticket in Burke's search for large props for the New Zealand Under 23 team.

Tokoroa has to be one of the coldest places on earth during winter and this night was no exception. The players looked huge in their Swanndri jackets, which they wore over their rugby jerseys to keep warm, but there was one who stood out as Burke and Simpkin peered through the mists of body steam drifting around the scrums. Not only did the team's prop look absolutely huge in his Swanndri, but he was also very good, they noted with satisfaction.

Paul 'Bam Bam' Koteka was promoted straight into the New Zealand Under 23s — he was on his way. Thanks to that tip-off, Koteka would become a Junior All Black in 1978, represent Waikato for seven years under coach George Simpkin, be a Maori All Black for five years and, at the pinnacle of his career, play two tests in his six matches for the All Blacks in 1981 and 1982.

Then, in 1984, Koteka received an offer to play with the Nedlands Rugby Club in Perth. He and his wife, Lieveling, chewed it over and decided he should accept. After all, he was 28, had no tertiary education qualifications and had played his final game for the All Blacks two years previously. A move to Australia would, they hoped, benefit the family by providing them with a degree of financial security in the future.

'I knew a little about the Nedlands Rugby Football Club because it was long established and considered the number one club in Western Australia. I was definitely interested,' recalls Koteka. 'I decided it would be a good move to accept and while I realised it would be a bit of a drop in standard, I had been there and done that in rugby and was ready for a change.'

When Koteka arrived in Perth with Lieveling and their five-year-old son, Josh, he brought with him a rugby pedigree as solid as his beefy arms, but just $500 in the bank.

In common with other long-serving players of his and previous generations, Koteka had been enriched by rugby in terms of experience and friendships but impoverished financially through playing commitments and the minimal allowances handed out by the New Zealand Rugby Football Union, in accordance with the stringent amateur code rulings of the time.

It was relaxing to be at Nedlands after seven years of immersion in the intense cauldrons of All Black and Waikato provincial rugby, but Paul was well aware that he could not operate in cruise mode. He had been brought in to help build the club. As the highest-profile New Zealander in Nedland's history, his name was used in advertising to encourage players to join the club. The strategy worked, with players of the calibre of Murray Watts (a former All Black from Taranaki) and Waikato mates such as Miah Melsom signing on from New Zealand — attracted as much to the Perth climate and lifestyle as to its rugby.

The premier side was coached by an able and dedicated Welshman, Viv Booker, and as captain of the team Koteka helped with the coaching and introduced the same level of training that he had been used to in New Zealand.

Nedlands flourished under Koteka's captaincy and, as one of the top West Australian clubs of the time, was frequently seen at the clubs' WA Grand Final competition. But the club's success brought with it a higher level of commitment and intensity. It became serious rugby and that was far too serious for Koteka, who had reached the age of 34.

'I thought I don't need that sort of rubbish any longer and I also decided I had had enough of team sport,' says Koteka. 'I took up triathlons and ended up doing about 14 of them. I thought that was a great sport.'

For Koteka, triathlons had the significant advantage of starting at about eight in the morning and finishing by 10, which was an important consideration for the devoted family man. 'I did a lot of training, which could be fitted around my work and family. I would cycle and run at lunchtime and swim at night,' he says. 'By contrast, when playing rugby, the whole day was stuffed up because you were preparing yourself for the game and when the game was finished, most of the time was spent with your mates. I discovered that individual sport was the one for me. It was the one I really enjoyed.'

He admits that at first he found it hard to switch his allegiance to

Australia. There had always been a rivalry between the trans-Tasman neighbours and it was hard to escape it. He was to learn, however, that the rivalry affected New Zealanders more than Australians.

'When you've lived over here for a few years you see that people don't really worry about that sort of thing. Rugby's our number one sport in New Zealand, but in Australia there are so many number one sports — like cricket, Aussie Rules and league — that rugby's not the same big deal.'

Later, Koteka became an Australian citizen out of loyalty to a country which had been good to him since his arrival. The Tokoroa boy, whose first job was in the bush working for New Zealand Forest Products (his nickname 'Bam Bam', of *Flintstones* fame, dates back to 1973, when members of his bush gang were introduced to the very large 'baby' of the team), is today a rigger, scaffolder and crane operator on an off-shore oil platform.

'I started from the bottom as a labourer here and worked my way up from that,' Koteka recalls with pride. 'New Zealand will always be my home but Australia has really looked after me and my family and I am very grateful for that.'

He works on a two-weeks on/two-weeks off cycle which suits him down to the ground. When he's at home he can devote himself to his family — Lieveling and Josh, now 23 and 1.93 metres tall and playing senior rugby for Nedland, and his three Australian-born daughters. Work and family are the main things in life for Paul Koteka.

A couple of years ago he came back to New Zealand for a family celebration and suffered a severe bout of homesickness. Paul and Lieveling again wondered whether they should switch countries but, against that, they weighed other considerations which had become important to them. Their children are now firmly established in Australia, their home and friends are there and it's only a few hours on the plane to come back to New Zealand for holidays.

In 2001 their youngest daughter, 10-year-old Mikayla-Ruth, was diagnosed with a serious and rare condition, and although her health is improving, the treatment she requires is at the Princess Margaret Children's Hospital in Perth. And so thoughts of New Zealand have been put on hold for the time being. Koteka reflects on the notion that had he been playing for the All Blacks in the 1990s rather than the 1980s he would probably never have left his home country.

'I think that even back in the 1980s a lot of us realised that changes had to come to the game. Guys like [former All Blacks] Andy Haden and Graham Mourie tried to bring in professionalism while I was there, but we still had those old fuddy-duddies in the Rugby Union who thought it wasn't to be.

'Players like myself have helped make the Rugby Union profitable and what we got out of it was basically nothing. On the other hand, I definitely believe that since the game has turned professional, people don't play as much for the pride of their country as we did. Today they have dollar signs on their chests.'

Koteka retains his interest in the Perth rugby scene. Along with many Australians he was disappointed that Australia wasn't given a fourth Super 12 franchise and points to the large number of New Zealanders, South Africans and English living in Perth whose contributions have lifted the level of rugby locally. He is still involved with the Nedlands Rugby Club and is to be seen on the sidelines watching Josh play as blindside flanker for the seniors.

But his rugby soul rests firmly with the red, yellow and blacks of his old home union, Waikato, which he first represented in 1978. 'Nothing will ever match those memories,' reflects Koteka. 'For me, the best years were '81, '82, when we held the Ranfurly Shield.

'I remember with affection my front-row mates, Foxy Bennett and Kiwi Searancke, and also Miah Melsom, Hud Rickit and Arthur Stone, who won the Ranfurly Shield off Auckland for us in 1980 with that awesome intercept try of his.

'What a moment that was for the guys and everyone who supported Waikato that afternoon. I've still got that video and sometimes I play it. I sit in Perth and have some lovely memories about my days with the Mighty Mooloos . . .'

For the record

Player
- New Zealand Juniors, 1978–1979 (6 games)
- Waikato, 1978–1984 (93 games)
- New Zealand Maori, 1980–1984 (11 games)
- New Zealand, 1981–1982 (6 games, 2 tests)

FIJI

The tropical South Seas islands have a special passion for rugby and have produced many talented players. While its greatest accomplishments on the international scene have come in sevens, Fiji has made its mark in the traditional game, thrilling audiences worldwide with its carefree, entertaining approach. It was only in 1938 that the national team took to wearing boots and in 1939 Fiji completed a full-scale tour of New Zealand undefeated, a feat not equalled before or since. Fiji participated in the 1987, 1991 and 1999 World Cups, qualifying for the quarterfinal repechages in 1999.

Founded
1913
IRB member
1987
Clubs
600
Players
55,000 men, 100 women
Rugby Nomad
Brad Johnstone

Brad Johnstone

When Brad Johnstone hung up his boots in 1981 after a celebrated playing career that embraced 13 tests for the All Blacks and 122 outings for Auckland, he never imagined the adventures, dramas and intrigue that would be packed into the next two decades.

'When I decided to try my hand at coaching,' says Johnstone, 'I think I expected it would anchor me close to my home territory on Auckland's North Shore. But life's full of surprises and I received tantalising offers to coach in exotic places which I found impossible to turn down.'

From preparing clubs in Sydney and L'Aquila, he went on to coach the national teams of Fiji and Italy, in the process picking up the coach of the tournament award at the 1999 World Cup. And but for a cockroach, he might have taken Italy to the 2003 World Cup. But we'll come to that later.

In his lengthy and distinguished playing career with Auckland and the All Blacks, Johnstone picked up the rudiments of coaching from such luminaries as J.J. Stewart, Jack Gleeson and Eric Watson and in his final season with Auckland he helped Bryan Craies, who hadn't co-opted a forward coach.

Johnstone had established a network of friendships during his rugby travels and on his retirement from representative play he was approached by the St George club in Sydney, which invited him to join as a player-coach.

'Sydney appealed, so I took up the offer,' says Johnstone. 'Those were the true-blue amateur days when you couldn't be paid in cash. What I got instead was a lawnmower, a washing machine, a dishwasher, a tumble dryer and a microwave! The washing machine and microwave are still doing good service at our holiday home. They also arranged a job for me, getting me into a position as a building foreman for a construction company.

'They were a couple of enjoyable years. We hammered Bob Dwyer's Randwick team by 40 points and the next year beat Alan Jones' champion Manly team. We were competitive but didn't possess the necessary depth to go all the way.'

In 1984, Johnstone returned to Auckland and took over the coaching of his old club, North Shore, the following year offering himself as

coach of North Harbour in its inaugural season. That appointment
went to Peter Thorburn, who
would remain in the position for
seven years.

Johnstone did get to work with
the union's Colts and B team, until
another interesting overseas offer
lured him away, this time to coach
the Scaviline club in L'Aquila,
Italy. It was the club All Blacks
Mike Brewer and Frano Botica
played for, with Springbok Joel
Stransky arriving during Johnstone's second year there. It proved
an enlightening experience for
Johnstone. 'That's where I learnt

Fijian coach Brad Johnstone.

that our way is not the only way,' he says. 'New Zealanders get rather
closeted over their rugby, but when you travel you appreciate that
players in other countries are just as passionate about the game. At
Scaviline there were problems with money and player strength, but
they were as passionate as any team in New Zealand.

'The motivational side was a bit of a challenge. You automatically
won at home and expected to lose away. That was ingrained in them.
We beat Roma at home by 60 points but as we prepared for the return
game, the players talked about what they would lose by. They were
convinced the Roma players were stronger than them in Rome! In the
finish, we beat them by a point.

'It's an Italian thing. Italians don't travel well. We'd be an hour out
of L'Aquila, travelling to our next match venue, and players would be
phoning home assuring their parents everything was all right.'

One of the away matches was against Catania, in Sicily. For that
game, in Mafia territory, Johnstone found he had difficulty establishing a starting XV. 'It's amazing how many mysterious injuries came up
on the Friday!' he said.

After two seasons at L'Aquila, where winter temperatures often
plunged to minus 15° C and his team trained in snow and ice, Johnstone
returned to the gentler climate of Auckland, where he took out the

senior championship with his old club, North Shore, in 1992. In his absence, Thorburn had finally relinquished the Harbour coaching role (to join Laurie Mains on the All Black panel) and been replaced by Brad Meurant. Johnstone picked up the North Harbour B job but didn't find it particularly satisfying.

'Standing in front of committee men, many of whom had never played the game and who made decisions based on club politics, not on your coaching ability, didn't do much for me,' says Johnstone. 'I wasn't prepared to wait forever and when the opportunity arose to assist Fiji, I grabbed it.'

Fijian rugby was at a particularly low ebb in 1995 after the national team had failed to qualify for the third Rugby World Cup, in South Africa. Samoa and Tonga would be there, but not Fiji. The sevens team was prospering, as always, but the fifteens side had lost its way.

Johnstone came on board in 1995 as a technical adviser. Still based in Auckland, he made 14 return trips to Fiji that year, helping turn round the team's fortunes. A victory over Samoa, the first in six years, restored confidence and resulted in Johnstone, who was effectively coaching the team, winning a permanent appointment. But being based in New Zealand wasn't a satisfactory arrangement for Johnstone, who realised the players weren't adhering to their fitness programmes in his absence. So he confronted the FRU, who put together a package which allowed him to be based in Suva, where he and his family relocated themselves in 1996.

Over the next four years, as Johnstone steered Fiji back to international respectability, would come many unusual and delightful stories. Rugby coaching, as he would soon discover, was only part of his responsibility.

Before one overseas tour he was required to broker a marriage settlement when one of the players' wives refused to release his passport. After Johnstone had arranged for half the player's tour allowance to be paid to his wife, the passport was handed across.

On another occasion, with the national team assembled at Nadi Airport in readiness for a flight to the UK, Johnstone was advised that one player was absent, having been arrested for not paying maintenance. His wife had read that he was departing the country and reported him to the police. Johnstone had to work his way back past the immigration authorities to the airport police station, where he contacted the local magistrate and put in place a deal that would allow a percentage of the player's tour allowance to be paid as maintenance. The player flew out to the UK 48 hours later!

Before a tour of Wales, Johnstone and the Fijian management became aware that there was a warrant out for the arrest of one of their players, who had been involved in a brawl on a previous visit to Swansea. Through the club and a lawyer, Johnstone brokered a deal that would allow the individual concerned to play two games in Wales, after which he would go to Swansea and pay an outstanding fine.

'It appeared a satisfactory arrangement,' says Johnstone, 'but after the second game, two policemen arrived at our hotel and took the player away. He was jailed for 21 days, which was a bit of a shock to us. He was released on bail after 16 days, rejoining us at Leicester a stone lighter. Incredibly, neither of the journalists on tour with the team noticed he was missing! At least he departed the UK with a clean slate, which allowed us to take him to the World Cup in 1999 without any complications.'

Outfitting Fijian teams presents unique difficulties because of the players' large feet. 'We really challenged the Mizuno people,' says Johnstone. 'About six of the players wore the largest size of boot that Mizuno made and another four or five had to have boots custom made, because there wasn't anything large enough in stock.

'Todd Blackadder was renowned for having giant feet. He wore size 16s. Well, there would be half a dozen players in the Fijian team with feet that size.'

Johnstone's duties included organising coaching sessions in Fiji's outlying districts, which presented special challenges for a New Zealander. 'Having faxed the school in one mountainous district, I duly arrived at 9 a.m. to find no one in sight. Eventually, someone appeared and led me to the chief, to whom I was obliged to present a bowl of kava. Following its consumption, I was accepted into the village, and the message went out for everyone to come to the school grounds. By soon after midday about 60 people had appeared, in a mix of bare feet and boots, and the session finally started. The three hours of coaching that followed were delightful.

'Some coaches would say "Stuff it" but I believe it's important to adhere to, and respect, the local cultures. In Fiji, it's important to involve the tribal side of things.'

Johnstone encouraged his players to drink kava in preference to alcohol.

'In the UK, they can go overboard on banquets following international matches,' he says, 'which don't really suit the Fijians. So once the food and speeches were finished, and the boys had presented a couple of songs, we would head for our hotel.

'There the players would provide their own music and drink kava, usually till they fell asleep. Generally speaking, they were bored with the UK style of entertainment.'

Under Johnstone, Fiji registered a series of significant victories, defeating Scotland for the first time, downing the powerful Leicester club on a bitingly cold night in the English Midlands and, best of all, smashing arch-rival Samoa by a staggering 60 points to nil at Nadi.

'Bryan Williams was coaching Samoa,' says Johnstone, 'and we used to joke that we were taking turns at winning, but that result came like a bolt of lightning. We clicked like never before, completely dominating them up front.'

The most important series of matches, however, was the World Cup qualifying games in Australia in 1998. Johnstone was prepared to shoulder the criticism that went with him fielding his B line-up against Australia. 'I didn't feel we had the depth of talent to survive three tough encounters,' he says, 'so I effectively sacrificed that game to target the Samoan and Tongan games, both of which we won.'

Unlike the major rugby nations of the world, Fiji had to operate on a shoestring budget. 'Fiji received a grant of $250,000 from the IRB plus $50,000 from Vodafone as a sponsor,' says Johnstone. 'That was it to run all rugby in the land, whereas Italy received $30 million. I can't help but feel if a comparable sum was made available to the Pacific nations of Fiji, Samoa and Tonga, it would achieve a lot more for the development of the game. The Pacific nations' problem is that there aren't enough television sets and modern sport is promoted by bean-counting businessmen.'

The other great challenge confronting Johnstone as he zeroed in on the 1999 World Cup was the Fijian preoccupation with sevens. Locals consistently referred to sevens events as 'tests' and to sevens tournaments as 'World Cup events'.

Johnstone was forced to play hard ball, establishing separate sevens and fifteens squads, which didn't make him popular either with the media or with multi-talented individuals like Waisake Serevi and Marika Vunibaka, whom he dearly wanted to take to the World Cup. 'Serevi walked on water, in the eyes of the Fijians, but he wasn't half as good at fifteens as he was at sevens. After appearing for a World XV in Australia and being named man of the match, the local newspaper ran a story declaring him the best rugby player in the world. Which didn't help me at all!

'Vunibaka didn't play for me for three years, even though I several times selected him. He just never turned up. Finally, he agreed to come on a tour of England and once he started demonstrating his fifteens skills, Robbie Deans targeted him for Canterbury.'

By the time Fiji began its World Cup build-up, Johnstone had successfully blended New Zealanders and Australians of Fijian blood — players like Alfred Uluinayau, Lawrence and Nicky Little, Greg Smith, Joe Veitayaki, Jacob Rauluni and Ili Tabua — with resident players, creating a group that, in Johnstone's words, became 'a big family'. Through Johnstone's initiative, Fiji completed its preparations by playing a four-nation tournament at L'Aquila, in Italy, scoring handsome victories over Spain, Uruguay and Italy. It was a result from which Italy never recovered, and would see Johnstone offered coach Massimo Mascioletti's job before the year was out.

At the World Cup, the Fijians, having been drawn to play in France, were quartered at Banyuls, a small town near Perpignan in the south west. They'd expressed a preference to be away from big cities and were delighted with the arrangement.

This contentment manifested itself in a series of excellent performances, Fiji crushing Namibia 67–18 and downing Canada 38–22, before almost pulling off the upset of the tournament against France at Toulouse.

Had New Zealand's leading referee, Paddy O'Brien, not chosen this occasion to deliver his worst display, Fiji would probably have advanced directly into the quarterfinals, for Johnstone's men had much the better of the game.

But poor Paddy and his touch judges made three calamitous blunders, all at Fiji's expense, disallowing a legitimate try by flanker Seta Tawake, awarding an undeserved penalty try to France and failing to detect a forward pass before Christophe Dominici scored. 'Paddy, who I rated one of the best referees in the world, had a particularly bad day at the office,' says Johnstone. 'Still, we won enormous respect and Alfred Uluinayau's try was a gem. Some critics were kind enough to name him the best fullback at the tournament.' The setback meant Fiji had to square off in the repechage round with England at Twickenham, a daunting assignment. On a bleak afternoon, the Fijians turned on plenty of razzle-dazzle before going down 24–45, their flamboyance earning them a standing ovation.

The Fijians headed home, their heads held high. Johnstone claimed the coach of the tournament award and individuals like lock Emori Katalau, centre Viliame Satala and fullback Uluinayau were rated among the best in their positions.

Back in Fiji, Johnstone was honoured with the Order of Fiji, presented to him by Ratu Mara.

After five years, it was the end of the road for Johnstone. But just as he was contemplating life back in New Zealand, he fielded a phone call from Rome. Following the disastrous performances by Italy at the World Cup, which included a 101–3 drubbing from New Zealand, coach Mascioletti had been sacked. The job was Johnstone's if he wanted it.

'They'd tried to play a French style and it hadn't worked,' says Johnstone, 'so now they wanted to go the New Zealand way. I couldn't resist the challenge and within a week I was in Italy to start the build-up for the Six Nations Championship.'

Johnstone was presented with a list of 60 names when he arrived to go into camp near Pisa. Twenty-two of them arrived with letters from their clubs or medical people saying they weren't fit to train. It was, Johnstone deduced, post-World Cup syndrome. The players had been so humiliated they didn't want to be part of the national scene. Mark Harvey, a former navy lieutenant who had been Johnstone's fitness trainer with North Shore and Fiji, linked up with him again and together they devised ways to inject enjoyment into the Italian camp. 'The mood the guys were in when they assembled, nothing was going to work,' says Johnstone, 'but gradually the 22 ripped up their letters.'

Johnstone's rejuvenated side pulled off a sensational victory over Scotland in its maiden Six Nations outing. The result brought ecstasy to the nation's rugby followers and was front-page news in the soccer-mad country, a rare happening indeed.

It spotlighted for Johnstone the Italian mentality regarding sport. 'If it's a tournament, it's important,' he says. 'If it's a one-off test, or a visit to the southern hemisphere, it's of lesser significance. That attitude comes from soccer where everything revolves around tournaments. But for rugby, it's wrong.'

Johnstone wasn't sure whether the victory over Scotland was a good thing or a bad thing. 'You take your victories, but it probably gave us a false impression of where we were at. Still, we were competitive throughout the Six Nations competition, even if we did still finish at the bottom of the heap.'

Mid-year, Italy was off to the South Seas to play Samoa and Fiji. What should have been a pleasant sojourn began to degenerate into open warfare, after a split developed between Johnstone and the Italian captain, Alessandro Troncon, along with half a dozen other internationals who were contracted to French clubs. They preferred to give priority to their clubs. Johnstone objected, insisting that their country had first call on them. When they resisted, Johnstone threatened to report them to the IRB. He prevented three from playing for their clubs, and the rest agreed to tour.

'It turned into a huge political thing,' says Johnstone, 'Troncon versus me. It was given wide publicity and I became the biggest arsehole in Italian rugby. But I was trying to set new standards and I genuinely believed Italy wouldn't be competitive internationally until it accepted these ideals.

'As it turned out, three French-based players and four Italian-based players didn't come on tour, leaving me with a seriously depleted team. We had eight or nine guys new to international rugby and, not surprisingly, we got towelled by Samoa and Fiji. I never recovered from that run-in with Troncon and lost a huge amount of face. He was from northern Italy and from that moment the northern clubs effectively rejected me.'

The first night in Apia, the Italians were shunted off to a university complex because the main hotel, Aggie Grey's, was full. Next morning the team doctor approached Johnstone in a state of agitation, advising him a player had suffered a panic attack during the night. The player, Andrea Scanavaka, who was being groomed to take over from Diego Dominguez at flyhalf, had woken to find a cockroach in his room, panicked, and spent the rest of the night walking around outside. 'He was in terrible shape,' says Johnstone. 'He wouldn't eat and was basically traumatised. He never recovered. He never participated in the two games in Samoa because he didn't eat and didn't train.

'When we returned to Italy, I dropped him from the squad, which caused a furore. Like Troncon, he was from Rovigo in the north, which further antagonised them.

'I took a hammering from the media, so I called a press conference and explained to them the reason I'd dropped Scanavaka. As far as I was concerned, I could never risk him again on tour. But the newspapers put their own spin on events, claiming I dropped Scanavaka because he doesn't like cockroaches!

'I suffered in Italy from telling the truth, I kid you not.'

Although Italy failed to win a match in the 2000–2001 Six Nations, it was generally competitive and the coach didn't cop too much flak. Instead, Johnstone's next crisis arose mid-year when Italy was scheduled to play in Argentina and South Africa.

'Being one of rugby's poor cousins, Italy has to take what it's offered and the Pumas and Springboks tests were a month apart. I felt we couldn't sit around doing nothing for a month, so I arranged matches against Namibia and Uruguay, plus games against South African Barbarians and Argentina A.

'I should have known a month-long tour wouldn't appeal to the Italians. Fifteen of the 32 squad members selected didn't arrive. All had excuses. By the time we were ready to depart, 27 of the 32 were unavailable! Their club contracts are more valuable than what the national body offers them, so they opted to stay at home.

'I went to Italy with a vision of building a squad through to the 2003 World Cup. I expected there would be some attrition, but to lose 27 players for a tour was unbelievable. I finished up taking kids who'd been sitting on the bench for their clubs.'

Although the Italians were surprisingly competitive in South Africa and beat Namibia and Uruguay, the team took two batterings in Argentina, results that caused dismay back home.

'Instead of criticising the 27 players who'd refused to tour, the media, and my arch-critics in the north, rounded on me.' While Johnstone was holidaying back in New Zealand, the northern clubs took matters into their own hands, deciding a new coach was needed. They offered the position to John Hart, with John Kirwan assisting.

'While in New Zealand, I ran into John Hart who showed me the letter he'd received. It was typical of the Italians that they would take that action while I was out of the country.'

When he returned to Italy, Johnstone found that the FIR had cancelled all the camps he'd arranged, with no one prepared to stand up to the clubs. He then confronted the Federation's president, who felt the northern club's rebellion was as much a reflection on him as on Johnstone. However, he had the power and Johnstone was reappointed through till the 2003 World Cup.

In November 2001, Italy hosted three internationals, beating Fiji but suffering heavy losses to South Africa and Samoa.

'The Italians find it hard to get up for two games in a row, let alone three. Nothing finds them out more than a sequence of matches. I knew we'd struggle against the Springboks, but I was confident we could put the Samoans away. Unfortunately, they attacked us physically in the opening 15 minutes, delivering a series of shoulder-high tackles.

'Although one player was sin-binned and another red-carded, psychologically they destroyed the Italians, who no longer wanted to play. We had 15 against 14, but our 15 walked around for the remainder of the game. They just gave in. It was described by one journalist as Italy's worst test performance.'

The fragility of Johnstone's status surfaced again after Italy lost its opening Six Nations encounter against Scotland in Rome in February 2002, a game many expected it to win.

'We performed disappointingly,' says Johnstone, 'and I did my balls at the team meeting afterwards, telling the older guys if they weren't interested, I'd bring in younger players to replace them.'

It was the beginning of the end for Johnstone. That evening Dominguez, Troncon and Kirwan held a meeting, which was followed by a newspaper article claiming 10 players would not front against Wales if Johnstone was still coach.

Seven of them, including the experienced Cristian Stoica, phoned Johnstone to say the story was wrong. Troncon also denied a story claiming he would never play for Johnstone again.

While Johnstone managed to placate almost everyone and complete the Six Nations competition, the fact Italy finished bottom again, without a victory, sealed his fate. 'At the press conference following the final game, against England, no one was interested in the game,' he says. 'All they wanted to know was when I was resigning.'

Johnstone didn't get the opportunity. The Italian Federation decided at an emergency meeting that Kirwan should take over as coach. Five days later, they notified Johnstone of their decision, a development he was already aware of, his daughter having read it on the Federation's website.

Where his association with Fiji had been a delight and concluded joyfully, Johnstone's Italian experience ended on a sad, disappointing note.

'With their Latin temperament, the Italians are so reactionary. After the first weekend of the national soccer league, three coaches were sacked. That's their mentality.

'Whoever the coach is, he's fighting huge odds and until the Italian Federation takes greater responsibility and stands up to the clubs, it's hard to see the national team improving. What may help in the future is that they are to receive a sixth share of the profits from the Six Nations Championship.

'The national rugby competition is much weaker than when I was coaching L'Aquila more than a decade ago. The 2002 club final between Calvisano and Viadanna featured only three native Italians. The rest were all second-tier footballers from New Zealand, South Africa, Australia and other parts of Europe.'

For the record

Player
• Auckland, 1971–1981 (122 games)
• New Zealand, 1976–1980 (45 games, 13 tests)

Coach
• Fiji, 1995–1999
• Italy, 1999–2002

JAPAN

Rugby has been played in Japan for more than a century but it wasn't until the 1950s that the game began to develop significantly. Now it is the third most popular sport behind baseball and sumo wrestling, boasting 4500 clubs and almost 150,000 players. Japan is by far the strongest Asian nation and has qualified for all four Rugby World Cups. However, it is not the national team but the clubs, representing the corporate giants, that create most of the excitement. It is these corporates that have lured dozens of international celebrities, a large percentage of them former All Blacks, to the country.

Founded

1929

IRB

1987

Clubs

4500

Players

146,000 men, 800 women

Rugby Nomads

Liam Barry, Kevin Schuler, Alan Whetton

Liam Barry

A corporate head of NEC who had flown from Japan for the interview leaned forward and asked, 'How would your grandfather [Ned Barry, All Black 1932–34] and your father [Kevin Barry, All Black 1962–64] feel about you going to play in Japan with so much New Zealand All Black history in your family?'

Liam Barry, New Zealand's only third-generation All Black, admits it was probably the last question he expected. 'I thought I would be asked about my track record or my reason for wanting to go there. Later, in Japan, I found that when they introduced me the fact that three generations were All Blacks meant a lot to them because of their traditions.'

Barry replied to his Japanese questioner that his grandfather, Ned, wouldn't mind because he was dead and his father was happy for him to play in Japan. 'Dad's actual reaction was "Yes. Go!", which would have surprised one old guy who came up to me in the Coroglen pub at Whitianga while on holiday two years into my Japanese contract. My brother, Tim, and I were having a couple of beers and this old stalwart walked up to us, didn't introduce himself, looked at me, and said, "Your father wouldn't have played for money", then walked straight out of the pub.'

In 1997 a combination of factors had driven Barry's decision to play overseas: he had missed the cut for the 1996 All Black tour to South Africa, had a troubling leg injury which he felt could limit his future playing career and was coming off his contract with the NZRFU.

'I was lucky not to have had a long contract. I'd only been signed up for one year. Maybe that was an administrative mistake on the NZRFU's part because the following year, when I announced my decision to go, the NZRFU said, "What do you mean, off? You're on a three-year contract." I said, "No, I'm not."'

The four-year contract from NEC, a large and long-established computer company just out of Tokyo, offered security, money and opportunity. Too good to turn down.

NEC's second recruit from the interview process was former All Black winger John Kirwan, and he and Barry were to join a third Aucklander, Ross Thompson (who had played for his old province at No 8), in the NEC corporate team.

Liam Barry, John Kirwan and Ross Thompson, with a fellow NEC player in Japan.

Daily training at either two or four in the afternoon, with little promotional or company work expected, was the norm for the team's three foreigners, along with the Japanese players employed by the company. Not taxing by any standards, but for this, as with other big Japanese corporates, Barry discovered a winning team performance was the all-important criterion. 'You were there to do your job well, and that was playing rugby. They didn't use JK or me for PR or training, they just wanted us to play, whereas *we* were always wanting to offer coaching advice.

'They saw the two roles as completely different. They don't mind taking the odd piece of advice but they employ their own coaches for that. And corporate rugby is so important; it's the biggest thing in Japan. The only other major force is the universities, where the rugby-playing students are head-hunted by the big corporates to play for their teams as soon as they graduate.

'It's really a cultural thing with the companies. They want to associate their plant or workplace with a sport. There's a bit of one-upmanship in having specific teams, such as a soccer team, or a baseball team. For big sports like this you are talking serious money. NEC had its rugby team based at the Abiko plant, a women's volleyball team at

39

Yokohama, while men's volleyball, tennis and marathon teams were at other NEC plants. All had foreigners in their teams and all teams were connected to those individual plants.

'A typical major corporate rugby team got by on an average budget of $US8 million a year. NEC carried a playing squad of 45 with 10 staff, which included a full-time physio and trainer. We spent $US40,000 a year on tape alone! Because they tape every day there would be a queue of about 10 guys waiting to be taped for training and if there was a knee injury they would tape the whole leg!

'The feel of the tape on the skin is part of the nerve stimulus, but they put a skinlike covering on first so the tape doesn't get stuck to their hairs. The actual stickiness of the tape is not in contact with the skin, which we found pretty odd.'

Attendance at big corporate matches would rival the turnout for New Zealand Super 12 games — up to 20,000 people — while it was not uncommon for 70,000 to 80,000 people to front up to big university games, where tradition was evident and much prestige rode on the result.

Despite the popularity of university matches, the real strength of Japanese rugby today lies in the corporates, where teams' foreign quotas of players contribute significantly to both performance and spectacle. For employees, whose lives revolve around their company, there are also career advantages in being seen by the boss supporting the team outside work hours.

Prestige was showered on Japanese companies who had All Blacks playing in their ranks, says Barry. 'In Japan, New Zealand's greatest export is the All Blacks. The Japanese associate New Zealand with the All Blacks, simple as that. Put a silver fern on any product and you'll do really well.'

Barry may have been admired, but for the Japanese 'JK' was a true legend. Crowds watched with awe as the big, blond winger shimmied effortlessly through opposition teams to touch down over the tryline.

Liam's wife, Sarah, recalls: 'I remember one Christmas I went shopping with JK to help him buy a present for his wife, Fiorella. We were in this little village about an hour north of Tokyo and a young Japanese kid came out of nowhere running up to us saying, "JK, JK. Great rugby All Black."'

Why do the Japanese like rugby?

Barry: 'They're fanatical about sport in general. Among the millions of Japanese sports-goers you get this relatively small group of regular rugby followers who are absolutely passionate about the game. It was quite something for me to experience a Japanese crowd for the first time — people yelling and screaming, flags flying — quite the opposite of the usual image we have of reserved Oriental people. They are far more outgoing than New Zealand crowds. It doesn't seem to matter that a lot of supporters don't understand anything at all about the rules of the game!'

But however good the imports were, a Japanese corporate team could only succeed if it had the best Japanese players on board. Barry cites the example of a talented Japanese No 8 who was chased by five clubs to join them after he had finished his university studies. Those studies led to a rugby scholarship at Oxford University, in England, which posed little problem for NEC's aggressive recruiter, a former salesman who was promoted to be the company's salesman for rugby. Twice the recruiter flew to England, travelled to Oxford and took the player out on the town to ensure he would sign up for NEC when he returned to Japan.

And in a rare concession, the company called in the services of Barry and Kirwan for a persuasive dinner with the player on his return. The No 8 joined NEC.

Late in 2001 Liam and Sarah Barry returned to New Zealand, where Barry played what many consider some of his finest rugby for his old province, North Harbour.

But in 2002 he missed a Super 12 berth for the Blues and again Japan beckoned. In March the Barry family, with the addition of baby daughter Esther, took up a two-year contract at Kubota, a heavy machinery company near their old stamping ground at NEC. That Kubota team, coached by Australian Matt O'Connor and including Wellington's Jason O'Halloran and former Wallaby Willie Ofahengaue, welcomed their foreign contingent with the same enthusiasm as had NEC before.

Barry has nothing but admiration for the Japanese attitude to outsiders. 'I don't know if I'd be as welcoming if some Japanese players came to North Harbour and got the treatment and rewards we get in Japan. The Japanese are so welcoming and so aware that it may help the team and therefore their company's cause. Quite awesome really.

'Japan look to New Zealand for training techniques all the time. We had Mark Shaw and Mac McCallion, but they wanted John Hart when he was coaching the 1999 World Cup team.

'They chased Hart for two months and were repeatedly told, "Look, he's coaching the All Blacks for the World Cup. Sorry, no." "We want John Hart!" "Sorry, you can't have him . . ." They have no qualms whatsoever about paying top money to get the top talent.'

For the record

Player
- North Harbour, 1991–1996, 2001 (83 games)
- New Zealand Colts, 1991–1992
- New Zealand, 1993, 1995 (10 games, 1 test)
- New Zealand Development Squad, 1994
- Waikato Chiefs, 1996 (8 games)

Kevin Schuler

A decade ago he was singled out as a future All Black captain, so it's no surprise to learn that in Japan today Kevin 'Herb' Schuler is accorded two leadership titles of respect — 'kantoku' (chief coach) and, more familiarly, 'Herb-san'.

The former New Zealand Colts, New Zealand Development, New Zealand Divisional, Manawatu and North Harbour captain first won All Black honours in 1989 at 22. He was a reserve for the home tests in 1990 and then, two years later, as an All Black loose forward noted for his rock-solid defensive qualities, astonished the pundits by moving his rugby career to Japan.

Schuler said he weighed up his options carefully before squandering the prized All Black jersey. 'I'd been in and out of the All Blacks since 1989 but I'd just got an injury and had always wanted to play overseas.

'I'd never considered Japan because in 1992 Italy and France were the places everyone wanted to be. Then someone came to me and suggested Japan so I said, Yeah, why not?'

To Japan he went, but three years later, in 1995, eager to be included in the World Cup he was back in New Zealand and playing once again for the All Blacks, describing as 'a competitive itch' the mood which impels leading players to return home to attempt to regain top honours.

His intention was to stay on in New Zealand, but the combination of a collapse of the proposed World Rugby Cup (WRC) circuit which he had anticipated joining, the advent of professionalism, an incomplete contract with Japan and 'terms that didn't meet' with the NZRFU forced the decision. He returned to Japan with his wife, Michelle.

Asked if much has changed in the 10 years he has lived there, Schuler is unequivocal in his belief that the international rugby fraternity has the wrong end of the stick where Japanese rugby is concerned. 'I think it's quite sad the world doesn't see the true level of rugby in Japan. The Japan national side is not a very good example of domestic rugby: it's the big companies that play really top rugby.

'Suntory is the best team in Japan; they were coached by Eddie Jones [current Wallaby coach] and they play an outstanding level of rugby in my opinion.

'The problem there is that the ultimate rugby goal is not playing for the national team. Most of the players' ultimate allegiance is to their company's side, which is not normal from our way of thinking, so it's a bit fractured at the top level. Also, a lack of direction and policy from the Japan Rugby Union has made the companies reluctant to release their players.' For example, the best flanker in Japan at present has been unavailable to play for All-Japan.

Schuler cites the 2001 tour to Japan by Wales B, when Suntory defeated the international side while the All-Japan team lost to Wales B by 40 points. Says Schuler, 'I believe that if Japan wants to get serious that upper echelon must get sorted out.'

Schuler's first contract as a star foreign player was for the Nisshin Steel team, centred in an industrial town where he and Michelle — with former New Zealand sevens player Scott Pierce and his wife, Jane — doubled the population of foreigners. The Schulers went whole-hog into a traditional Japanese lifestyle, learning Japanese and living alongside other employees in the company's concrete-box apartments. At that time there were about 20 foreign players in Japan — today that number has increased fivefold.

Nisshin had set up the platform. By the time Schuler had moved to Yamaha, initially as the team's player/coach, he was entirely comfortable with his new role and at a good level conversationally.

In 2002, at the time of writing, Schuler is head coach for Yamaha. He admits to dreaming in Japanese and has the undoubted respect of his home-grown players by speaking to them in their language.

What's more, he loves the country and that shows.

'When you're talking to a group of 40 players and you can babble away in Japanese it gives you confidence. I've just developed my own style in the little ways I communicate with them. I've had a good chance to evolve slowly and that's been of benefit to me.

'I try and say it like it is. Rugby's a fairly simple game and I just say the same thing over and over. The challenge is to keep their attention. Japanese players are generally rote-learned and respond well to a structured pattern.'

Schuler recalls how he and Pierce introduced grid skills used by Auckland's Jim Blair to the team. 'We did a slow-pace demo of a grid skill, got them to run through it and then told them we wanted to see it at full pace. Within seconds two of the Japanese players had knocked themselves out and had to be stretchered off the field.

'They'd run into each other at full tilt, whereas a Kiwi's natural instinct would have been to sidestep to avoid the collision. The natural creativity probably isn't there nor are their instincts when compared with a New Zealander. While we start playing rugby at six, most Japanese don't start until they are about 16 and they cram it all in. They overcoach to a degree and that can take away spontaneity. "We can't do that, we can't do that" — it's the psyche of the country.

'The really good players do stand out, those with rugby instinct.'

Yamaha's 2002 allocation of players known in New Zealand is Tabai Matson, Waisake Sotutu and Tim Henshaw from the Canterbury Development Squad. Other recent recruits have included Steve Surridge, Willie Lose, Norm Broughton and Rhys Ellison.

The question must be asked: have the Japanese really got value for the huge sums of money spent over the past decade in attracting these high-flying foreigners? 'Yes, they have,' insists Schuler.

'The influence of foreign rugby in Japan has been huge and that's lifted the domestic performance level dramatically. I have no doubt that many of the New Zealand players in Japan want to play well; they do not see themselves coming here in retirement mode.

'Most of the top overseas players are so innately competitive that they don't slacken off when they get to Japan. Far from it — some I've seen playing their best rugby ever here.

'A good example is Andrew McCormick, who went to Toshiba at the same time I went to Nisshin. Andrew went on to become famous as captain of Japan's rugby team for the 1999 World Cup — the first time a foreigner has ever achieved this. He was a guy who played consistently outstanding rugby at the same level in Japan as he had in New Zealand. Incidentally, he took to the culture full-on and published a rugby book in Japanese, which is unique to my knowledge.'

Telephone-book figures are bandied about; how well do these players really do? 'Pretty well,' Schuler says. 'The scene has changed since we first went to Japan, when things were good but not lavish. The top boys who go to Japan now do really well. On top of all their living costs average players can save more than $NZ100,000 a year, while top players are putting away $N250,000 upwards.'

But while this may be serious money by New Zealand standards, put into a Japanese context it is nowhere near the top level paid out to sports stars. Schuler speaks of a leading baseball player in Japan who earns more than US$5 million a year. 'The sums paid out to New Zealand rugby players would not be considered big by Japanese standards.'

However, he concedes that Japan's rough economic ride in 2002 will have an ongoing effect on many of the country's lesser teams, with a number having already gone to the wall.

'You get a lot of guys going up to Japan with big financial expectations and some of those companies are saying, "Hang on. We can't afford the big bucks now." There is still a big budget, but it's more constrained. I can see them targeting more Pacific Island players, where they're not looking at Super 12 salaries. So I think you'll see a big difference in the teams.'

On the home front, the Schulers now have four young children and are contemplating life after Japan. How their future in New Zealand will pan out is in the lap of the gods, says Schuler.

'I'd like to continue coaching and we also want to turn our energies into something outside rugby. But to what? We've got another year in Japan and then it's home. That's the challenge. I'm looking forward to it.'

('Herb' — Schuler senior's first name — was adopted as a nickname by Kevin, his sister and four brothers during their schooldays.)

For the record

Player
- New Zealand Colts, 1987–1988
- Manawatu, 1987–1990 (49 games)
- New Zealand, 1989–1990, 1992, 1995 (13 games, 4 tests)
- New Zealand Development Team, 1990
- New Zealand Divisional Team, 1990–1991
- North Harbour, 1991–1992, 1995 (20 games)
- Nisshin Steel, Japan, 1992–1995
- Yamaha, Japan, 1996–2002

Coach
- Yamaha, Japan, 1998, 2001–2002

Alan Whetton

'Weton-san, aaah Weton-san. Foto!'

As a high-profile All Black, Alan Whetton was hailed as a morale-boosting saviour when he arrived in the Japanese port city of Kobe in 1996, along with his wife and two young daughters, to take up an appointment as coach and recruitment officer for the international industrial corporate giant Kobe Steel.

In 1995, Kobe had been shattered by the *Hanshin dai shinsai*, one of the worst earthquakes ever to hit Japan. Six thousand residents of the city had been killed and thousands more injured, apartment blocks had come crashing down and the city's infrastructure had been devastated.

Fourteen months later the city was pretty much as it had been prior to the 1995 earthquake, with reconstruction work evident everywhere and the populace back to travelling on trains and using roads which had been virtually demolished. It said something about Kobe's resilience, but wounds to the spirit were harder to heal. Whetton recalls, 'A lot of the guys I played with, and some of the *gaijin* [foreigners], still have memories of being in their houses during that terrible shake. Considering the devastation, many were fortunate to survive.

'Kobe Steel is a substantial employer in the city and it was important for the rugby team to be successful at that time to raise morale within the company,' says Whetton. 'They wanted to utilise my profile and so we started . . .'

The 1995 World Cup final, in which the All Blacks had been edged out of the winning title by the boot of South Africa's Joel Stransky, was fresh in Japanese minds, not to mention New Zealand's 145–17 win over Japan at Bloemfontein! Whetton, claiming 65 appearances for the All Blacks, including 35 tests, was the highest-profile All Black ever to have resided, or played, in Kobe.

The respect for 'Weton-san' was huge in a country which recognises excellence in business and sport. He received saturation coverage in the local press and was pressed to attend many invitation dinners. Kobe Steel wanted to see their star in action, but at 37 Whetton, who had played his last game for Auckland in 1992, was reluctant to get physically involved. He had long hung up his boots. Initially he declined, preferring to settle for the roles of recruitment officer and coach, but eventually he relented and returned to action.

'My body took a bit of a pounding but I still had the basic skills I'd developed in New Zealand and played satisfactorily, which in turn lifted the level of the team. Probably my value was more in on-the-field leadership than in my contribution as a player. I struggled to survive the full 80 minutes!

'I was able to give direction to the Kobe players more easily on the field than as a sideline-based coach. That was an eye-opener for me. I thoroughly enjoyed being back in action again. If you're competitive, as I always have been, once you pull the boots on and immerse yourself in a couple of rucks, the old passion and enthusiasm comes surging back. It was good fun but by the time my contract was coming to a close I was nearing 40 and I just couldn't perform to the level I wanted in a competition that was quite intense. Besides, the Japanese love their tackling and my aging body didn't appreciate it!'

Whetton, at 1.91 m, was not the largest player in the Kobe Steel team. A couple of Japanese held that distinction, but his stature elicited excitement, especially when he was travelling on trains or was in the company of Japanese women, who are keen fans of the game.

'Japan's leading rugby personalities have a tremendous following among young females, who have an insatiable demand for pictures and autographs,' says Whetton. 'There's also a respect. They don't confront you personally, as New Zealanders would do. They prefer to go through someone else for an approach. Being an All Black certainly carried a lot of weight there.

'I always enjoyed my time playing overseas and being exposed to other cultures and meeting people. Japan was no exception. People there were probably more reserved socially, shy in some ways with foreigners. They kept their distance, but once they got to know you, they were fine. Japanese food I love, my children settled there very well and the people were most hospitable.'

As a player in New Zealand, Whetton had been an integral part of two phenomenally successful teams: Auckland, which successfully survived an incredible 60 defences of the Ranfurly Shield over an eight-year period from 1985, and the All Blacks, who got through 50 matches without defeat, starting at the 1987 World Cup.

Whetton initially distinguished himself by making his first four test appearances (against Australia three times and Argentina once) as a replacement, an oddity back in the 1980s.

'I was an All Black, but I wasn't really an All Black,' recalls Whetton. It was a frustrating time for the specialist blindside flanker, whose twin brother, Gary, was a regular in the All Black pack at the time, and life became even more frustrating when he was dropped for the 1986 tour of France.

That's when he approached his good friend Lee Wahlstrom, a fitness trainer, who quickly deduced that Whetton's major problem was that he wasn't fit. Under Wahlstrom's guidance that was remedied by the time the new season rolled around. It allowed Whetton to excel in the early-season fixtures and win selection in the World Cup squad, where he became a star.

Combining brilliantly with fellow loose forwards Michael Jones and captain Buck Shelford, Whetton created a special piece of history by scoring in five consecutive World Cup games, missing out in only the grand final against France.

He commanded the No 6 test jersey right through until 1991, surviving a torn calf muscle on the tour of Argentina, to participate in his second World Cup. Sadly, there would be no celebrations this time. The All Blacks' devastating loss to the Wallabies at Dublin would spell the finish of many celebrated players' international careers, Whetton's among them.

He was recognised as the finest modern-day exponent of the blindside flanker's role and as someone who fearlessly put his body on the line. Following his first tour as an All Black, to Australia in 1984, it was written of him: 'Often looked like a losing heavyweight boxer, so regularly was his face patched up, which only served to underline his dedication to duty.'

In Japan, Whetton found the language a barrier and he feels that perhaps he should have tried harder. 'There were certain topics I wanted

Alan Whetton, who shared the glory at the first World Cup, ready for action in 1991.

to converse in, but I found it difficult to express myself. It's all about the basics, because a good understanding of the basics leads to everything. It's like a five-year plan. I look at Kevin Schuler, who's done exceptionally well over there, and Scotty Pierce. It's a time thing. In three years I was just starting to come out of my time.'

Whetton took the decision to return to New Zealand when his contract expired. 'My team had a proud history in corporate rugby in Japan, but they had struggled in the years before I arrived, with Suntory and NEC so dominant. Hopefully, the basics I helped put in place will help them recapture their previous status. The year after I left, Kobe Steel went on to take the title. In some ways that was disappointing, because I would have loved to have shared that success with them, but maybe some of my input was starting to pay dividends.'

Whetton had helped changed Kobe Steel's mind-set and introduced players who could contribute and win games, an improvement on its previous pattern of recruiting big bruising forwards purely because of their physical stature.

'They need players who are going to make a difference, like the former Bay of Plenty first-five Andy Miller, who is now kicking the goals and winning the games for Kobe. Creativity is the key.'

For the record

Player
- Auckland, 1981–1992 (150 games)
- New Zealand, 1984–1991 (65 games, 35 tests)

Coach
- Kobe Steel, Japan, 1995–1999

ARGENTINA

Argentina is often referred to as an emerging rugby nation, but the game has been played there since 1873, introduced by British engineers working on the railways. The establishment didn't take too kindly to the physical nature of rugby, being horrified at the number of broken limbs, and it was banned for nine years. It re-surfaced in 1882 with the River Plate RU (now the Argentinian RU) being formed in 1899. However, it wasn't until Danie Craven invited the Pumas to tour South Africa in 1965 (the team winning 11 of its 16 matches) that Argentinian rugby came of age. Then came Hugo Porta, one of the most accomplished footballers ever to wear the No 10 jersey. Complementing the nation's giant forwards, he guided the Pumas to genuine world status for more than a decade from the mid-1970s, including a famous 21-all draw against the 1985 All Blacks.

Founded
1899
IRB
1987
Clubs
280
Players
70,000 men, 200 women
Rugby Nomad
Alex Wyllie

Alex Wyllie

Alex Wyllie had no intention of coaching rugby outside New Zealand until a group of South African sporting enthusiasts got in his ear at Lancaster Park, in Christchurch, during the 1992 Cricket World Cup. 'Come and spend some time in sunny Port Elizabeth, the Friendly City,' they implored him. 'Lovely climate — and you can work with the Eastern Province Currie Cup team.'

Wyllie, or Grizz as the whole rugby world knows him, was receptive to the idea because he was still smarting over happenings before, during and after the second Rugby World Cup. That tournament, hosted by England and eventually won by the Wallabies, should have been the pinnacle of Wyllie's coaching career, but instead everything turned sour.

Having guided the All Blacks through one of the most successful phases in their entire history (his record coming into the 1991 season was 46 wins, a draw and a loss from 48 matches), he suddenly found himself, at the insistence of NZRFU chairman Eddie Tonks, saddled with John Hart as a co-coach. It wasn't what Wyllie wanted. His term as coach, having started in 1988, was scheduled to run through till the end of 1991 and incorporate the World Cup. But he was vaguely aware of factions apparently displeased with his coaching performance during the tour of Argentina.

'It was obvious Hart was using the media to stir things up,' says Wyllie. 'There was a lot of nonsense being talked. I just sat back and largely ignored it. With hindsight, I wish I'd done something about it.'

The dreadful truth was revealed when Wyllie and Hart were summoned to Wellington, where they were advised by Tonks that, starting with the Bledisloe Cup contest at Eden Park and extending through to the World Cup, they would be operating together as co-coaches. 'It was bloody ridiculous,' says Wyllie. 'You can't have joint coaches.

'I'd been with John during the 1987 World Cup and on that occasion Brian Lochore was in charge. He was the boss, we were his lieutenants. Collectively, we got on famously and won the World Cup. But here was Eddie Tonks saying we had to operate as joint coaches. I was unhappy with the arrangement right from the start, but what made me really furious was when Mike Brewer was told, soon after the team's assembly in Auckland prior to departure for the World Cup, that because he wouldn't remove strapping from his foot to undertake a particular fitness test, he was to be replaced.

'He was a vital member of the squad and should have made the trip. The same week we played our opening fixture [against England] at the World Cup, Mike was captaining Otago in an NPC champion- ship match at Carisbrook. How bizarre was that?

'Following the Brewer fiasco, I said to our manager, John Sturgeon, that I'd had enough. I wanted out. Too many things were going on behind people's backs, which was never going to create a healthy at- mosphere in the UK.'

Sturgeon worked overtime to convince Wyllie that he should remain. While recognising that Sturgeon was operating with the best interests of New Zealand rugby at heart, as he always did, Wyllie says he wishes he had followed his instincts. He says it's the only regret he retains from a career in rugby spanning four decades. 'I should have got out straight after the Brewer affair,' says Wyllie, 'and left Hart in charge. Then he could have stuffed things up all on his own, as he did in 1999.'

Wyllie acknowledges that his relationship with Hart was strained, at best, and that although they had a common goal of wanting to win the World Cup for their country, their philosophies on how to achieve this were poles apart.

'When you see an Auckland clique heading out for a meal, accom- panied by Hart, you know it's not doing much for team spirit,' he says.

After the All Blacks had come crashing down against the Wallabies in the semifinal at Dublin's Lansdowne Road, Wyllie drop-kicked the co-coach agreement out the window. 'Hart seemed to lose interest with the glory gone, and I selected and prepared the team for the play-off against Scotland.'

The recriminations were many in the wake of the World Cup disas- ter, with the nation unanimous on one thing: the co-coach concept had failed dismally.

Individually, Wyllie and Hart were determined to re-establish their reputations and both allowed their names to go forward in 1992 for the All Black selection panel. But Wyllie withdrew after a comment by chairman Tonks that he was only getting involved again to pro- mote his book (*Grizz The Legend*, which had been launched immediately following the World Cup).

'I felt I hadn't been given a fair go at the World Cup,' says Wyllie, 'and was keen to have another crack. We're talking the old amateur days, of course. None of us was in it for the money, but purely for our love of rugby.'

And so in 1992, as Laurie Mains, Earle Kirton and Peter Thorburn were being installed as New Zealand selectors, Wyllie headed back to his farm at Omihi, in north Canterbury, believing that that would be his focus for a good many years. But then came the South African cricket supporters, who convinced him otherwise. Well, one individual, solicitor Emile Greyvenstein, did. Wyllie had already had a fax from the Eastern Province union, enquiring if he would be interested in a coaching role. By the time he replied, the position had been filled.

Greyvenstein confirmed that Willie Viljoen had won the Eastern Province coaching role but said he had negotiated an involvement for Wyllie. He would assist Viljoen and be responsible for the B team. Eastern Province had special appeal because its colours were the same as Canterbury's — red and black!

'I wasn't looking to coach overseas so soon,' says Wyllie, 'but South Africa, where I had first toured as an All Black, appealed as a country. I felt I'd done everything I could in New Zealand.'

On that score, Wyllie wasn't kidding. He'd made a massive 210 appearances for Canterbury in a celebrated career spanning 17 seasons, captaining the red-and-blacks on 108 occasions. He'd also played 40 matches, including 11 tests, for the All Blacks.

That was Grizz the player. Grizz the coach then emerged. He took over a forlorn Canterbury team in 1982 and produced instant results, winning the Ranfurly Shield that first season (and defending it a record-equalling 24 times) and claiming the NPC first division title in 1983. Canterbury remained potent until he pulled out after the 1986 season.

In 1987 he coached the New Zealand Colts (to a handsome victory over Australia), then stepped up to the All Black panel. He was associated with the World Cup-winning side in 1987, then was in charge for the next (stunningly successful) three-and-a-half seasons — until people like Eddie Tonks and John Hart started to intrude!

After Eastern Province finished last in the Currie Cup first division in 1992, Wyllie was installed as coach, with immediate success. A perennial struggler among the republic's rugby provinces, Eastern Province came third in the Currie Cup, ahead of Northern Transvaal and Free State, which qualified it to represent South Africa in the 1994 Super 10 (the forerunner of the Super 12).

Eastern Province, Transvaal and Natal did battle with North Harbour, Auckland, Waikato and Otago from New Zealand, Queensland and New South Wales from Australia and Western Samoa. Although Wyllie's men didn't win a game, it was still an achievement to be participating in such illustrious company, especially given the province's record over the previous decade. Not many of the Province players had travelled far, so it was a thrill for them to be taking on Otago at Carisbrook.

The lifestyle and climate in Port Elizabeth appealed to Wyllie, but he became disenchanted in 1995 following a change in administration. His job sheet, in addition to coaching the Currie Cup squad, now involved assisting the B team and schoolboys and working in the black townships. 'I was happy enough to do all those things,' says Wyllie, 'but I would have needed 15 hours a day and eight days a week to make it all happen. When I complained, they suggested I finish up, which I did. I was ready to move on. Following my departure they went through three coaches in two seasons.'

The split freed up Wyllie, allowing him to follow the third World Cup and take a break from coaching. But it wasn't long before he was being tempted with offers again, as rugby advanced into the professional age. Andre Markgraaff, then coaching Griqualand West and later to take charge of the Springboks, invited him to Bloemfontein to assist him at the start of the 1996 season. Wyllie took the Griquas sevens team to the national tournament and was having a major input into rugby in the area when he received an unexpected call from Louis Luyt, the big boss of Transvaal (and South African) rugby.

Transvaal had made a disastrous start to its Super 12 campaign, losing all four matches in Australia and New Zealand, under ailing coach Kitch Christie, who 12 months earlier had been a national hero following South Africa's World Cup triumph.

Luyt bore no compassion. He asked Christie to resign, creating a vacancy which Luyt offered to Wyllie. 'It was a hell of a challenge to take on players who, a year after winning the World Cup, were languishing in the Super 12,' says Wyllie. 'Something was dreadfully wrong.'

Taking over a team occupying bottom place meant there was only one way for Wyllie and his Transvaalers to go. Although they never threatened to make the play-offs, there was the satisfaction of registering victories at Ellis Park against the Auckland Blues (Graham

Henry's team, which went on to win the competition), the Waikato Chiefs and the Canterbury Crusaders.

What Wyllie hadn't bothered to mention to Luyt was that he had committed himself to coaching in Argentina from the end of 1996, having been approached by the Argentine union's president, Luis Gradin, who as Puma coach four years earlier had 'borrowed' Wyllie to run a coaching clinic. He thought it was probably timely to drop it into a conversation he was having with the South African rugby boss in the boardroom at Ellis Park midway through the Currie Cup, Wyllie's involvement having spilled over into the domestic competition.

'You know I'm going to Argentina at the end of the season, Louis?'

'That shouldn't be a problem. Which team are you going to coach?'

'The national team.'

'The national team? You realise they are playing the Springboks in November? I want you to think again and change your mind. I want you to stay here and coach Transvaal.'

'I'm sorry, Louis, but I've made a commitment to Argentina.'

'Then you can't carry on coaching Transvaal. I'll have to find someone else.'

And with that, Wyllie's association with Transvaal ended. It was Big Louis' way of doing business. 'We actually got on well together,' says Wyllie. 'We parted amicably. Goodness knows how our relationship would have developed had I stayed. But I had business in another country.'

Wyllie arrived in Buenos Aires as the Pumas were preparing for two tests against the Springboks — games they lost decisively. The day after the second test, they flew out for a nine-match tour of England, Wyllie instantly involved as a technical advisor. The team developed mightily on tour and after sweeping aside all the lesser opponents narrowly lost the international to England at Twickenham 18–20.

A fascination for Wyllie, especially having come from South Africa, was the realisation that Argentina was resisting professionalism. 'This was because the power base, the Buenos Aires union, didn't believe in professionalism,' says Wyllie, 'to the extent that not until 1995 did they accept sponsors' logos on the players' jerseys.' Because of the union's entrenched amateur attitudes, Wyllie found himself labelled a technical adviser, not a coach, of the national side.

'That was so I could be paid as an employee of the union, because in 1997 Argentina still wasn't into paying its coaches. In some ways they were better off, because they took their time to adapt to professionalism, although nations like New Zealand, Australia and South Africa couldn't have done that. They wouldn't have had any players left!'

In 1997, the Pumas embarked on a daunting five-match, two-test tour of New Zealand with Jose Luis Imhoff as coach and Wyllie still in his advisory role. He knew what was in store for the tourists and tried to prepare them for the onslaught, but they insisted on adhering to their traditional game plan.

'They wouldn't allow me to change their defensive system,' says Wyllie. 'I warned them that all they'd see against the All Blacks would be Christian Cullen's backside. Which is exactly what happened in Wellington, where they conceded an embarrassing 93 points. A call came from the field during the game: "What do we do?" I sent back a message telling them it was too late.

'In some ways, that crushing defeat was the best thing that could have happened. After that, once we got back to Buenos Aires, we changed a lot of things, the defensive pattern in particular.'

One trait among Argentinians that Wyllie never adjusted to was their lateness. Grizz is a punctual person. In Argentina a noon meeting means 12.15 or 12.20, but with Grizz it means 11.55! The Pumas pretty soon got the message.

Upon their return from New Zealand the Pumas scored a notable test victory over the Wallabies, but in 1998 they were on the receiving end against France (three times), Japan, Italy and Wales, after which Imhoff was sacked as coach and Hector 'Pipo' Mendez brought in. Mendez and Wyllie had operated together most successfully with the Argentinian Under 21 team, Mendez as coach with Wyllie his assistant. That was the arrangement for the home series against Graham Henry's Welsh tourists in June 1999. But further disappointing results saw the UAR despatch the Pumas to the UK in August, only two months before the World Cup, with Mendez and Wyllie as joint coaches.

For Wyllie, the co-coach arrangement was an ominous reminder of 1991. And it didn't work any better this time. He and Mendez were soon at odds over team selection. For the Irish international, Mendez insisted on using Nicolas Fernandez Miranda at halfback ahead of Agustin Pichot, who Wyllie regarded as one of the best in the world.

The tourists achieved an excellent victory over Scotland, 31–22, which perked everyone up, but without Pichot they went down to Ireland 24–32, and that was followed by a 23–18 loss to Wales.

As the Pumas returned to Buenos Aires, Wyllie made a fleeting visit to New Zealand to attend to some business matters. He was back on the farm at Omihi when he heard a radio news item that Mendez had resigned, having advised the Argentine union that he wasn't prepared to operate as a joint or assistant coach. He wanted to be the main coach or nothing.

That evening, Wyllie fielded a call from UAR headquarters in Buenos Aires. Was he prepared to coach the team at the World Cup, on his own? Naturally, he accepted. It was a luxury he hadn't enjoyed as All Black coach.

At the three previous World Cups, the Pumas, while always highly regarded, had seriously underachieved, managing just one victory (against Italy in 1987) while registering eight losses. They had never qualified for the play-offs.

Wyllie saw his team's prospects against Wales diminish before kick-off at the magnificent Millennium Stadium in Cardiff. The players had tears in their eyes. 'Their minds were blown,' he says. 'The whole occasion got to them.'

But against Samoa and Japan they were far more composed and completed comprehensive victories. The win over Samoa was especially satisfying as they had gone down to them in 1991 and 1995.

That put Argentina into a repechage contest against Ireland at Lens in France, where the environment was decidedly more conducive to the Pumas' Latin temperament than to the Irish.

Wyllie was quietly confident. He felt Argentina should have defeated Ireland in Dublin six months earlier, and probably would have had Lopez not insisted on playing his best friend's son at halfback ahead of Pichot.

At Lens, Pichot was the pivot. With 20 minutes to play, Wyllie introduced Filipe Contepomi at flyhalf, moving prolific-scoring Gonzalo Quesada to fullback, a brave strategic move that caused alarm among the Argentine management. 'What are you doing?' they asked him.

'Filipe's a play-maker — we need him,' Wyllie assured them. And sure enough, in the desperate final quarter, it was Contepomi who created the match-winning try for winger Diego Albanese. At the final whistle, Argentina had pulled off the biggest upset of the tournament, eliminating Ireland to set up a quarterfinal clash with France in Dublin.

The players, Wyllie says, were 'unbelievably happy'. They had broken into the top eight teams in the world, previously uncharted territory for the Pumas.

Soccer is the only winter sport that regularly commands front-page headlines in Argentina, but when the Pumas defeated Ireland the nation went wild. 'When a goal is scored by Argentina at the soccer World Cup, car horns toot throughout Buenos Aires,' says Wyllie. 'Well, when Albanese scored his match-winning try at Lens, the same thing happened.' Wyllie's men weren't able to quell the French to the same degree in their quarterfinal clash, even though they had the Irish crowd resolutely behind them at Lansdowne Road. The French, who had been decidedly ordinary in pool play, began to recapture their finest touches — form that would see them sensationally bundle the All Blacks out of the tournament a week later.

The Argentine players returned home to a heroes' welcome. Wyllie wasn't with them. During the tour of Ireland earlier in the year he'd been approached by officials of the Clontarf club, inquiring what his plans were following the World Cup. 'I didn't have a contract with Argentina and so I said I would be free. A couple of seasons in Ireland, given their legendary hospitality, seemed an appealing way to round out my career.

'I always said I'd never coach in the UK because of the lousy winter weather there, but Ireland is a bit different. The hospitality compensates for the climate.'

Clontarf turned out to be a greater challenge than Wyllie anticipated. Brent Pope, the former Otago player who'd been working with them, took himself off to another club after seeing his job advertised and the person chosen to replace him caused a revolt among the players. By the time Wyllie arrived, Clontarf had lost 15 of its senior squad. 'It was mildly hard working with what was left,' says Wyllie. 'We managed to survive relegation, but were damned lucky to do so.' The following year, Wyllie embarked on a policy of building for the future, introducing several of the club's colts. While this wasn't appreciated by the more mature squad members, it got Clontarf back to the middle of the table.

Not even Ireland's hospitality and the appeal of their most famous beverage could lure Wyllie back for a third northern-hemisphere winter. After a decade as a rugby nomad, he was content to become a farmer again. Until Marlborough came knocking on his door, that is! 'I really thought the curtain was down on my rugby career after Ireland. But my philosophy has always been that you get out when you're getting tired, and I'm still enjoying the involvement.

'Hopefully, I can put something in place with Marlborough. It's a progressive rugby union, an area that has produced Anton Oliver, Leon MacDonald and David Hill in recent times. I'm concerned at what's happening to the smaller unions in New Zealand. If the NZRFU isn't careful, it's going to seriously damage its base. That's why I'm happy to put something back into the game.

'Because the players aren't professional, it means we can't train during the day, and until the NPC started, I was commuting from the farm, about two-and-half-hours' drive away.'

There's a certain irony about Wyllie rounding out his career coaching Marlborough for it was the Red Devils who caused him, as captain, so much anguish when they whisked the Ranfurly Shield away from Canterbury in a daring raid on Lancaster Park in 1973.

On the way home, the exuberant Marlborough supporters stopped at Wyllie's driveway at Omihi and decorated his letter box in Marlborough colours. 'Mmmmm, I think I remember that,' says Wyllie, who's not really grizzly any more.

For the record

Player
- Canterbury, 1964–1980 (210 games)
- New Zealand, 1970–1973 (40 games, 11 tests)

Coach
- Canterbury, 1982–1986
- New Zealand, 1988–1991
- Eastern Province, 1993–1995
- Golden Lions, 1996
- Cats, 1996
- Argentina, 1997–1999
- Marlborough, 2002

SOUTH AFRICA

The most demanding of all countries to tour has always been South Africa, because the venues vary from sea level to 6500 ft. The All Blacks had toured there since 1928 but it wasn't until 1996 that they finally claimed a test series on South African soil. Traditionally, All Black–Springbok clashes have been the ultimate in rugby contests, with each trying to outdo the other physically and strategically. South Africa's apartheid policies resulted in it being isolated throughout the 1980s and it was only in 1992 that tours of the republic resumed. The Springboks rebounded in time to win the third World Cup, in 1995, having been locked out of the 1987 and 1991 events. The game's headquarters are in Cape Town with the other main test centres being Durban, Johannesburg, Pretoria and Bloemfontein.

Founded
1889
IRB
1949
Clubs
1116
Players
361,300 men, 600 women
Rugby Nomads
Grahame Thorne, Kevin Putt,
John Plumtree, Laurie Mains

Grahame Thorne

Defections overseas by players of international status are commonplace these days but in 1970, when Grahame Thorne announced he was returning to South Africa only weeks after performing heroically on tour there for the All Blacks, the nation was aghast.

It didn't matter that Thorne had fallen in love with a South African lass and was heading there for personal reasons. He was an All Black, a bloody good one at that, aged just 24 and in his prime, and he was quitting New Zealand.

To most New Zealanders, Thorney's defection was incomprehensible. All Blacks just didn't pack up and head overseas. Not to South Africa, the land of the arch-enemy, for goodness sake.

But Thorne had always been a free spirit. On and off the field. And he'd played many great hands in his comparatively brief All Black career.

He had returned from that tour as the leading try-scorer, with 17, surpassing the record set by Lions winger Tony O'Reilly in 1955. Against the Gazelles at Potchefstroom he had even taken over the goalkicking duties, having been advised only at 11.30 a.m. on match day of this new responsibility. Thorne dragged himself out of bed and went down to Olney Park, where he attempted four shots at goal from the centre of the 22. Three went over, after which he returned to his hotel and went back to bed. Like most international players when they're on tour, Thorne liked to sleep as late as possible on match days. Not that it ever cured him of the pre-match nerves that caused him to throw up throughout his rugby career. He was, he readily acknowledges, one of the game's 'great chunderers'.

'I dry-retched before my senior-club debut for Auckland University, and from that day till I retired I never played without chundering!' Before the North Island trial in Palmerston North in 1967, Thorne was so uptight he vomited in the dressing room, to the horrified looks of team-mates such as Colin Meads, Waka Nathan and Mac Herewini, and also threw up on the field after scoring a try.

Anyway, at Potchefstroom on that 1970 tour, he slotted four conversions and a penalty goal, helping the All Blacks escape a ferocious challenge from what were effectively the best under-23 players in South Africa. The busiest All Black on the field, with 19 appearances out of

24, Thorne was also fully preoccupied off it. He met Jenny-Lynn Busby and fell in love. Which presented an ever-so-delicate complication when he returned to New Zealand, because he was engaged to be married to a Christchurch girl.

'Suddenly, South Africa seemed a very appealing country,' he recalls. 'For the first time in my life, I ran away. I ran away to South Africa, one month after arriving home with the All Blacks.'

Thorne thought he knew South Africa. But three months cocooned in the All Black environment didn't fit anyone for actually living there, as he was to discover. As an English-speaking outsider, he would see the place in an entirely different light.

The arrival in the republic of a high-profile, high-quality All Black provided newspapers with a rich source of material. They spared no detail for readers, who avidly soaked up everything they could on Thorne, who had won selection for his country before representing Auckland and who had sacrificed a broken-hearted fiancée in New Zealand for a South African beauty queen.

Some writers were scathing. One accused him of sitting on his chair in Johannesburg expecting people to grovel for him to play for their team. The 'inside word' was that he would join the fashionable and exclusive Wanderers club.

Thorne's marriage to Jenny-Lynn and the summer recess meant he didn't have to rush into any rugby decisions. 'Because I resented newspaper claims that I was being precious, I decided not to play in Johannesburg at all, but to join the university club in Pretoria, which was known to everyone as Tukkies.'

While it fitted in well with his new job as manager of the Pretoria office of National Mutual Insurance, his decision stunned many, especially the English-speaking fraternity in Johannesburg. How would the high-flying Thorne cope in the dour Afrikaner environment he was placing himself in?

Tukkies was one of the strongest teams around, boasting 16 members of the Northern Transvaal squad; in Thorne's time with them they would lose only two matches. The game of rugby is universal and presented no complications for Thorne, who was soon back to his dynamic best, even taking over the goalkicking responsibilities for the side.

Despite his success he found the Afrikaner mentality hard to breach. 'All the team talks and announcements were in Afrikaans,' he says, 'which was a challenge for an English-speaking New Zealander. I picked up a spattering of the language, enough to get by.'

However, he was surprised at the hostility shown towards him by the womenfolk. 'The wives hated me,' he says. 'They were more nationalist than their husbands and they saw me as married to a very pretty English-speaking South African who had never been to Pretoria. We were different. We were considered a beautiful couple, so they told me, and therefore not trusted.'

Thorne would have loved to have become a dual international, but he concluded that that was an impossibility as long as Ian Kirkpatrick, who had toured New Zealand with the 1956 Springboks, remained as a selector. 'He hated New Zealand because of that '56 tour and he was never going to offer me a Springbok jersey.' That didn't stop Thorne participating in the Springbok trials, disappointingly in 1971 but with great impact the following year.

Between seasons, Thorne, for the first time in his life, went to a gym, where he worked on weights and his fitness generally. He complemented the gym work by playing soccer during his lunch breaks, resolving to make 1972 a year to remember.

Fitter and more determined, he returned to Tukkies. It proved a liberating experience for the now 25-year-old. Thorne was given control of the backline, and although the forwards stubbornly persisted in talking in Afrikaans, he plotted moves with the English-speaking backs. The result was that Tukkies won the Carlton Cup, Thorne clinching the title with a 60 m intercept try in the final game. His achievements for Tukkies saw him promoted to the Northern Transvaal Currie Cup side.

Thorne had regularly been in the headlines back in New Zealand and nothing changed in his new country. On the last Friday of September, his son, Bruce, was born. Thorne celebrated by drinking a bottle of former Springbok Chris Koch's three-year-old brandy, after which he performed 'like a dog' against Rhodesia the next day.

The following Tuesday he was ordered off, by Max Baise, in an inter-varsity match between Tukkies and Ikeys at Newlands, ostensibly for fighting.

'In fact,' says Thorne, 'I was trying to break up a fight. But the referee didn't see it that way. I don't think I was ever involved in a rugby fight in my entire career.'

Some days later Northern Transvaal's celebrated coach, Colonel Bierman van Zyl, summoned Thorne and said to him, 'Grahame, you were drunk when you played against Rhodesia on Saturday and then you were ordered off on Tuesday. What have you got to tell me?'

'All I said to Bierman was, "Well, just don't pick me then. It's no problem. If I'm not good enough, don't pick me!" That was the great thing about being an amateur. You could do what you liked in those days, within reason. I don't think you'd be so cavalier now, or you'd jeopardise your major source of income.'

Thorne believes van Zyl was close to dropping him for his behaviour but retained him for the Currie Cup final against Transvaal, a match that ended in a draw, largely, in Thorne's opinion, as a result of the 'incompetent' refereeing of Piet Robbertse.

Thorne backed up his stunning games for Tukkies and the Blue Bulls with outstanding performances in the trials. At both Pretoria and Johannesburg, his B1 team defeated the selectors' A1 side, but it mattered not. He missed Springbok selection, along with his fellow stars of the B1 team, centre Peter Swanson and No 8 Morne du Plessis. In protest, they all grew their hair long, radical behaviour in that conservative climate.

Thorne wasn't the only individual who believed he was harshly treated by the selectors. Norman Canale wrote in the *Sunday Times* that 'Kiwi Thorne has replaced Frik du Preez as the Idol of Loftus. He has proved himself the best centre in South Africa, so an ominous political spectre looms in the background whenever the Thorne case is discussed.' And Marshall Wilson wrote in the *Rand Daily Mail* that 'Thorne was without doubt one of the two best centres on view in the trials.' Late in 1972, Thorne farewelled his Tukkies and Northern Transvaal team-mates and moved south to Durban, to become a partner in a wholesale liquor outlet with his brother-in-law.

He found life in the tropical seaside city of Durban vastly different from Pretoria. Durban was, and still is, the most British of the South African cities and, accordingly, all the players spoke English. Thorne, who was made vice-captain to Tom Bedford, one of Natal's favourite rugby sons, enjoyed the relaxed and congenial atmosphere, although, paradoxically, he says that as a serious rugby player he preferred the intensity of playing for the Blue Bulls more than the laid-back approach of the Natal side.

In 1973, for the third year in succession, Thorne was chosen as a trialist. But the essentially Natal team he captained was overwhelmed 55–6. 'Oh well,' thought Thorne, 'that's that. If I wasn't wanted previously when playing for winning sides, I'm certainly not going to feature this time.'

But to his astonishment he was named in a South African XV chosen to play matches against Northern Transvaal, Transvaal and Free State, fixtures arranged because the Springbok tour of New Zealand had been cancelled for political reasons.

'It was a sop for leaving me out in 1972,' says Thorne, who withdrew, accepting a rival invitation to play for the New Zealand President's XV — an exotic mix of international celebrities (including Pinetree Meads and Super Sid Going) — against the All Blacks at Wellington and Auckland. 'I decided, during that trip home, that New Zealand was the country in which I wanted to live and so, in March 1974, I returned with my wife and son.'

Thorne departed South Africa with mixed feelings. He says he had no regard for either the Springbok selectors or the country's biased referees. But he had grown to quite appreciate the 'gritty old Afrikaners'.

'I had some wonderful mates; not many, I concede. Individuals like Jappie Bekker, Louis Mulder and Jan Oosthuizen. But most Afrikaners just had this big chip on their shoulders. We live by the New Testament and they live by the Old.

'I loved South Africa in many ways but even though I'm a right-wing reactionary, I couldn't get to grips with people not being treated equally. Although Pisceans like me can just drift away and keep the blinkers on, it was an unreal society in which to live.'

Thorne would later become a local and national politician in New Zealand, and with that track record would revisit South Africa as a member of the New Zealand Parliamentarians rugby team during the 1995 Rugby World Cup in South Africa.

Thorne's son from his first marriage, Bruce, who stood a towering 1.98 m and was later to become a Junior Springbok and play Currie Cup for Transvaal, made a special guest appearance for the New Zealand Parliamentarians.

The reality of modern-day life in Johannesburg hit home when Thorne and fellow New Zealander Alan Trotter were mugged a few days before the World Cup grand final.

Having arrived at Trotter's home in one of Johannesburg's affluent suburbs, they were ordered out of his car by a gun-wielding robber who made them lie on the footpath while he stole their wallets, watches and cash.

'It was,' says Thorne, one of countless overseas visitors held up during the tournament, 'a frightening experience. You just prayed he wasn't going to pull the trigger after he'd taken what he wanted.'

Grahame Thorne and his second wife, Briony, now live in Blenheim, where they have established the Thornedael Olive and Wine Estate and provide a retreat for visitors in their homestay. They have four children: Gareth, 20, Hannah, 18, David, 16, and Hamish 14.

For the record

Player
- Auckland, 1967–1970, 1974 (20 games)
- New Zealand, 1967–1970 (39 games, 10 tests)
- Northern Transvaal, 1971–1972 (10 games)
- Natal, 1973 (6 games)

Kevin Putt

For the wiry kid growing up in Waikato in the late 1970s there was a single aim in life: when he grew up he was going to be an All Black. But in 1994, when halfback Kevin Putt ran onto the field for his international debut, he was wearing the green and gold of South Africa. It was a considerable irony for Putt, who, as the kingpin of a crack Waikato side and an All Black trialist, had come so tantalisingly close to achieving his childhood dream.

Putt's provincial rugby career began under Laurie Mains while he was studying physical education at Otago University. A decade later Putt, a player noted for his cannoning dive pass, shrewd game analysis and hyperactive energy on the field, had made it to the top.

Today, there are few regrets about the twist of fate that saw him become a Springbok rather than an All Black.

The uniqueness of becoming the first New Zealander to be selected to play for the Springboks was a more than adequate compensation, says Putt. 'It was a bit of an odd feeling at first to be representing the old enemy,' he says. 'However, I regarded it as a great honour to have made the transition into the conservative culture of South African rugby and to have been accepted. When I made the Springbok team in 1994, I regarded it as an equal achievement to winning selection for the All Blacks.

'I have great memories of playing for Waikato and the New Zealand Sevens team but that's what they are, memories. I operate on the basis that if you keep looking back you will never go forward.'

Life-changing moments seldom come in isolation. Two of Putt's friends would shape his destiny: his old Waikato team-mate Warren Gatland and a president of the Natal Rugby Union, Chris Edwards.

In 1991, Gatland, later to become an inspirational coach of Ireland, suggested Putt should apply for the position of coaching co-ordinator at Terenure College club in Ireland. Putt says that thanks to Gatty's advice he would later meet the club president's daughter, Louise, who is now his wife. At the conclusion of his first season in Ireland, Putt was invited to Natal for a five-month playing stint for the Empangeni club, where he met Edwards, who later became his mentor.

That period in Natal would have a major effect on Putt's life. In the final two months of his initial contract he went to a Zulu township to work as a teacher at Tisand Technical High School. The school had been given money to invest in a gymnasium and needed someone to initiate a physical education curriculum.

'There was no curriculum when I arrived, no PE of any kind operating in any of the black schools, no facilities,' says Putt. 'That's when I made a commitment to myself to return to this fascinating land and endeavour to get PE up and running.'

But first there was unfinished business in New Zealand. Putt still hankered after an All Black jersey and with the appointment of a brand-new selection panel — Laurie Mains, Peter Thorburn and Earle Kirton coming in following the disasters of the 1991 World Cup — he sensed an opening.

'Laurie said he would be starting from scratch,' says Putt, 'so I figured I had as good a chance as anyone of winning selection.'

Putt featured in the early trial at Napier, opposite Stu Forster, and although he was one of the standout players, the selectors went for Graeme Bachop and Ant Strachan.

That was when Putt decided to quit New Zealand. He was only 26 and he felt he had something to offer as a halfback, but his positive appraisal of his own talents wasn't shared by the selectors. And they were the ones who made the important decisions.

Although sad to be quitting New Zealand, Putt could reflect on a marvellous few seasons with Waikato, vintage times in which the Mooloo men defeated Wales and Australia, twice won the CANZ competition against Otago, Canada and the Argentinian sides Banco Nationale and San Isidro, and twice — in 1989 and 1990 — finished in the top four in the Air New Zealand NPC.

Through '89 and '90 Putt operated behind an awesome pack, one captained from No 8 by John Mitchell, anchored by

Kevin Putt in action in his debut game for the Springboks.

69

its All Black front row of Richard Loe, Warren Gatland and Graham Purvis and which also included such talented individuals as Brent Anderson, Richard Jerram, Duane Monkley and Richard Coventry. Little wonder that in three seasons, from 1988, Putt scored 20 tries. (Mind you, that statistic pales a little alongside the achievements of Mitchell, who scored 27 tries in just two seasons off the back of the scrum.)

Probably the closest Putt came to All Black selection was in 1989, the year in which he was selected for the successful North Zone team, where he opposed Bruce Deans and Jason Hewett. Notwithstanding Putt's enterprise and great ability on the burst, the selectors stuck with Deans and a very young Bachop.

A year after returning to South Africa, Putt won selection for Natal, and he shudders as he recalls that he nearly blew it with his team-mates in his first provincial match.

'Although Natal was an English-speaking province, Afrikaans was the predominant language when I first joined the team.

'Wahl Bartmann, the captain, had got everyone together in a huddle before the game and I was expecting the usual New Zealand pre-match carry-on with a lot of cursing and heavy language, head banging and so on.

'I was all ready to yell out a motivational "C'mon, you bastards" when I heard a chorus of "Amen". I hadn't realised that they prayed before every match.'

In 1992 he honoured the second commitment he had made to himself the previous year — that he would work as a PE teacher in the Zulu townships. His first day at school was a shocker. An introduction to Hlamvana School's principal was cut short when an army van pulled up outside the school spilling out fully armed soldiers after the discovery of an arms cache in the school's roof. Putt lost no time in making himself scarce.

'I wondered what I was letting myself in for. Fortunately, I found such incidents were isolated.'

At the school Putt had 100 pupils per class and the only recreational facility was a concrete slab which had been created for school assemblies.

He painted lines on the slab, converting it into three volleyball courts that could also double as a full-size basketball court. Another innovation that he dreamed up, and which proved immensely popular with the basketball-crazy populace, was to attach backboards with basketball hoops to the townships' light poles.

Soccer also ruled the African townships and Putt admits he grew frustrated with his volleyballs being used for kicking practice. 'One day a teacher came up to me after I'd admonished a kid, suggesting to him that kicking the ball was not a smart thing to do.

'"Can't you see he's wearing blue pants?" the teacher asked me.

'I looked around. Of the 100 or so kids there, probably four were kitted out in blue pants. "Do the blue pants have some significance?" I asked, innocently.

'"Sure do," he replied. "In the ANC outfit these kids belong to, blue pants signify they've killed a person."'

Putt considers he was fortunate to be a foreigner and therefore not implicated in South Africa's sins of the past. 'I was out playing with the kids the whole time and I'm sure my safety was never in doubt.

'Through rugby, I had a high profile and although Zulus tend to be small physically and not greatly interested in the game, it helped to get my message across to them. I was told that the kids were pretty chuffed that I was there. "This guy isn't just in it to take bucks out of companies. He's a star and he's chosen to work with us."'

Sport was the one way Putt could help pupils in Zululand's townships achieve a level of success in life. Through sporting achievements and better facilities both the socially disadvantaged and non-academic could experience satisfaction and self-worth, he explained to his South African colleagues.

'Experience some sort of success and it gives value to your life,' he told them. 'That's ultimately what we're all looking for.'

From that first black-township school Putt progressed to the wider community and on one unforgettable occasion, he recalls, an athletics day he organised was attended by 24 schools.

It wasn't without its moments. 'A race was about to start and this starting gun goes off and then it goes off again. I thought it must be a false start until I realised I was hearing automatic gunfire. All the kids dropped to the ground, trying to hide from whatever was going on. Fortunately, no one was injured. There were three white teachers and we all raced off to where our cars were parked and got out of the place. It wasn't a time for heroics.'

Putt was seconded by the Zululand Sports Development Project,

ZSDP, for 'the upliftment of sport within the greater community, including the promotion and development of sport in the under-privileged areas of Zululand'.

His brief included the initiation of a sports' training centre to empower coaches and administrators from the disadvantaged areas to uplift their communities through sport. In association with the local government of Kwa Zulu Natal, Putt would initiate and implement PE into 14 schools in the area. He was then appointed the Zululand Rugby Development Officer for the Natal Rugby Union, linking it with his ZSDP co-ordination and coaching roles throughout the Zululand region.

In all, Putt spent five years from 1992 as the co-ordinator of the ZSDP in South Africa, leaving it in far better shape than he found it. The decision to leave a country he and Louise liked was forced on them in 1997 when their young daughter was diagnosed with a metabolic disorder known as PKU, stemming from a recessive gene which both parents carried. At that time the treatment she needed was unavailable in South Africa and so the Putt family returned to Ireland, where Kevin took up a coaching position at Terenure College.

Five years on, their daughter's condition has improved more than they could ever have wished for, says a delighted Putt.

'The danger was she could have been retarded,' he says, 'but somehow she fought it for two years before being diagnosed. There are not many instances of kids of that age with that particular disorder turning out normal, but she's now in mainstream school and doing fantastically well. We have to adhere to a protein-free diet, which is a bit hard in a barbecue-mad country like South Africa, but otherwise she's fine.'

In March 2002, Putt received a call from his old friend Chris Edwards in South Africa. Would he put his name forward for the position of chief coach of the Sharks and, in tandem with that, the Natal Currie Cup team? The Super 12 was already under way and the Sharks were languishing at the bottom of the table; with Rudolf Straueli having been promoted to the Springbok coaching role the job was up for grabs.

Putt flew from Ireland for the interview process, was the management's surprise choice and on 1 April 2002 officially took over as chief coach of the Sharks.

Five days later, to the delight of the fans at Kings Park, Putt's Sharks pulled off a shock victory over the Blues and a week later downed the Chiefs.

For the record

Player
- Otago, 1984–1986 (14 games)
- Waikato, 1987–1990 (52 games)
- New Zealand Sevens, 1989
- Natal, 1992–1999 (128 games)
- South Africa, 1994–1996 (11 games)
- South African Sevens, 1995
- Leinster, 2001 (European Cup)

Coach
- London Irish, 1998–2000 (youth and school teams)
- Terenure College RFC 2000–2002 (director of rugby)
- Leinster, 2001–2002 (skills coach)
- Sharks Super 12, 2002
- Natal Currie Cup, 2002

John Plumtree

Different people reacted in different ways to the unauthorised Cavaliers tour of South Africa in 1986. While many were outraged by the subterfuge and scheming that circumvented officialdom and reactivated an association with a country considered 'out of bounds' because of its racist policies, thousands of rugby traditionalists followed events as closely and enthusiastically as if it was a genuine All Black tour.

One of those was John Plumtree, a 20-year-old freezing worker in the Taranaki township of Hawera. The political ramifications washed over Plumtree, who had made a handful of appearances for the Taranaki representative team the previous year. Like most of his mates, he was interested in sport for sport's sake. Events on the Cavaliers' tour would have a profound influence on him. Not the outcome of the series, not the controversial refereeing, not even the fact that the players involved would face suspension from the NZRFU on their return. It was the country itself that impacted on Plumtree. As he monitored the Cavaliers' progress, which culminated in an almost inevitable test series victory to the Springboks, he was fascinated by the rock-hard surfaces on which the matches were staged, the massive size of most of the Cavaliers' opponents and the South Africans' obvious passion and enthusiasm for the game. South Africa, Plumtree remembers thinking, was a country he'd love to experience.

The opportunity arose three years later. Although Plumtree was by then an established member of the Taranaki NPC team, claiming 37 appearances, most as a lock although some as a loose forward, he felt in need of greater challenges than Hawera and Taranaki could provide.

He'd always aspired to become an All Black and when in 1986 he'd attended the New Zealand Colts trial at Lincoln College and rubbed shoulders with emerging stars like Michael Jones, Zinzan Brooke and Stephen Bachop, he wondered whether he might possess the qualities that would take him right to the top.

However, by 1989 he was fast concluding that a century of appearances for Taranaki would be his lot. Satisfying as that might be, he knew there had to be greater, more rewarding challenges. He felt he was in a rut at the freezing works and not developing as a person.

Plumtree had a kindred spirit in Chris Sutton, who, as a midfield back, was also representing Taranaki. In the company of Roy Wetini, a

John Plumtree demonstrating his try-scoring action for Taranaki.

cricketer, they considered various OE options. This was when rugby was still amateur, when players went overseas because a particular country beckoned, not because lucrative contracts were on offer.

It was the cricketer who suggested South Africa. Plumtree recalled the fascination the country had always held for him. 'Yeah,' he recalls, 'South Africa was the place, we decided.'

'Everything just fell into place from there,' says Plumtree. 'With an introduction from Colin Meads, we were met at Durban airport by Robbie Savage of the High School Old Boys club, a delightful individual who'd served as liaison officer for several overseas touring teams. We stayed with him for two months until we moved into a flat overlooking Kings Park. We didn't have much money, but the rent was modest and the club arranged part-time jobs for us. There was a car available but Chris and I preferred to run to training at Kings Park and bum a ride home.'

Plumtree and Sutton had reached Durban in October, timing their arrival so they would have the summer to settle in before getting serious about rugby. The coastal city with its tropical climate had instant appeal, Plumtree recalling how, during that first summer, he and Sutton lived in shorts and T-shirts and made extensive use of Durban's gorgeous beaches.

Plumtree, realising he was of modest proportions by South African standards, committed himself to the gym. When he arrived in Durban he weighed in at about 98 kg. By the time the rugby season rolled around, he had bulked up to almost 110 kg. It was his intention to stay just 12 months in South Africa before heading back to Taranaki. But a fellow called Ian McIntosh would change all that.

Natal had traditionally been one of the also-rans of the South African Currie Cup rugby scene, capable of the occasional upset but not a force to rival provinces like Transvaal, Northern Transvaal, Free State and Western Province. For a large part of its history Natal had languished in the second division.

It irked faithful Natal followers that in 99 years the province had never once won the Currie Cup. But 1990 was the union's centenary and coach McIntosh was determined to make it a season to remember. McIntosh, quite revolutionary in his approach, didn't hesitate to strengthen his team with outside players. Former Wallaby tighthead prop Tom Lawton became a key component of the Natal pack and after a modest number of performances for the Old Boys club side Plumtree found himself in the Currie Cup squad, named as a blindside flanker.

'It was all pretty overwhelming for a boy from Hawera,' says Plumtree. 'The first pleasant surprise was the brown envelopes given to us under the table, after training each week. These were the days of amateurism, of course, but we received about $60 or $70 a week, which made for comfortable living. Once I'd made the Natal team, there was a car as well.'

Natal possessed special strengths behind the scrum, where Craig Jamieson combined with Joel Stransky, and in midfield, where Dick Muir and Jeremy Thompson formed a potent partnership. Lawton's arrival made a huge difference to the scrum and McIntosh was delighted to welcome Wahl Bartmann also, a powerhouse No 6 surprisingly unwanted by Transvaal.

Northern Transvaal, captained from flyhalf by Naas Botha, were the dominant side in the competition throughout the 1990 season, with Natal, responding to McIntosh's inspirational guidance, a clear second.

By chance, Northerns and Natal were drawn to play each other in Pretoria a fortnight before the final. Northerns had already beaten

McIntosh's men during the first round in Durban and this time inflicted a 28–6 drubbing, which, naturally, meant it went into the final an overwhelming favourite. As far as the Pretoria media were concerned, it was almost a waste of time Natal even turning up.

But McIntosh was a shrewd campaigner. In the first meeting in Pretoria he'd told his players he didn't want any of them missing the final because of being suspended through retaliating, regardless of the provocation. He was later quoted as saying that he only instructed them not to retaliate, not to 'play like schoolgirls'.

Plumtree vividly recalls McIntosh's brilliant planning in the fortnight leading up to the final. 'He'd spent time with Australian Rod Macqueen between seasons and taken on board some of his methods. He called in a psychologist and built belief in every player. There wasn't one player who didn't believe we could win at Pretoria.'

Plumtree featured prominently in McIntosh's strategic approach — unexpectedly, off the bench. He was used as a tactical replacement before it was fashionable and legal to use impact players. McIntosh preferred to start with the 115 kg Steve Atherton at No 6, giving Natal one of the biggest packs ever fielded in South African rugby. Plumtree's impact was immediate once he took the field. He secured the ball from a breakdown to help set up winger Tony Watson's match-winning try, Natal hanging on to win 18–12.

'It was an astonishing result. Northern Transvaal were so confident of winning they'd even had wine labels printed in advance,' says Plumtree. 'Our scrum was magnificent and put halfback Robert du Preez and flyhalf Naas Botha under relentless pressure. The Northerns fans couldn't believe what they were seeing, for their forwards had annihilated us a fortnight earlier!'

For Plumtree, whose biggest moment in New Zealand had been winning promotion with Taranaki from second division, the Currie Cup victory was like a fairy tale. The players were fêted with a ticker-tape parade through the streets of Durban and then flown overseas for a skiing holiday.

It might have taken Natal 100 years to claim their first Currie Cup, but before he finally quit South Africa Plumtree would share in two more championship victories. Not in 1991, which was a disappointing season; nor, through circumstances, in 1992, when the McIntosh magic saw Natal triumph again.

Plumtree flourished under McIntosh's coaching and is proud to list himself among the survivors of Mac's gruelling pre-season activities.

'He'd have us assemble on Durban beach at 7 a.m. and go through various exercises before the trainer would go out and tread water and we'd all have to swim out and around him. On other occasions, he'd make us jump off the end of the pier and swim into the beach. Given that Afrikaners are not natural swimmers, that there was a current sucking you back towards the pier and that there was a shark net within sight, it was amazing we never lost anyone! The lifeguards used to keep an eye on us, but there were some pretty exhausted individuals dragging themselves up on to the sand, I can tell you!'

For variation, McIntosh would then make the players run up the (awfully steep) grandstand staircase at Kings Park.

Plumtree wasn't the only New Zealander making an impression in Natal in the early '90s. Grant Ross, a lock from Wellington, and Ross Knight, an outside back who'd played for Counties Manukau, were quality performers, but the individual who would go furthest was halfback Kevin Putt, a proven NPC performer unwanted by the All Black selectors. While Plumtree had the distinction of representing South Africa at sevens, Putt achieved the ultimate, becoming the first Kiwi to win full Springbok honours.

In 1992, Plumtree, uncertain whether his future as a player lay in South Africa or New Zealand, returned home, quietly hopeful an All Black jersey might still be within reach. With Taranaki back in the second division, he headed east, opting to play for Hawke's Bay, then coached by Graeme Taylor.

Although the team scored stirring victories over Wellington and North Auckland, they lost all their remaining first-division fixtures and were fortunate to survive in the premier grade. While Plumtree enjoyed the season, he could not resist the lure of Natal, where there was 'unfinished business'.

Responding to the positive environment in Durban, Plumtree enjoyed his finest season in 1993. By now, Noel Olivier was coach of Natal, McIntosh having stepped up to take charge of the Springboks. Plumtree proved himself an artful exponent of the sevens game. After helping Natal win the national title, he earned selection in the South African Sevens team for a couple of seasons, along with such distinguished individuals as Chester Williams, Andre Joubert, Adrian Richter and Henry Honiball. They had the satisfaction of getting through to the semifinals at Hong Kong, losing narrowly to Fiji.

'Once I made the South African Sevens team, I was accepted by everyone, it seemed. I was then seen as an adopted South African.'

Although Plumtree was obviously highly respected by the South African selectors, he was in competition with some extremely talented loose forwards during his time in the republic — players such as Bartmann, Ian Macdonald, Rudolf Straueli, Tiaan Strauss, Adrian Richter and Francois Pienaar.

'I don't think it counted against me, being a New Zealander; after all, Kevin Putt made it. With a bit of luck, I could have got there.'

Plumtree had greater luck in romance, meeting Lara in Durban, where they were married in 1994. She accompanied him on his summer trips back to New Zealand and they now live in Hamilton.

An exciting innovation in 1993 was the Super 10 (the forerunner of the Super 12), involving the leading provincial teams of New Zealand, Australia and South Africa. Natal did well, losing only to Graham Henry's crack Auckland team during the first season, while progressing to the final in 1994, where they went down narrowly to the Queensland Reds in Durban (the game in which Wallaby midfielders Tim Horan and Jason Little both finished up in plaster).

One of Natal's finest Super 10 victories was against Waikato in Hamilton, where Plumtree opposed John Mitchell, who, as All Black coach, is now his boss. 'I remind him of that result occasionally!' says Plumtree.

Natal's good form didn't extend to the Currie Cup in 1994. Under Olivier, the team performed dismally, finishing well down the field, which rendered them ineligible for the Super 12 in 1995.

Olivier came under fire, as losing coaches always do, and was sacked. His replacement? Who else but Ian McIntosh, who was also suddenly on the list of unemployed rugby coaches following his Springbok team's failures in New Zealand. Infamous Louis Luyt didn't tolerate losers. So McIntosh was pitched out and Kitch Christie brought in to prepare the team for the World Cup.

All of which was good news for Natal. Under McIntosh, they were soon humming along again and would claim Currie Cup victories in 1995 and 1996. Natal were once again the undisputed kings of South African rugby.

As the 1997 season approached, Plumtree was contemplating fresh challenges. The knee injuries which had troubled him for some time were now a major concern.

'I was sick of trying to fight back to fitness,' he says. 'Besides, Mac had Gary Teichmann in his team and I wasn't going to oust him. Approaching 32, I felt the writing was on the wall, so I pleaded with Mac to release me from his squad. He valued my experience but was prepared to let me go.

'I'd had an offer to coach Swansea, which came about after I rented my house to a group of Welshmen during the Lions tour of 1997. One day I had a long talk at the gym with Scott Gibbs, which was a bit of a laugh because he finished up playing for me.

'My only coaching experience was with a school team in Durban, but I felt confident in the role. All those years under Ian McIntosh had prepared me well.'

McIntosh was sorry to see Plumtree go, releasing him on the strict condition Swansea utilised him exclusively as a coach. 'He was still a valuable member of my Natal squad,' recalls McIntosh. Swansea would have been in breach of contract if they'd put him on the field.

'John gave an immense amount to Natal over the years. He was one of the best carriers of the ball we ever had and he presented it so well, in true New Zealand fashion. He was also a great personality and character who set fresh standards in our beer-drinking competition!'

From the tropical climate of Durban, Plumtree suddenly found himself rugging up in the valleys of Wales. The winters were dramatically different, he quickly came to appreciate, but the passion for rugby was the same.

With a quality assistant coach in Kevin Hopkins, a full-time trainer, and internationals of the calibre of flyhalf Arwel Thomas, midfielders Gibbs and Mark Taylor, hooker Garin Jenkins and No 8 Stuart Davies, Swansea had the potential to succeed. And Plumtree made it happen, winning the championship at his first attempt.

Suddenly a two-year contract was extended to five years but, like Graham Henry with the Welsh national team, Plumtree would find that five years was too long to remain involved with one team in the cauldron that is Welsh rugby. He claimed the Welsh Cup knockout title in 1998 (the year Swansea and Cardiff split from the Welsh union and played in the English championship) and lost the 1999 Welsh club final to Llanelli, only to triumph again in 2000.

By the time 2001 rolled around, Plumtree was ready to come home. 'I'd turned my back on New Zealand as a player and now felt I wanted to give something back as a coach.'

He applied for, and was appointed to, the post of rugby development officer with Waikato and had also applied for the assistant coach's position with the Wellington NPC team when he received 'the call' from new All Black coach Mitchell.

'He offered me the position of analyst with the All Blacks, which was simply too tempting to turn down. It was hard to believe, really. One minute I'm development officer for Waikato, which was appealing enough, and the next I'm involved with the All Blacks.

'Mitch and Robbie Deans want feedback on players and opponents they'll be encountering. It's my role to give them as much information as I can. It's a unique opportunity and one I'm really looking forward to.

'I'll be involved at all the camps and will travel with them to all their matches in 2002.'

Plumtree couldn't wait to get started.

For the record

Player
- Taranaki, 1985–1988 (37 games)
- Natal, 1990–1991, 1993–1997 (80 games)
- Hawke's Bay, 1992 (11 games)
- South Africa Sevens, 1995

Coach
- Swansea, 1997–2000

Analyst
- New Zealand, 2002

Laurie Mains

As a rugby coach, Laurie Mains has never accepted the easy option. He's always preferred to start from scratch with underachieving teams, relishing the challenge.

He first rejuvenated his own club, Southern of Dunedin, then brought Otago back from the dead and finally restored the All Blacks to greatness after some depressing performances at the 1991 World Cup. After coming agonisingly close to success at the 1995 World Cup in South Africa, Mains, mentally drained, quit. He wrote his biography the next year, married South African Anna-Marie and refocused on a couple of business deals — plus fishing, which he loves.

Many, probably including Mains himself, regarded his distinguished active coaching career as being at an end. But there were challenges afresh beyond New Zealand's shores. And Mains was made aware of one such opportunity while being entertained by friends in Brisbane in 1998. When the phone rang, it was Mr Rugby from the Golden Lions (formerly Transvaal) Rugby Union in South Africa, Louis Luyt.

'How on earth he ever tracked me down at that home, I'll never know,' says Mains, 'but he did. He said the senior coaching position with the Golden Lions was available and was I interested?

'I guess I was looking for a fresh challenge in rugby because I replied in the affirmative. Two trips to Johannesburg later, we stitched a deal together. From the beginning of the 1999 season, I was in charge of the Golden Lions.

'I was mindful that South Africa had been something of a graveyard for New Zealand coaches. The Golden Lions had gone through six coaches in four years and when my appointment was announced the media asked me how long I thought I would last. I responded by saying that I enjoyed a challenge and that I did not intend to fail. That was conditional, I might add, on me being left alone to coach the team on my terms, with no administrative interference.

'Given the talented players available, I knew I could make the Golden Lions successful, doing it my way. Louis Luyt and the Lions' president, Jomo King, gave me their assurance there would be no interference from them, and they were true to their word.'

Mains was to be responsible not only for the premier team, the flag-bearing side which would compete in the Vodacom and Currie

Cups, but all four professional teams within the club, starting with the Under 19 side.

Available for the Golden Lions were several members of the champion Springbok World Cup team of 1995, the side which had caused Mains, as All Black coach, such anguish on the day of the final. Hennie le Roux, Hannes Strydom and Balie Swart were still going strong and were joined for the Currie Cup campaign by Japie Mulder and James Dalton once their test commitments were completed.

Mains, aware that the Lions had been seriously underachieving, introduced them pre-season to what he terms 'good old-fashioned Otago-style training sessions', of the type that traditionally made the blue-and-golds so formidable.

'In my book, the game is about getting your techniques right,' says Mains. 'In the first few weeks, I made huge changes to their play, particularly in their approach to rucks and mauls, not to mention the set pieces. Once they realised they weren't going to break me down, they knuckled down to their work, with startling results.'

Part of Mains's brief was to develop coaches and after about half a dozen games he identified prop Balie Swart as having immense potential. 'He was coming up 35, so I removed him as a player and took him under my wing as an assistant coach, having identified his leadership and communication skills.

'Of all the young coaches I worked with, he was the best. He grasped the discipline and work ethics, which are so important. At the beginning of 2002, he moved to New Zealand to coach Nelson Bays, where I'm sure he'll be successful.'

After one loss, the Lions went through to win the Vodacom Cup, a subsidiary competition which runs concurrently with the Super 12. Next up was the Currie Cup, the main focus of the South African domestic season.

While the Golden Lions were

Laurie Mains and Lions captain Hannes Strydom are all smiles after winning the Currie Cup in 1999.

pleased to welcome their Springboks back from international duty, these high-profile players first had to undergo Mains's initiation. 'We couldn't have one-third of the team playing the Springbok way and the rest my style,' he says, 'so it was back to basics for these guys.

'There were a couple of problem players, most notably James Small, who had been a champion performer but who was past his best. He didn't stay with us for long.'

Although there were sceptics who questioned what a New Zealander was doing coaching a Currie Cup team, Mains says that from the start he received great support from former Transvaal (now Gauteng) players and administrators. 'People like Syd Nomis, Corrie Pypers and Kevin de Klerk gave me every encouragement,' says Mains. 'They wanted their team back on the road.' Mains also found that because of his association with the All Blacks of 1992, who had beaten the Springboks at Ellis Park, and 1995, when his team had been edged out in a dramatic World Cup final, he had a huge following among the black and coloured communities, which increased as the Golden Lions went from victory to victory.

The Golden Lions became a superefficient unit, finishing as top qualifier. In New Zealand that would have guaranteed them a home final, but South Africa operates a different system. There, the venue for the final is the opposite of where the two teams last met. So instead of playing in front of more than 50,000 of their own fans at Ellis Park, the Golden Lions had to contend with the supercharged atmosphere of Kings Park, in Durban, the home ground of the Natal Sharks.

As if that wasn't advantage enough, the Sharks had motivation galore because the occasion marked the farewell appearances of three of Natal's favourite sons — coach Ian McIntosh, captain Gary Teichmann and fullback Andre Joubert.

'There was,' says Mains, 'an awful lot of emotion, which we managed to snuff out. The first 30 minutes were fiercely contested, but then our forwards' repetition play, involving a pick-up-and-drive approach through the middle of their pack, took them out of the game.

'That style of play is not a strength in South Africa. It forced their forwards to commit themselves to the tight, which created room for our backs, who were especially sharp and who scored some memorable tries.' The Golden Lions were ahead by seven points at halftime and cruised to an overwhelming 38–9 victory, five tries to none, a surprisingly one-sided result for a final. The scoreline exceeded the expectations of even the most parochial Lions supporters.

Mains says that South Africans know how to celebrate and his players partied worthily, toasting the Currie Cup a few dozen times more than was absolutely necessary.

A victory parade through several of Johannesburg's shopping centres in an open bus capped a memorable year for the Golden Lions Rugby Union. As the Currie Cup was nearing its end, Mains was approached by officials of the Cats Super 12 franchise, inquiring if he would be prepared to extend his expertise to their team. The Cats had been underachieving on an annual basis. After finishing a promising fifth in 1997, they had saddened their fans by coming in twelfth and eleventh the previous two years.

It was an ideal scenario for rugby's champion fix-it coach, who couldn't resist the challenge. All the teams he'd coached had been in identical situations, underperforming despite being blessed with quality players.

'The Super 12 had always excited me and I was thrilled to have the opportunity to be involved,' he says. 'It was obvious that many of the Cats' problems stemmed from the fact that the three unions comprising the franchise, Free State, Griqualand West and Golden Lions, had been anything but compatible.

'The franchise had its headquarters in Johannesburg and it was plain to see Free State and Griqualand West viewed their big city cousins with a fair degree of suspicion. I believed the players were there for the team to be competitive, but obviously we had to get the three unions working together.

'Being a New Zealander, and therefore neutral, certainly helped. I appealed to the three unions to set aside their parochialism and trust the people running the team. We had excellent support from Free State, who were allocated two home matches.'

Mains says he was excited about the quality of individuals he found himself working with, establishing a particularly close bond with loose forwards Andre Venter and Andre Vos. Mains ensured his players put in plenty of hard work pre-season, which brought handsome rewards when the competition started.

An away victory over the Bulls and a thrilling home win against the much-vaunted Stormers gave Mains' men the best possible start to the competition. 'Percy Montgomery almost brought us unstuck in the Stormers' game with two massive dropped goals, but we scored the tries to get home narrowly.'

The wins were achieved at a cost, test midfielder Japie Mulder sustaining a serious injury. Mains regarded him as a crucial member of the backline. It was a frustrating blow as the Cats headed for New Zealand and Australia, where their record across four Super 12s couldn't have been worse — 16 outings, 16 losses.

'The Transvaalers are not good travellers. They don't like being away from home,' he says, 'until they become hardened through experience, that is. The younger players tend to lack confidence when they're on tour.'

With Mains trying to function as a psychologist and a rugby coach, the Cats turned in massive performances against the Highlanders and the Hurricanes, winning both games everywhere but on the scoreboard. They lost the first 33–31, the second 29–23. 'At least,' says Mains, 'we snared a couple of bonus points, which were to prove valuable later.' The exertions in New Zealand took their toll in Canberra with the front-running Brumbies inflicting a 64-nil drubbing on the tourists. 'The guys had had enough by then,' says Mains. 'They just wanted to get home.'

Miraculously, Mains managed to restore the players' belief in themselves within a week, for six days later they nosed out the Sharks in Durban, 28–27 — a remarkable achievement.

The Cats then embarked on a spectacular sequence of performances that carried them into the play-offs. In succession, at home, they defeated the Crusaders 54–31, the Reds 36–32, the Blues 34–27 and the Chiefs 53–3.

'They were really good wins,' says Mains, 'particularly for the Cats, who'd never beaten the Queensland Reds and hadn't enjoyed success against the Crusaders or the Blues since 1996.'

The good news was the Cats finished fourth, one point ahead of the Stormers. The bad news was they had to journey back to Canberra for their semifinal, to tangle with George Gregan's Brumbies again. It was a dramatic turnaround in fortunes for a team that had finished second to bottom the previous season. What a boilover if the Cats could now topple the Brumbies, who'd humbled them a month earlier. Mains says they were closer to winning than the scoreline of 28–5 suggests. 'There was nothing in it at halftime, but then we lost Japie Mulder, injured. That was a big loss, for he had been hugely disruptive of their backline.

'When Thinus Delport was pulled down near the goalposts, the game hung in the balance. The Brumbies survived and came away with two late tries. We lost, but the belief was there. We could look forward to the next season with optimism.'

The stunning success of the Cats not unexpectedly led to a much greater representation in the Springboks, which, while satisfying for Mains and the faithful fans, impacted on the Golden Lions.

'The 2001 Currie Cup campaign started disastrously,' says Mains. 'Now we had nine or 10 away on international duty and with others injured we were bowled over by a couple of the lesser sides.

'Once the Springboks returned, we picked up momentum and managed to qualify for the semifinals. But we were drawn against Western Province — who were responding well to Gert Smal's coaching — at Cape Town and we were beaten. Western Province went on to win the Currie Cup.'

Mains had installed Andre Vos as captain but when he broke his cheekbone playing for the Springboks, the leadership passed to fellow loose forward Rassie Erasmus. It would be a fateful decision.

Mains says he couldn't put his finger on the problem at the time, but the spirit that had existed in the Golden Lions the previous season was diminishing. 'We were losing unity; there wasn't the spirit of the previous year,' he says. 'Something wasn't quite right. On the field, I sensed Erasmus was changing the game plan to suit himself. It was something that would spread to the Cats.'

When the new season rolled around, essentially the same players comprised the Cats Super 12 squad. And, as the incumbent, Erasmus was reappointed captain. It was a decision that would come back to haunt Mains.

'Initially,' he says, 'things seemed to be coming together well. I personally was unaware of any problems. Erasmus missed some training after undergoing blood tests, but we seemed on track for another good campaign.'

Once again the Cats made a flyer, beating the Stormers at Cape Town — a 'bonus' win, in Mains's mind — and putting 56 points on the Highlanders in Johannesburg. But then they were tripped up, at Ellis Park, by the Brumbies.

'It was the first evidence of a breakdown in the captaincy,' says Mains. 'We had a good lead, but blew it. I put it down to tactical misjudgement by the skipper. But it became apparent as the competition progressed that Erasmus was changing the onfield game plan because he, himself, was being shown up by his direct opponent. On this occasion, George Smith was beating him to the breakdowns.'

In the next game, against the Waratahs, the Cats again squandered a handsome lead, but held on for the victory. Again, there were adjustments to the game plan from Erasmus, who this time was beaten for pace by Phil Waugh.

'I still naively believed it was through misjudgement rather than disobedience that our game plan was going awry,' says Mains. 'After all, Rassie was a Springbok of good standing.'

Two hard-fought victories were then ground out in heavy conditions in Bloemfontein, against the Hurricanes and the unbeaten Sharks, the second of those a massive grudge match, with many of the players in direct competition with their main rivals for test selection. Thanks to Louis Koen's goalkicking, the Cats got home 26–25. Erasmus held his own in the conditions and the Cats flew off to New Zealand a point behind the competition leader.

With the bogey of having never won outside South Africa hanging over them, the Cats kicked off their away programme against the Chiefs at Tauranga. 'To this day,' says Mains, 'I don't know how we lost that match. We dominated the opposition but finished behind on the scoreboard, having blown five tries. We took a bonus point, but it was a frustrating outcome.'

Against the Blues at Whangarei, Mains again witnessed his game plan being altered by Erasmus, on this occasion, he presumed, because he was being shown up in the loose by Matua Parkinson. This time he didn't hesitate. He pulled Erasmus from the field at halftime, replacing him with a 'New Zealand-style flanker', Piet Krause, and transferring the captaincy to Andre Vos.

The switch worked. The Cats, 10–nil down early, came back to snatch a famous late victory, their first outside South Africa. Mains was now fully aware of Erasmus's attitude as the touring party headed for Nelson and the Crusaders game. 'I wanted to send him home from Nelson,' he says. 'He was being treated for depression by the team doctor.

'However, the other management were concerned about the reper-
cussions and convinced me we should allow him to remain on tour. I
relented, but said I didn't want him playing against the Crusaders.
Again, my fellow management, eager to avoid controversy, talked me
out of it. I yielded to their wishes, but only on the condition that Vos
captained the team, which they agreed to. Although Rassie was outplayed again, this time by Scott Robertson, we achieved another fine
victory. We'd extracted 10 points from our three matches in New Zealand and although we were beaten by the Reds in Brisbane, rather
predictably for we were carrying several injuries, we returned home
poised to secure a home semifinal.

'For that to happen, we had to defeat the Bulls, who were languishing at the bottom end of the points table.'

The Erasmus Factor was now a source of major concern to Mains.
'His attitude was undermining the team effort,' he says. Under pressure from his managers, Mains selected Erasmus to play at Pretoria.
The outcome was a disaster. 'We led by 12 points but Erasmus turned
down five opportunities to kick penalty goals. Had we taken those
points, it would have stopped their infringing and probably put us
beyond reach. We didn't score any tries as compensation and, in the
finish, lost the match by two points, which cost us a home semifinal.'

Instead of hosting the semifinal in front of their own fans, the Cats
had to journey down to Durban to do battle with Rudolf Straueli's
Sharks. Mains knew it was a mission impossible. 'Team morale was
shot to bits,' he says. 'We were on a hiding to nothing in Durban and
lost by 30 points to 12.

'It was a tragedy, really, because we had positioned ourselves to
advance to the final, where we would have given the Brumbies a major
shake-up.

'I take the responsibility for not acting when I knew I should have.
But being a New Zealander, an outsider effectively, I was reluctant to
impose my will on others. If it had been a New Zealand team, I wouldn't
have hesitated to act.

'Had I banished Erasmus from the team when we were in Nelson, I
believe we could have recovered. We had a bye after returning from
Australia and could have come out firing again in the last two matches.'
It all meant that Mains's South African sojourn ended a little
frustratingly, for the Cats should have gone on to the final. Having

accepted a coaching role with the Otago NPC team, he headed for Dunedin immediately following the Super 12.

The Erasmus affair aside, Mains says he loved his time working with the Golden Lions and the Cats and developed close, lasting friendships with individuals like Hennie le Roux, Thinus Delport, Andre Venter and Andre Vos.

'They were a committed, hard-working lot,' he says. 'It's so disappointing that one guy ruined it for a lot.'

Mains says he can't speak highly enough of the Lions' president, Jomo King, chief executive officer, Johan Prinsloo, and the assistant coach, Gysie Pienaar. He even speaks fondly of the infamous Louis Luyt. 'He supported me all the way, which I appreciated. Ninety-five per cent of the time, I had absolutely no problems with him.

'Unfortunately, his son, Louis Luyt junior, who was the marketing manager for Ellis Park, felt it necessary to stick his finger into everything and caused some strife. Blood being thicker than water, Louis senior felt obliged to take his side!'

Mains departed South Africa with the opinion that the country possesses an abundance of quality footballers. 'If they can pick their best XV, they'll be the equal of any nation.'

Mains returned to New Zealand midway through 2001 and was immediately into resuscitation mode. Having salvaged the Cats, he promptly got Otago, which had disappointed in 2000 and 2001, back into the top four and, predictably, did the same with the Highlanders when that coaching post was offered to him for 2002.

For the record

Player
- Otago, 1967–1975 (115 games)
- New Zealand, 1971, 1976 (15 games, 4 tests)

Coach
- Otago, 1983–1991, 2001–2002
- New Zealand, 1992–1995
- Golden Lions, 1999–2000
- Cats, 2000–2001
- Highlanders, 2002

ENGLAND

Although they have yet to succeed at the World Cup or achieve more than fleeting success against other major nations like New Zealand, South Africa, Australia and France, England can lay claim to being the 'home' of rugby. The game was supposedly born at Rugby School in 1823 when William Webb Ellis disregarded the laws of football as they existed and ran with the ball. England formed the game's first governing body in 1871 and shaped the early laws and until comparatively recently the IRB always met in London. Eight of England's founder clubs still survive, including Blackheath, Richmond and Harlequins. England has won the International Five (now Six) Nations championship most times, 33, although it was unsuccessful from 1893 to 1909 and from 1964 to 1979 (save for 1973, when there was an amazing quintuple tie).

Founded
1831
IRB
1890
Clubs
2049
Players
419,000 men, 122,000 women
Rugby Nomads
Josh Kronfeld, Kevin Boroevich, Earl Va'a

Josh Kronfeld

Cool is a word Josh Kronfeld likes to use.

So it's fair to ask — is playing for the champion Leicester Tigers club in England cool or uncool? One of the world's greatest modern flankers hesitates.

It would be cool — if he could get onto the field of play. It's pretty frustrating to be hammered by a combination of bizarre accidents and managerial stand-offishness, he admits.

'Yeah, I suppose I'm a bit cynical about it all. The way I see it is, if they want to play me, they'll play me. If not, it's another game where my body hasn't been bashed around. Don't get me wrong,' he adds hastily. 'I'd rather be playing, but come Monday I've got over it.'

Not that he's criticising the Tigers themselves, whom he describes as great guys and some close friends. Or Leicester's, England's and Lions' captain Martin Johnson, who wins the highest Kronfeld accolades for his inspirational leadership. His uncompromising approach to the game reminds Kronfeld of two superb former All Black captains, Shelford and Fitzpatrick.

'I rate Johnson as one of the finest players I have ever encountered. He leads by example, he never misses training and he's there week in, week out for his club.

'Martin says what needs to be said, doesn't wash around with fancy birds, try to look cool or create an image. He doesn't have any shortcomings and he's such a powerful figure in English rugby.'

Johnson and Kronfeld have similarities. Both espouse the game's traditional virtues and both have always been prepared to lay their bodies on the line. So it was natural that when Kronfeld decided to leave the All Blacks in 2000 after his outstanding 56-match, 54-test career for New Zealand he would choose Johnson's club, England's champion side for 2001 and 2002.

In Kronfeld's reckoning Leicester resembles New Zealand's Canterbury Crusaders or his own old unit, the Otago Highlanders, performing better in some areas, but languishing 'miles behind' in others. Like the time shortly after he arrived when he gave the Leicester squad his views on the tackle-ball: how they could make their tackles and, as a specialized skill, how some tackles could be used to win ball.

It opened their eyes, Kronfeld noticed, and made him realise how New Zealand players take such skills for granted. Overall though, he regards Leicester as a very good, very professional outfit, always on the lookout for improvements — which may be why the club invited him on board in May 2001.

At that time sports sections of newspapers in Britain and New Zealand led with the news: 'Premiership champions Leicester Tigers have secured their biggest signing of the professional era after capturing the services of All Black Josh Kronfeld.'

A year on, Leicester won the 2002 Heineken Cup in Cardiff, making history as the first side to retain the premier European rugby trophy, with a 15–9 win over Munster. Kronfeld cheered on his team from the sidelines.

The after-match celebrations carried on until the early hours. Then, just a short time after staggering home from the festivities, a bleary-eyed Kronfeld took a phone call from Barbarians coach Rod Macqueen: 'Can you be at Twickenham in two hours to play England?'

It wasn't the ideal preparation for an international, but Kronfeld was superkeen to get back on the field. He hopped in a taxi and journeyed to London.

Josh Kronfeld in limbering-up mode while the anthems play.

'I felt as excited as a young kid,' he murmurs. 'I enjoyed just getting on the field and was so damn thrilled to be playing again.'

Kronfeld acknowledges that Leicester was always going to be a hard nut to crack in the flankers' department, having in his specialist openside position the long-serving England and Leicester incumbent, Neil Back, and an exciting prospect in the outstanding young blindside flanker, Lewis Moody.

Kronfeld says he chose Leicester because it was a champion side and a great team and has no regrets on that front. Whether he makes the starting line-up or not, his commitment to training and fitness is as strong as ever it was in his All Black days, he says.

'But in some areas you tend to become a bit wary, especially over here because they're keen to bash the hell out of each other and maim each other at training. To be honest, I'd say it is a bit more physical in England than it is at home.

'I think that is mainly because of the poor playing conditions and perhaps a more limited skill base. The physical thing can dominate, because things are a bit slower so the knocks are a bit more intense and the pitches are pretty bad, which doesn't allow for attractive rugby.'

Since joining Leicester, Kronfeld has had an 'incredible spate of really crazy-type injuries' like popping his ribs, bending his fingers back, which caused his hand to split open, and, on his first outing for Leicester, having his ankle seize up as he was about to run onto the field of play. It hurts the pride, too, that he hasn't been able to show the Brits how he can play. Not that one of the world's top flankers really needs to prove himself.

'I've had to revert to where I was as a young fellow and accept the situation, and at my age [31] and with the things I've done, it's something I didn't expect.'

He claims to be in the dark about where he stands in the scheme of things with Leicester's director of rugby, Dean Richards, who heads the coaching panel.

'I'm obviously pretty happy about being in England for all sorts of reasons, like the shows you go to in London, that's pretty cool, and also the fact that you can get on a plane and go all over the place.

'I've thought about switching clubs, and had plenty of offers with more money and whatnot, but I guess I'm a loyal sort of person so will stay with Leicester. However, if I really get pissed off there's a good headline at the end of it all! In the meantime, I'm frustrated at sitting on the bench and I don't know really what the guts of that is . . .

'Dean is the top coach, top selector, manager — the whole shooting works. He is quite calculated and doesn't give much away, so I don't know what he wants from me, because he's never talked about it.

'It's a pretty strange situation to be in, after spending your life with New Zealand and All Black coaches who left you in no doubt about their opinions on your play.'

Laurie Mains, 'an intriguing character' who demanded discipline from his players, was probably the best, Kronfeld reflects. John Hart had his moments although the two frequently clashed, while Wayne Smith and Tony Gilbert were a 'great combination and I think hard done by' when the NZRFU replaced them with John Mitchell in 2001. But ask Kronfeld which New Zealand coach has most influenced him and he immediately replies 'Gordon Hunter' — the former New Zealand selector and Otago coach who lifted him out of Dunedin's University club team and into his Otago squad in 1992.

Kronfeld had played age-group rugby in Hawke's Bay but as a PE student in Dunedin couldn't progress into representative Otago sides, until Gordon Hunter watched him play one afternoon in 1992 and followed up with a call.

As Kronfeld recalls it, he picked up the phone in his student flat and heard a rather growly voice at the other end say, 'It's Gordon Hunter here, lad . . .' (silence) '. . . the Otago coach, lad. I want you to come along to training.'

'Aw, aw, yeah, yeah,' a stunned Kronfeld replied.

Hunter would later say that he saw Kronfeld as clever and 'amazingly flexible, very good at getting hold of the ball and staying on his feet', while for Kronfeld, the phone call marked the start of his Otago and All Black career.

That year Kronfeld played a few games for Otago Seconds and at the end of 1992 had a game for the President's XV followed by a trial for New Zealand Colts — missing team selection, he was later told, because one of the selectors was aghast at the sight of his hair, which had been plaited with coloured rubber bands to hold it in place.

From Otago to All Black turned out to be a natural progression for Kronfeld, who places much of the credit for his international career at the feet of his old Otago coach.

'Gordon was very much my mentor and I learned so much from him. You could say whatever you wanted to say, and you might get a bit of a cryptic answer but you came out of it with a lot more confidence. He was a unique character; even players who had been under him for just one or two games felt his mark. Many, many were stories told about him in changing rooms, in the pubs or at dinners — all with respect, which was cool. He was a legend really. I've never heard anything against him. To me, looking back, Otago was Gordon Hunter.

'I wish he'd been given the chance to be the All Black coach because I think he would have done a great job. I had him for four seasons at Otago and although he never really had the full fire-power team, he knocked over some of the big dogs, like the Lions and the Springboks. The following that he had in the rugby network through-out the world was huge. He was a principled man, who stood by his word. I respected him so much and that's a big part of a player–coach relationship.

'I was out of the country when he died in 2001, and in some ways it was just as well not to be there, because it would have been a night-mare.'

In 1995, Hunter's last season as Otago coach, Kronfeld inherited the No 7 jersey from All Black great Michael Jones — the player he'd al-ways idolised as a kid — and within a season had established the same devoted following as his predecessor.

Over the next half-decade, in his 50-plus test matches and two World Cup tournaments, Kronfeld would come to be considered the best open-side flanker in the world: a fearsome tackler and scavenger for the ball, a mighty runner and, if uninjured, a certainty when every All Black side was named.

But he was also an unusual kind of bloke, his fans agreed. Like the odd way he jiggled his head during the playing of the national anthem before test matches.

It wasn't that he was being disrespectful or unpatriotic — it was just that it got in the way of a ritual he had formulated early on, the kind of superstitious routine so many sports stars follow when com-peting at the top level.

The jiggling was an outward sign of the release of inner tensions for Kronfeld, allowing his muscles to relax and his thoughts to break free from everyday life, to focus on the match ahead. Get that prepara-tion wrong and his game was adversely affected. Kronfeld grins in recollection. 'Unfortunately when I got into the All Blacks you've got this anthem, which gets in the way of this preparation, but it's even more frustrating when you've got to stand there through the playing of two anthems!

'Everyone's got their hands on their heart or singing and I'm shak-ing my head. It's not that I'm not patriotic, nor because I don't love our anthem or anything like that — it's just me personally — I'll sing the praises and the accolades and the greatness of our country and all

At the remarkable age of 91, Grant Holms kicks off the season for Hervey Bay in Queensland.

Brad Johnstone pegging out his Italian jersey. Eventually, it was Johnstone the coach who was hung out to dry.

Jeremy Paul, the New Zealander who represented the Wallabies before he played state rugby.

Alan Whetton challenges American Eagles halfback Mark Pidcock during the 1991 World Cup at Gloucester.

Liam Barry hot-footing it for NEC during an athletics day in Japan.

Kevin Schuler on the burst for his Japanese club, Yamaha.

Kevin and Jan Boroevich, on their winter honeymoon in France.

Lions coach Graham Henry commiserates with his captain, Martin Johnson, after the deciding test in Sydney, 2001.

Grahame Thorne (right) and his son Bruce after playing for New Zealand Parliamentarians at the time of the 1995 World Cup in South Africa.

A team with bite! Natal Sharks team-mates Kevin Putt (right) and Mark Andrews with a team sponsor at King's Park, Durban.

John Plumtree, representing South Africa, heads for the goal line during the Hong Kong sevens tournament in 1995.

Laurie Mains in reflective mood as Cats coach in 2001.

Josh Kronfeld decked out in the Leicester gear he hasn't got to wear often enough.

Earl Va'a . . . back home in Wellington after sojourns in England, Italy and Southland.

Alex 'Grizz' Wyllie in his role as technical advisor to the Pumas.

that off the field. It was the disruption to my focus that created the stress for me.'

It even got to the point where the haka got in the way, but after having its symbolism explained, Kronfeld managed to successfully weld it in to make a positive contribution to his ritual build-up.

Otago was plunged into deep mourning in 2000 when the province's two All Black superstars, Jeff Wilson and Josh Kronfeld, announced they were retiring. Wilson later missed the game so much he returned to play a further season for Otago and New Zealand, but Kronfeld stuck to his original decision. Not that the NZRFU went out of its way to keep him. Kronfeld had given the rugby union a year's notice that he was going to have a look at playing elsewhere and says he was told: 'Be nice for you to stay, but you probably realize that we won't be able to pay you what we paid you before.'

'You think, *Hold on, I'm still the recognized AB flanker, I've played all the tests this year*, and that was frustrating,' he reflects.

Kronfeld took an eight-month break from rugby, surfed till he dropped from his Raglan beach-front home and finally got the call.

The All Blacks had registered a win and a loss in France at the end of 2000 and things had not gone so well in the first Tri-Nations games of 2001. The NZRFU was keen for him to stay on. Was there any way they could keep him, they asked?

The commitment to England had been made, Kronfeld replied, and he had already given the NZRFU a year to think it over.

'They had made it very obvious to me that they were keen to find someone new and younger. In New Zealand you don't have that hierarchy format any more of senior players versus the juniors.

'You come in at 19 and you're expected to be a senior player right away, but you're a kid. I think of myself as a 19-year-old compared to what I was like at 26 and they're two different people.

'At 29, I didn't consider I was over the hill by international standards. Look at my Leicester counterpart, Neil Back, who in 2002 is England's openside flanker at the age of 33.'

Kronfeld watches test matches on his TV and thinks, *God, I wish I was in that game*, while simultaneously reflecting that he's glad to be out of it. It would be easier, though, if he wasn't continuing to play at top competitive level.

Josh Kronfeld shrugs when asked what the future holds. Following the end of his contract with Leicester in 2003, he may opt to continue playing — France is a favourite — or he may return to New Zealand and Auckland University to study for another degree.

Whichever path he chooses, Kronfeld says he'll enjoy it. 'You soak up everything, and while you have to filter out a bit of shit, all input's good for you. I'm a pretty relaxed kind of person, I guess, and I like facing new challenges.'

For the record

Player
- Otago, 1992–2000 (69 games)
- New Zealand, 1995–2000 (56 games, 54 tests)
- Highlanders, 1996–2000 (42 games)
- Leicester, 2001–2002

Kevin Boroevich

The story goes that when Richmond RFC was formed in 1861, 10 years before the Rugby Football Union was established, one of the club's founders looked out of his window in The Strand and saw the Belgian army marching past. His eye was taken by Belgium's boldly coloured red, yellow and black flag. That would do for Richmond's colours, he decided, and more than 150 years later, Richmond Vikings still play in those distinctive red, yellow and black hoops.

Richmond, in Surrey, has always attracted London's affluent middle and upper classes. The River Thames winds lazily through the ancient borough, past the former palace of King Henry VIII, Royal Richmond Park, where the monarch once hunted deer, romantic centuries-old waterside pubs and, across the water, the tall stands of Twickenham, England's home of rugby, which dominate the skyline.

As with other middle-class bastions of 'rugger' in England, Richmond's supporters are distinguished by a dress code of cavalry twills, cravats, hacking jackets and well-polished tan brogues, a far cry from the garb worn by the average New Zealander at a rugby match.

It was in this rarified atmosphere that two New Zealanders, Kevin Boroevich and Earl Va'a from the uncompromising backgrounds of the Waitete club in Te Kuiti and the Wainuiomata Rugby League Club of Lower Hutt, would, perhaps surprisingly, find themselves totally at home . . .

When he was nine Kevin Boroevich composed a love song, 'Janeo', for Jan Cressy, his girlfriend and classmate in Standard Three at Te Kuiti Primary School. And, at the same age he fronted up every Saturday for two games with the local Waitete club.

In the morning he played for the Under 10s, and in the afternoon he was fullback for Waitete's third grade (Under 19) side. The third-grade team was always short of players, his three older brothers were there to protect him and he learned to run fast.

Those early lessons in hardening-up would be put to a stern test just eight years later, when as a 17-year-old Boroevich was selected to prop for King Country in its 1978 pre-season match against Auckland. Against him was Brad Johnstone, 10 years his senior and current All Black prop. After the game he reflected that he had done pretty well; he had suffered nightmares before the match at the task ahead of him, but he felt that he had held his own against Johnstone and King Country had only narrowly gone down to Auckland, 18–24.

He was therefore totally unprepared for the blasting he received in the dressing room after the match from the team's coach and his mentor, Colin Meads. He had not done well enough, he was told; he'd let the team down. Boroevich went home distraught, ripped the curtains off his bedroom windows and vowed he would never have that accusation thrown at him again. In his next match for King Country a couple of weeks later, he was sent off for punching and the 'wild-man Boroevich' legend was born.

At 23, Boroevich was an All Black, with six years' senior experience behind him, and would later claim the unusual distinction of being selected for the All Blacks from three separate provinces — King Country, Wellington and North Harbour — in his 19-year career of first-division rugby. In 1986 he made his first move — from King Country to Wellington — with considerations other than rugby driving him south. He had married Jan in February that year and when she was transferred to Wellington for cabin work with Air New Zealand, naturally he went too. But he recalls it was a dodgy move from a rugby perspective because Wellington's two props, Scott Crichton and Brian McGrattan, were the All Black incumbents at the time.

Boroevich shone in that competitive climate and his dynamic play

so impressed coach Earle Kirton that he made him captain, a timely and astute decision, as Boroevich would lead Wellington to first-division victory later that season.

At the end of the year he toured France with the All Blacks. He was then joined by Jan for a four-month honeymoon, during which he played a game a week for the Voiron club and the happy couple skied in the mountains nearby and enjoyed 'cruising around' in their new environment.

Kevin Boroevich in France.

He returned to New Zealand in an unsuccessful attempt to make the 1987 World Cup team, but the following year, 1988, he was back in the All Blacks, on tour to Australia — and playing provincial rugby for North Harbour.

That was to be his last tour with the All Blacks. Two years on and still playing for North Harbour at the age of 30, it was time to consider what he was going to do with his life.

'I hadn't done much about a career,' he reflects, 'and I needed to do something, because I was always broke. They were amateur days; I suppose I could have been wealthy if it had happened for me 10 years later. But I don't carry a chip about it — our generation were rich with experience.'

But fate was to take a hand. During an enforced lay-off with a slipped disc in his back, Boroevich was lying down and watching the Gulf War unfold on the TV screen when the phone rang. On the other end of the line was David Hilliard, a business consultant from England, who said he was looking for an All Black to go over as captain/assist-ant coach for the Richmond club in outer London.

Was Boroevich interested, he asked, and how soon could he get over there? 'I'm a little bit busy at the moment,' Boroevich said, de-ciding he would play hard to get. They kept talking, Boroevich named a price, Hilliard named a price and they ended up somewhere in be-tween. There were some loose ends to tie up, Kevin prevaricated: it would be at least six weeks before he could get there.

'That's fine,' said Hilliard, and to Boroevich's relief the gamble paid off.

'My back came right. It was amazing luck really, the injury could have gone either way and wrecked my career. Jan was keen to go too, because at the end of 1990 things here were a bit depressed and so we flew off to our new life at Richmond.'

It was a sharp learning curve for both sides as Richmond and their new captain/assistant coach came to grips with each other. At the first training session Boroevich stood open-mouthed as he heard Richmond's inside centre call, in piping tones, 'Could you please pass the ball out to me?'

Says Boroevich, 'I thought, *Man! Unreal!* I was blown away.'

And from his Richmond team-mates there was stunned respect as they were introduced to their New Zealand captain's unique post-match bonding sessions in the Sun Inn, recalls one of the team's locks, Martin Slagter.

'The guys were pretty awe-struck by Kevin and his personality. After the game, he would sit everyone down at the Sun Inn, where we drank, and the young guys, in particular, would be literally crapping themselves as they faced up to Kevin's beer-drinking sessions.

'There were a few occasions when Kevin certainly commanded a lot of respect. He was a lovely guy, but I have to say he was really quite a culture shock for the lads.'

The technical ability of England's props, and Jason Leonard in particular, impressed him but Boroevich was less enraptured with the style of play in vogue at that time.

'English teams' problems lay in their mentality and I think a lot of their coaches let them down. They prepared their teams for game-styles that were quite negative,' he says.

'At Richmond, we had Dave Hilliard as coach and he was an exception. He was great. His only shortfall was a professional attitude that just didn't wash really — the guys weren't committed enough.' Hilliard, in those final amateur years, was also 'right up there' with the physical preparation of the Richmond team, who had their own physiotherapists, nutritionists and trainers.

Each player was handed an individual training manual describing techniques for his position — an initiative well in advance of anything in New Zealand, Boroevich was told when he later handed his manual to the All Black selectors. The Richmond team was taken to Bath University, in the west of England, to use the university's facilities for studying the human body and this proved a revelation for Boroevich.

'It was the first time I had ever worked at different energy levels and it made me the fittest I had ever been. I was technically fit, because I was employing different muscle groups,' he recalls. 'They worked at specific energy levels for your position. I learned a lot. I wished I'd known that stuff when I was in my early twenties because it would have helped my career so much.'

At the end of 1992 Peter Thorburn, an All Black selector, came to stay with the Boroeviches at their home in St Margarets, Twickenham. Richard Loe was in trouble and had been suspended for eye-gouging, Thorburn said, and the selectors wanted Boroevich to come home so

Kevin Boroevich, English version, arriving at his new home near Twickenham.

that they could look at him again for the All Blacks.

Boroevich had loved his two years at Richmond, but the lure of pulling on the black jersey once more was irresistible.

So, in 1993 at the age of 33, and having played his last game for the All Blacks five years earlier, Boroevich lined up for the All Black trials once more.

The All Black selectors warned him in advance his position could not be guaranteed, and Boroevich missed the team for the home series against the Lions. He admits he wasn't too perturbed at being brought home on a wild goose chase as he had the consolation of playing twice in one week — for North Harbour and New Zealand Maori — against his old friends from England days. A few days later Kevin and Jan headed off to join the Begles-Bordeaux club for a two-year stint in France.

Says Boroevich: 'Those two seasons we spent living in Bordeaux are amongst the most treasured memories of our rugby travels. We made wonderful friends, people like the legendary Moga family, who had made such a contribution to Begles-Bordeaux, and the hospitality was stunning.

'I even invented the "Borok" lineout machine there, which is probably still in use!'

That was almost it for the Waitete man's playing days, but in 1998 there would be a further joy for Kevin Boroevich when, 12 years after they had married, Jan gave birth to their only child, a daughter — Amy Elizabeth Poppy Boroevich.

In his two years in England, Boroevich made a huge impact on the Richmond club, recalls Slagter, who now lives in Austin, Texas.

'We won promotion while Kevin was there; he was great for the players and he was great for the character of the side, but unfortunately he didn't stay on the pitch enough!

'The word got around that he was pretty wild and provokable and he got sent off a couple of times, which was a major frustration from his point of view and the committee's!

'He was quite soft-spoken off the field, but slip the shirt on and the eyes start rolling! Apart from that, Kevin was a joy to be around, a straight-up, straight-down guy.

'What you saw was what you got from him and we became very good mates. He was a top guy.'

For the record

Player
- New Zealand Colts, 1978–1979
- King Country, 1978–1985 (83 games)
- New Zealand Maori, 1980, 1982–1983, 1985–1986, 1993
- New Zealand, 1983–1984, 1986, 1988 (26 games, 3 tests)
- Wellington, 1986–1987 (31 games)
- North Harbour, 1988–1991, 1993 (22 games)
- Richmond, England, 1991–1993
- Begles-Bordeaux, France, 1993–1995

Earl Va'a

This has got to be some kind of New Zealand sporting record — a five-year international and overseas playing career launched on the strength of just 100 minutes of senior rugby.

First-five Earl Va'a would be the first to admit he's been tinny, and being in the right place at the right time has certainly paid off handsomely for this personable former league player.

It came about this way. In 1996 the Wellington league season had finished early and Va'a, a representative for his province, turned out to play a social rugby game in Lower Hutt for his mate's Paremata-Plimmerton Senior 4ths team. It was the first game of rugby he'd played since his first XV days as a pupil at St Bernard's College in Lower Hutt and he quite enjoyed the experience.

'I grew up in Wainuiomata, which was real league heartland, and so when I left school I just carried on playing league along with my mates,' he explains. 'I was vaguely thinking about switching to rugby the following year, but events overtook me.'

Wayne Guppy, the mayor of Upper Hutt, who was also coach of the Wellington Development team at the time, heard that Va'a had played a game of rugby, rang him and drafted him straight into his Wellington Development team.

Va'a was on the field for five minutes in Wellington's match against the Auckland Development XV, a full 80 in the next against Otago Development and a further 15 when the Wellington and Counties Manukau Development teams played a curtain-raiser for the Wellington versus Counties-Manukau NPC match at Athletic Park.

In that last game he had a cracker and Manu Samoa's coach, Bryan Williams, who was seated in the grandstand, had no hesitation in drafting Va'a, of Samoan parentage, into his team for its end-of-season tour to the United Kingdom.

Then, on tour, the run of fortune continued when Manu Samoa's regular first-five Darren Kellett was injured. Va'a leapfrogged into the starting line-up for Manu Samoa's test against Ireland and had a huge game. Sitting in the stand were officials from the Richmond club in England, who had come to spy out the Samoans' talent in preparation for their club's match against Manu Samoa three weeks later, and they were mightily impressed by the team's zippy replacement inside back.

Richmond was the final game on tour and Va'a, who got a knock on the head early in that match, didn't remember much about the game thereafter.

'But I suppose I must have done a few good things,' he recalls, 'because that night, after the game, Richmond approached our Manu Samoa agent and the next morning they offered me an enticing three-year contract with the club.'

'Gee, I'm onto something playing rugby,' Va'a thought to himself. He returned to New Zealand with the team, chewed over the proposal with his wife, Ngaire, and telephoned his acceptance. Within a month of boarding the plane at London's Heathrow Airport, Va'a was back on the rugby field — in England — and ready for the challenge.

His first impression on arrival at the Richmond club in January 1997 was one of astonishment. 'I hadn't had any senior rugby club experience at all, but all the same I was surprised at how poor the skill levels were. That changed during my time, partly due I think to the influence of overseas players and coaches,' he says. 'Playing standards had lifted dramatically by the time I left three years later.

'The old pint in the pub after training had given way to a far stricter regime on the correct way to treat the body and there was more discipline imposed through the professional climate which came into full force while I was there.'

Va'a had by-passed the normal player's route to an overseas career and so he doubly relished the opportunity to play alongside international stars, including the likes of the Richmond captain, England's Ben Clarke, Australia's Matt Pinney and Welsh international brothers Scott and Craig Quinnell as well as Adrian Davies, who generously shared with Va'a much of his knowledge on first-five play.

In that first season, Richmond made it to the first division, beating a couple of England's 'top dogs', Leicester and Harlequins, in the process.

'There were great celebrations, but we could never repeat that success,' he says.

'Thinking back on those times, I'm very grateful to Richmond, because it changed my life. It turned me into a committed rugby player and our family grew to love the place.'

Italy followed when the Richmond contract ended, and Va'a joined the Mike Brewer-coached Scaviline club in L'Aquila for the 1999–2000 seasons. As with Richmond, Va'a says that one of the biggest thrills came from being in a team which achieved above its expected level.

'We were a club of nobodies and we ended up making the finals of the Italian competition. To get there we beat Benetton away, which was huge. They needed a last-minute conversion to draw the match and failed. To win at Benetton was the highlight of Italy for me.'

In 2001, Va'a and his family returned to New Zealand to live, waving goodbye to five years in Europe. They had loved the leafy greenness of Richmond and Kew Gardens, their home in St Margarets, Twickenham, the City of London, their new English friends and the solid grounding Va'a had received in rugby. While at Scaviline they had acquired a working understanding of Italian, a new-found skill at skiing and a fondness for Italy — 'pity about the rugby' and the autostrada system.

Va'a had learned his rugby overseas, and at 29 moved to Southland in 2001 for his introduction to the NPC competition. A knee injury wrecked that season, which was a cause of deep regret to Va'a and the Southland RFU, says its 2002 manager, Craig Morton.

'Earl was very dedicated and professional and he was an inspiration to the younger players. It was a real shame that his NPC season was cut short and quite staggering to think that a guy with this amount of ability was playing his first season of New Zealand rugby at the age of 29!'

In 2002, Va'a is employed by the Wellington Rugby Union, plays senior rugby for Hutt Valley Marist and internationally for Manu Samoa. His sights are firmly set on making the Manu Samoa team for the 2003 Rugby World Cup. 'I'll be 30 then, but I aim to give the young guys a bit of a hurry-up.'

It might be rugby these days for Va'a, but he still likes to turn out to support his old league club, Wainuiomata, along with a close mate from those early league days, Tana Umaga.

'The league boys supported me in my switch and, to me, rugby's like one big game of league anyway,' says Va'a. 'I owe a lot to my league background and guys like Ken Laban, my old captain, who was a big influence on me. I still pick his brains for moves.'

Oddly, his mentor has travelled a similar path. Laban, who played provincial league and rugby for Wellington, and holds coaching certificates for both codes, is today a rugby commentator on radio and television and says he has become more union-oriented.

'It's really not such a big deal because the two games are so closely aligned now. The biggest influence in rugby has been the 'use it or lose it' rule, which has made the game far more fluid. Players are reluctant to commit themselves in the ruck and maul in big numbers and that has freed the game up.

'As John Mitchell said to me: "Rugby is league with the lineouts!"'

For the record

Player
- Manu Samoa, 1996, 2002 (26 games)
- Richmond, England, 1996–1999
- Scaviline, L'Aquila, Italy, 1999–2000
- Southland, 2001 (8 games)

Postscript: After Va'a's departure, Richmond RFC embarked on some expensive player-purchasing contracts, which led to its bankruptcy. However, the club, threatened with extinction, was saved when former players and supporters rallied around. The club's headquarters, the Richmond Athletic Ground, was bought back by the club, but the glory days have gone. Richmond Vikings now compete in the lower London Division South League competition.

SCOTLAND

For a country which refused to play against the All Blacks in 1924 because it was unhappy with the financial arrangements, Scotland has come to display a deep affection for New Zealand in matters of rugby. It has toured down under regularly in modern times, inculcating All Black strategies and style into its own game. Simultaneously has come a modern phenomenon: Kilted Kiwis, New Zealanders who have broken into the Scottish national team. It started with Sean Lineen and latterly there have been Glenn Metcalfe, John Leslie, Martin Leslie, Gordon Simpson and Brendan Laney. While the game's headquarters are in Edinburgh, where Murrayfield can accommodate almost 70,000 spectators, rugby now flourishes in the borders, in towns like Hawick, Galashiels and Melrose.

Founded
1873
IRB
1886
Clubs
276
Players
10,303 men, 600 women
Rugby Nomads
John Leslie, Brendan Laney

John Leslie

John Leslie had anticipated Gregor Townsend's delicate chip-kick in the 1999 World Cup pool match against the Springboks at Murrayfield so perfectly he was able to gather the ball on the run and make a bee-line for the goalposts.

The Scots had been rank outsiders to win this contest against the reigning champions but having operated with enormous commitment and passion for more than 50 minutes, they were level pegging when Leslie latched on to Townsend's kick.

A seven-pointer would have given Scotland a vital advantage over the South Africans. It might even have provided the inspiration for a sensational upset. But all the hopes, all the dreams, were shattered when Leslie was 3 m short of the goalposts. That's when Springbok Deon Kayser thwacked into him.

Had Kayser driven into Leslie, he has not the slightest doubt his momentum would have carried him through to the goalline. But instead, the Bok effectively threw himself over the top of Leslie. It had the effect of stopping the former New Zealander dead in his tracks. Worse, Leslie's left ankle took the entire weight of both himself and his tackler. He went down in a heap. Leslie had broken his leg as a 14-year-old when playing in a fourth-form trial. This felt horribly similar. As play continued, he sat forlornly out from the goalposts waiting for Scotland's medical men to arrive and assess the damage.

Play seemed to take ages to come to a halt and when it did, it was because Scotland had been awarded a penalty. As the South African players retired to await the kick, they discovered Leslie parked there. Pieter Rossouw and Robbie Fleck inquired of his wellbeing. 'No good, mate,' came back Leslie. 'I'm out of here.'

Out of here, indeed. Leslie had popped the tendons in his left ankle. It would require two operations and the insertion of a pin before the ankle would finally regain its original strength and allow Leslie to recapture the form that, based on his performances for Otago at NPC level and Scotland in the Six Nations over the preceding 15 months, had had many critics branding him the most accomplished midfield back in the world.

It was a monumentally disappointing occasion for Leslie. His parents were at the ground watching, he was operating alongside his

John Leslie couldn't have marked his final appearance for Otago more appropriately, the team securing the NPC trophy with a crushing win over Waikato in 1998.

brother, Martin, in the Scottish team and this was the important opening fixture of a campaign that, hopefully, would see the Scots, with the home advantage, progress to the semifinals again, as they had in 1991. Given the severity of the injury, there was never a possibility of Leslie taking any further part in the tournament. World Cup rules demanded that before a new player could be introduced, the original had to withdraw.

And so, a once-in-a-lifetime opportunity to participate in rugby's greatest show, including, as it turned out, a quarterfinal clash with John Hart's All Blacks, was shattered. 'It was a wrench to have that opportunity taken away,' says Leslie, who, with his foot in plaster, witnessed the All Black game from the radio commentary box as Graeme Moody's comments person. Mission unaccomplished, Leslie hobbled off to Fukuoka, in Japan, to begin his commitment to the Sanix club.

Achieving in Japan and the UK would bring its satisfactions, not least in monetary rewards, but Leslie had dearly wanted to be an All Black, like his father, who had captained New Zealand with huge success from 1974 to 1976.

Given Otago's spectacular success in 1998, when the team averaged 60 points a game through the final six weeks of its successful NPC campaign, with Leslie a major contributor, he was quietly optimistic about his prospects of promotion. However, he was ignored by the All Black selectors, whose chief at the time was John Hart. When Leslie realised that he and Tabai Matson were the only two Super 12 midfielders unwanted, he knew it was time to look elsewhere.

'Every other midfielder had been given encouragement,' says Leslie. 'When I couldn't even make the reserves for the All Black trial or New Zealand A in a year when the selectors were obviously considering fresh talent, I knew I was never going to achieve international honours in my own country.'

Further dampening his enthusiasm was a comment from one of the selectors that, approaching 28, he was considered too old. 'That annoyed me,' he says. 'Surely, if they were selecting the best players, age, within reason, was irrelevant. Joe Stanley and Frank Bunce were 29 and 30 when they entered the international scene, and you'd have to say they were pretty successful. I felt that, like them, I'd become stronger and better with age. I believe I'd been classified for my performances when I was younger. But rugby is one big learning curve. I was seeing the game quite differently since I'd entered the first-class scene seven years earlier.'

During a trip to Japan to visit his old Otago buddy Jamie Joseph, Leslie had been offered a three-year contract by the Sanix club of Fukuoka. Now that it was apparent he wasn't appreciated by the All Black selectors, he decided to accept the deal.

Like countless other quality New Zealand players who'd either ended their international careers or never been granted the opportunity to launch them, Leslie could have become an almost forgotten figure in the Land of the Rising Sun but for a chance encounter with a Scottish friend of his father, John Thorburn, who was on a fleeting visit to New Zealand.

Aware of Leslie's talents, Thorburn, upon learning he was heading for Japan, asked what he was doing between the conclusion of the NPC and his exit from New Zealand.

'Nothing much,' replied Leslie.

'Then why not come to Scotland and play the off-season there,' said Thorburn.

'Sounds a good idea,' said Leslie.

And so it came to pass that Leslie, blessed with Scottish ancestry (his grandfather had played soccer for Hibernian and Scottish school-boys) flew out for Edinburgh in the first week of November 1998. Thorburn had acquainted Scottish coach Jim Telfer of the development, which thrilled Telfer. He couldn't believe his good luck.

There were no contracts drawn up, no payments. For Leslie, it was purely a rugby experience. But what an experience it would become! Within a week of arriving in Scotland, he found himself wearing the Glasgow Caledonians' jersey against the Springboks, something he describes as 'a terrifying experience'.

'We had one brief training run the day before the game, then assembled 90 minutes before kick-off,' says Leslie. 'We had almost no moves organised and little combination. Not surprisingly, the Springboks put 60 points on us.'

Notwithstanding the Caledonians' hiding, Leslie was fast-tracked into the Scottish test team, which obviously didn't surprise Springbok coach Nick Mallett, who went on record as describing him as the best inside centre in the world.

If Leslie needed a reminder that rugby attitudes in Scotland would be poles apart from those in New Zealand, it was provided by a colleague only 30 minutes before the bus departed for Murrayfield for his test debut, against the Springboks.

'I'd only been in the country 11 days,' says Leslie, 'and was sitting on my hotel bed contemplating the game ahead, trying to focus on what life would be like at test level against the Boks. Suddenly, into my room walks one of my new team-mates. "John, my boy," he says in jovial fashion, "only three-and-a-half more hours." "Three-and-a-half more hours to what?" I asked him, just a little bit confused. "Three-and-a-half more hours till we're on the piss!"'

The Scots didn't win that game but, through a sequence of remarkable events five months later, they did take out the Five Nations Championship, nosing out the raging-hot favourite, England, having been quoted at odds of 100 to 1 before the competition had started. Equally as unlikely was Leslie's participation in the triumph.

Leslie should have been playing for Sanix in Japan through that period, but following some delicate negotiations, with a boss who, fortunately, had his best interests at heart, he was released for the duration of the championship.

For the final round of matches, Scotland was drawn to play France in Paris, a daunting challenge for any team, while Wales (steadily improving under new coach Graham Henry) was hosting unbeaten England at Wembley.

Everyone predicted victories to France and England, which would secure for Clive Woodward's Englishmen a glorious double, the Grand Slam and the Triple Crown. Displaying not a little arrogance, the English media dismissed Wales as a serious contender at Wembley. One commentator suggested it was scarcely worth their while even turning up!

Well, Scotland produced a boomer in Paris to bound to the front of the competition, a lead which was expected to evaporate within 24 hours. Among those who thought Wales had no show was Leslie. He was back in Edinburgh, watching the Wembley game on television as the impossible began to unfold.

'I didn't give the Welsh a chance,' says Leslie. 'England seemed to be all over them, but they hung in tenaciously and when Scott Gibbs scored just before full time, I was jumping around shouting uncontrollably. When Neil Jenkins added the conversion, I bolted down to the pub to join the guys to celebrate.'

Leslie had enjoyed international rugby and his association with Scotland to such an extent that he was now reluctant to abandon it. So back in Fukuoka, he described his feelings to the president of Sanix. Obviously, if the president had been a mean-minded individual, Leslie would have had to sacrifice his burgeoning international career. 'But the president of the club was a fantastic man, a real rugby enthusiast,' says Leslie. 'He admires New Zealand and Scotland and he understood my dilemma.

'A couple of UK clubs were chasing me and although I thought life in Japan was great, at 28, I realised I wasn't ready to abandon rugby at the highest competitive level.

'The president understood and wished me well. I keep in touch with him and send him a bottle of whisky each year.'

Leslie took up the offer to join the Newcastle Falcons club in the north of England, from where he could commute easily to Edinburgh. The 1999–2000 rugby season had the potential to become his most memorable. He was enjoying his new club, and Ian McGeechan, who'd succeeded Jim Telfer as Scotland's coach, appointed him captain. If that wasn't good enough, in January 2000 he married Carmel

O'Loughlin, a girl from Timaru who he'd met at Otago University.

A rugby star John might have been, but Carmel came with pretty impressive credentials herself. As a gymnast, she had represented New Zealand at the 1990 Commonwealth Games, finishing fourth in the floor event and tenth overall, and participated on the world circuit. Such was her athletic ability, she became screen heroine Lucy Lawless' stunt double in *Xena: Warrior Princess*.

There, the good times ceased for Leslie in 2000, the rest of the year producing frustration after frustration. The ankle continued to trouble him, but he preferred to ignore it as he led Scotland into the Six Nations Championship.

Scotland's first opponent was the competition's new chum, Italy, in Rome. To Leslie's dismay, Scotland suffered an embarrassing defeat, followed by losses to Wales at Cardiff and France at Murrayfield. Skipper Leslie's record was a dismal three losses from three outings. Although he came through the Italian match unscathed he says he was fighting injury throughout the 2000 championship. 'I should never have taken on the captaincy, but it was such a privilege to be offered it, I didn't feel obliged to turn it down. We've all played on with dodgy legs, convinced that eventually the problem would come right. Well, this time it didn't.'

X-rays revealed a piece of cartilage floating in the ankle, which necessitated a second operation and brought Leslie's season to an abrupt finish. It also cost him the Scottish tour of New Zealand, which was an obvious disappointment. He was beginning to think he would never play against the men in black.

The summer was one of 'huge rehabilitation', getting the ankle right. Just when he felt he was recapturing full fitness and, with it, all his old confidence, Leslie was summoned to appear before Newcastle Falcons' chairman Rob Andrew.

He was completely unprepared for what eventuated. 'Rob said he wanted me to leave the club, saying I would never play again for the first or second team. He had his reasons. I asked him to give me the opportunity to train hard and prove my fitness and worthiness. He said it didn't matter what I did, I would never play for the Falcons again. He assured me it was not a disciplinary matter, but he gave no reasons for my sacking.

'It was bizarre. And it left me shocked. I had a wife and five-month-old son and a house in Newcastle. What was I going to do?'

Leslie says that in the week that followed, while he contemplated his options, Andrew told the local newspaper that he (Leslie) had demanded a first-team spot. 'That was completely untrue,' says Leslie. 'He was making excuses for letting me go. And I was the one getting all the bad publicity. It was very embarrassing and upsetting.

'There was a clause in my contract that said if by speaking out publicly I brought the club into disrepute they could withhold my earnings. As they owed me a considerable amount of money, I was effectively gagged.

'The whole affair was horrible. I'd never experienced anything like it in my life. But I had to move on.'

What appeared a disaster at that time was to become, in Leslie's words, 'a blessing in disguise', for he was soon snapped up by Northampton, a flourishing club 150 kilometres south of Newcastle. The contrast, he quickly appreciated, was vast. Northampton possessed facilities which Leslie describes as 'fantastic'.

'They have a super stadium with a capacity of 13,000, one which would be an ideal model for modest-sized unions in New Zealand. The pitch is beautiful and the locals get right in behind their team; in fact, they're rugby mad, whereas rugby means nothing in Newcastle.'

Unburdened by leadership, Leslie returned to Six Nations action in 2001, featuring in the entire campaign, which stretched out over eight months following the outbreak of foot and mouth disease.

Then he finally got to confront his countrymen, appearing opposite Aaron Mauger when John Mitchell's touring side played at Murrayfield in November. A typically defiant Scottish effort kept the All Blacks tryless until the 70th minute, when the floodgates opened. In a flash, Mitchell's men had bolted from 18–6 (six Andrew Mehrtens' penalty goals) to 37–6.

Leslie missed the opening two matches of the 2002 Six Nations with a strained calf. Although he declared himself available for the Irish match, the selectors opted to keep their winning combination intact. But Leslie was back for the France and Wales games, the latter producing a thrilling victory at the Millennium Stadium in Cardiff.

And that was it. Following the Welsh game he announced his retirement from international play, content, at the age of 31, to concentrate on club rugby with Northampton. In four seasons, he'd made 23 test appearances and also appeared twice for Scotland against the Barbarians. Not bad for a player the New Zealand selectors weren't remotely interested in.

While Leslie says he enjoyed every minute of his association with Scotland, and describes Jim Telfer as 'a wonderful man, right up there with Gordon Hunter, someone you'd go to war for', he concedes that the rugby culture there is vastly different from that of the country in which he grew up. 'In the changing room before Six Nations encounters at Murrayfield, it's not unusual to have guys in overalls, usually with a broom, come in and walk about. No one seems to mind. I could imagine how Grizz Wyllie would have reacted! In New Zealand there are certain protocols before a game, but things are much looser in Scotland.

'On another occasion, at a team meeting before an international, no one had noticed that there were no chairs in the team room. We all just stood there. We short guys at the back couldn't see anything that was going on!

'In 2001 after two really physical games against Tonga and Argentina, we started training for the All Black game. The boys were sore, so a light training would have been appropriate. But the forwards were assembled in four corners, each group with a ball. They were told to face out — 'to the four corners of the earth' — then on command to turn and sprint hard to the opposite corner, without slowing down or sidestepping. Predictably, all four collided in the middle. Miraculously, they all survived. That particular exercise went on for about five minutes, which left me wondering . . .'

Northampton was one of English rugby's also-rans when Leslie arrived but by the end of the 2001–2002 season the club had improved to fifth in the premiership and positioned itself for prestigious European fixtures. Behind the marked improvement was the New Zealand connection. No, not just John Leslie, but a coach named Wayne Smith and a former All Black flanker named Andrew Blowers.

Smith arrived at Northampton in November 2001, having failed to win the support of the NZRFU for a third term as All Black coach. The man who'd guided the Crusaders to successive Super 12 victories in 1999 and 2000 made an instant impact.

He certainly won over Leslie. 'It was great to be operating under a quality New Zealand coach again,' he says. 'Wayne has a fantastic knowledge of the game and gives you sharp coaching instructions. He provides maximum description in few words, so you know exactly what he means. And after the game he'll comment on your personal play, which is mighty. It's what every player wants, I'm sure.

'Now matter how old you are as a sportsman, you never stop learning. And thanks to Wayne Smith, I'm still learning plenty.'

Besides the Kiwis, the Northampton team of 2002 featured Scottish internationals Budge Poutney (as captain) and Tom Smith, Frenchman Olivier Brouzet, England test players Matt Dawson, Ben Cohen and Nick Beale and former Australian Peter Jorgensen.

Ask Leslie to nominate the most treasured memories of a first-class career that stretches way back to 1991 and he unhesitatingly singles out his time with Otago.

Of his experiences in the Otago jersey, he says they made him the player and the person he is today. 'Those marvellous years with Otago provided me with the rules on how to behave and how to go about life. I do want to go back and live in Dunedin and be an Otago person. I'm looking forward to that when my UK rugby experience comes to a close.' The onfield highlights from his 120 games for Otago were the 1991 NPC success under Laurie Mains (in his debut season), the victories over the Lions in 1993 and Springboks in 1994, and the 1998 season when Otago, under Tony Gilbert, swept everything before it.

To those, he would add Scotland's stunning victory in the 1999 Five Nations.

For the record

Player
- Otago, 1991–1998 (120 games)
- Otago Highlanders, 1996–1998 (32 games)
- Glasgow Caledonians, 1998
- Newcastle, 1999–2000
- Northampton, 2000–2002
- Scotland, 1998–2002 (27 games, 23 tests)

Brendan Laney

It was an unreal situation, for sure. Brendan Laney had only been in his newly adopted country for four days and there he was getting ready to play for Scotland A against the All Blacks at Perth.

Perth? He didn't even know where Perth was. 'When we boarded the bus in Edinburgh to travel there,' he says, 'I had no idea whether we were heading north, south, east or west!'

Then when he took the field at Perth (which is actually about 70 kilometres north of Edinburgh), Laney says he recognised every player in a black jersey opposite him, but was largely unfamiliar with his own team-mates.

The so-called 'enemy' included Paul Miller, Simon Maling, Pita Alatini, Kees Meeuws and Tom Willis, who had been his brothers-in-arms just 17 days earlier when Otago had taken on Canterbury in the NPC final. Laney, still wearied through jet lag, watched with fascination as Miller and Maling, two of his great mates and newcomers to the international scene, went through the haka routine. Maling made the mistake of winking at Laney, thereby losing concentration and, to Laney's glee, 'completely cocking up' the haka.

Scotland A went down 35–13 and Laney concedes that he spent most of the game chasing the guys in black around Perth's McDiarmid Park. On the rare occasions he needed to communicate with his own players, he just referred to them as 'mate' because, with one or two exceptions, he didn't know any of their names.

If that wasn't weird enough for the man they call Chainsaw, immediately after the game the Scottish selectors were inviting him to join their squad the following morning for the coming Saturday's international at Murrayfield.

Four days off the flight from New Zealand, he was being asked to play a test against the All Blacks. He was having trouble getting his head around everything. Life was advancing at a giddy pace. Naturally, he accepted the selectors' invitation to join the party at Murrayfield — who wouldn't? — but he sought a dispensation from coach Ian McGeechan.

Might he, upon the team's return to Edinburgh, spend one evening at home with his wife, Miranda? Fresh from Dunedin, having never previously set foot in the UK, she was feeling just a little lonely and bewildered. She hadn't seen much of her husband since their arrival.

McGeechan consented and Laney spent a relaxing evening with his wife, the pair of them trying to absorb all that had happened within a week of departing Dunedin.

The naming of Laney at fullback for Scotland precipitated something of an uproar. Critics and former Scottish internationals alike criticised the selection. He expected there would be a backlash. 'After all, I had come straight from NPC to test selection for my adopted country,' he says. 'I could see where the critics were coming from. It didn't worry me. I'd long ago learnt to absorb bad publicity.

'Besides, I hadn't made the rules. My ancestry entitled me to represent Scotland, and the selectors said they wanted me. I wasn't going to give up that opportunity in a hurry.

'Naturally, there followed a flurry of media interviews. In all of them, I said if there was someone better than me for the position, then let the selectors pick him. I advised the media to stop whinging and to get in behind the team. Generally speaking, they were very good about my selection but, as you would expect, there were a few who resented another Kiwi bolting into the side.'

Like any New Zealander, Laney had wanted to be an All Black. His best opportunity had been in 1998, when he scored 16 tries as Otago took a stranglehold on the NPC. But the selectors of the time, headed by John Hart, ignored him, as they had John Leslie, who had preceded Laney into the Scottish team.

'It probably counted against me that I finished up as a utility player, someone who could operate as happily at first-five as fullback and wing. Twenty years earlier, there was a demand for utilities on All Black tours, but the modern game is all about specialists. And I guess I wasn't one of those. I wasn't angry I never became an All Black, just disappointed.'

It was Marie Strang, his grandmother on his mother's side, who qualified him for test selection at Murrayfield. She was born at Lesmahagow, in Scotland, in 1932.

Unlike Shane Howarth and Brett Sinkinson, who'd played a couple of seasons for Wales before it was disclosed that they had no Welsh ancestry whatsoever, Laney was genuinely of Scottish descent. He had every right to be standing on Murrayfield opposite Anton Oliver's men as the band launched into 'Flower of Scotland', which he sang heartily. He remembers thinking during the preliminaries what a lucky guy he was to be there.

His team-mates included fellow New Zealanders John Leslie, who'd broken into the international scene in equally dramatic circumstances three years earlier, and Gordon Simpson.

Predictably, the All Blacks won the game decisively, 37–6, but Scotland had the satisfaction of keeping them tryless until the final 10 minutes.

There could have been a fourth try, but Laney prevented his old Otago buddy Oliver from forcing the ball over the goalline. Laney had invited him to 'have a go' as he surged towards the goalline. Denied the five-pointer, Oliver made no comment, just tendered a wry smile towards his former colleague. Another time Laney gave Kelleher a friendly tap on the head, but Kelleher just ignored him. 'Obviously, the Otago boys were under instructions not to get friendly with me,' says Laney.

For Laney, the test dinner was truly special, with Scotland's grand old traditions being preserved. He loved it as the haggis was piped in and he allowed himself to sample a wee dram of finest Highland whisky. It was, he reflected, a long way from Temuka, in South Canterbury, where his rugby career had started.

Brendan was just four when the Laney family settled in Temuka, where his father, Joe, a policeman, soon became a local identity. Although Joe was a rugby devotee, and was soon intimately involved with the Temuka club, Brendan initially played the round ball code. That's because the Laneys lived opposite the soccer ground.

He was 10 when he first sampled rugby action, but it wasn't until he was in the sixth form at Timaru Boys' High School that rugby started to receive his undivided attention. Until then, he'd had a go at most sports — 'tennis, golf, cricket, anything but schoolwork!'

So that Brendan could negotiate the 15-kilometre daily trip between Temuka and Timaru, his father bought him a Hillman Imp, which became as much a part of him as the nickname Chainsaw that he would later acquire. The Timaru High first XV coach, Grant McFarlane, who would become a lifelong friend, and who was assisted in 1991 by the South Canterbury representative coach, Kevin Gloag (later to coach Laney with Otago and the Highlanders), soon appreciated that in Laney he had tapped into a rich rugby talent. Laney became the catalyst for one of the school's most successful seasons.

Operating mostly from the wing but occasionally at centre, he scored an astonishing 64 tries in the one season as Timaru put away such traditional rivals as St Andrew's College and Southland Boys' High School and ran Otago Boys' High School to one point.

On Saturdays, Timaru competed in the local Under 20 competition, where it twice hit the century mark and exceeded 50 points on most occasions. Laney recalls that, after a while, most opponents were reluctant to play them. The team also included Tevita Vaikona, another wing, who now plays professional league for Bradford in the UK.

'Brendan was a self-motivated player,' says McFarlane, who still teaches at the school. 'He combined a mix of skill, vision and understanding, a player who was a champion at making something out of nothing.'

Against Otago Boys' High, Laney attempted a penalty goal from halfway, out of the mud. 'We thought he was dreaming,' says McFarlane, 'but the ball grazed the upright, almost snatching a fairytale victory for us.' Gloag felt he could not ignore Laney's skills, and even though he was only 17 he selected him on the wing for South Canterbury against John Hart's New Zealand Colts.

Laney didn't allow the occasion to faze him. In fact, he played in an interschool fixture the day before, then proceeded to celebrate his rep debut with a try, but it wasn't enough to stop South Canterbury going down 46–14. He marked Damon Kaui, who'd run in four tries against North Otago, and had the satisfaction of keeping him tryless.

Gloag decided to release Laney for the Under 18 representative side, recalling him for the all-important promotion-relegation match at season's end against Marlborough in Blenheim — a winning performance that elevated Gloag's men to the second division for 1992. Laney was on his way. For the next three seasons, he was a permanent fixture in the South Canterbury team, mostly in the No 13 jersey, missing only one of 40 matches. Both he and the rep team prospered.

In 1993, South Canterbury overachieved, finishing second only to North Auckland in the NPC second division and ahead of Counties and Bay of Plenty. Unfortunately, it was still the amateur days, when the NZRFU insisted that the venues for semifinals should be the reverse of what happened in round-robin play. And so South Canterbury had to trek to Pukekohe to tackle Ross Cooper's Counties team. The challenge was beyond them.

Still, the match was telecast live throughout New Zealand and gave a great lift to South Canterbury rugby, which had been pretty much in the doldrums since the side had been relegated from the first division in 1980. Laney had his eyes opened to the opportunities available through rugby when he toured the United States and Wales in 1992 with the New Zealand Youth team, a tour on which all the players were sponsored by their clubs. Temuka raised the necessary funds to get him away. His consistently high-quality performances at NPC level were recognised in 1994 when he was invited to attend the New Zealand Colts coaching school and trials at Porirua College in Wellington.

He couldn't believe it when his name was read out for the three-match trip to Australia. 'I was blown away,' he says. 'I phoned my old man and gave him the great news. What a buzz for both of us.' Among the players at Porirua, and subsequently named in the team, was Jonah Lomu, who as a 19-year-old had just made his test debut.

Laney's major concern at Porirua was how he would fare in the dreaded beep test. He was amazed when Lomu, who went before him, conked out at level six. The next guy made it to level 10.

'I was determined to better both of them and I made it to level 12, which I don't think I've managed since!'

Laney found himself in some pretty august company, with many of his team-mates having already aspired to Super 12 level.

The backline selected for the international against Australia in Sydney read like this: halfback: Justin Marshall; first-five: Carlos Spencer; second-five: Daryl Gibson; centre: Brendan Laney; wings: Tana Umaga and Jonah Lomu; fullback: Adrian Cashmore.

Andrew Mehrtens and Todd Miller, who would both go on to represent New Zealand, could only make the reserves bench!

The team was captained from No 8 by Taine Randell, the pack also featuring Kees Meeuws and Anton Oliver. Another who took his place on the reserves bench was Jerry Collins.

Not surprisingly, that team, coached by Lin Colling, beat the Aussies in the test, 41–31, having racked up scores of 76 and 60 in the lead-up games. Laney returned home, his reputation enhanced, as the equal top try-scorer along with Lomu and Umaga.

A vivid memory is of Lomu, before the first game, speaking reverently of the moment he received his first All Black jersey. 'It was inspirational stuff and I know we all regarded the black colts jersey we pulled on as the equivalent of the real thing.'

Upon his return, Laney received a call from Gerald Simmonds, manager of the Otago team, inquiring if he would be interested in an off-season sevens trip to Sri Lanka. It was an offer he found impossible to refuse.

On tour, the team's coach, former All Black Arthur Stone, convinced Laney that there was a future for him in Otago, where he would be more in the limelight, which was important now that he had reached New Zealand Colts status. He linked up with Stone's Kaikorai club.

Stone 'mothered' Laney during his initial months in Dunedin. 'I was only three hours' drive from Temuka,' he says, 'but suddenly I was away from my family and friends, flatting for the first time. I was out of my comfort zone. I know my mother was terribly concerned. People in flats in Dunedin didn't have good reputations!'

Gordon Hunter, the Otago coach, used Laney sparingly in 1995, preferring John Leslie and Marc Ellis in the centres, Paul Cooke and Jason Wright on the wings and Jeff Wilson at fullback. Laney was on the reserves bench for the NPC semifinal at Pukekohe, getting 'a taste' of first-division rugby.

The next year, when Glenn Ross took over the Otago reins, Laney featured at both fullback and wing and shared the goalkicking duties with Tony Brown, although for much of the NPC campaign he bided his time on the reserves bench.

It was more of the same in 1997 — two games at fullback, four on the wing and a bunch on the reserves bench. Until the final fixture against Canterbury at Carisbrook, that is, when Ross phoned Laney and asked him if he would like to play at first-five.

'Hell, I'd never played there in my life, except for the final 10 minutes of the Auckland game the weekend before, when Tony Brown was off the field. I was shocked, but I was prepared to give it a go. Mind you, I'd have played hooker if he'd asked me to. I just love to be involved. I bet I featured prominently in Canterbury's pre-match planning; a rookie first-five — you always target them!

'Although I was as nervous as hell, things worked out pretty well. The main requirements of a first-five are being able to kick and pass and I was fortunate to possess those basic skills.'

Although Otago pulled off a crushing victory, costing Canterbury a home semifinal, it would be another four years before Laney's talents as a flyhalf were fully utilised. With Brown away on All Black duty for much of the 2001 season, Laurie Mains, back in Otago after a four-year stint in South Africa, handed Laney the No 10 jersey.

It was his performances with Otago during 1998, when Tony Gilbert's team reached stellar heights, that really put Laney on the map, pushing him close to All Black selection.

One evening he was in a pub in Dunedin — drinking orange juice, of course — a place popular with university students, commonly known among the rugby fraternity as scarfies. One of them acknowledged Laney. 'G'day, Chainsaw, how are you going?'

Chainsaw? What's he on about, thought Laney?

A little later, Laney, returning from the bar, accidentally knocked this fellow's glass out of his hand. He apologised profusely.

'I'll get you another one,' said Laney.

'No worry, Chainsaw. I'm fine.'

'Why are you calling me Chainsaw?'

'Because you cut through backlines.'

If Laney thought that was the end of it, he was in for a rude shock when he turned out for Otago the following weekend. It was at the time of the mayoral elections and draped across the fence at Carisbrook was a sign declaring Chainsaw for Mayor.

Whenever play went his way, he could hear shouts of, 'Go, Chainsaw!' Team-mate Reuben Parkinson, enthusiastic about the new nickname, suggested to Laney that if he scored a try, he should then pretend to start a chainsaw.

All of which happened. 'I never thought it would stick,' says Laney, 'but it sure did. It's even followed me to Scotland. In my first outing over here people were barracking for Chainsaw.'

The 1998 season was one of spectacular achievement for Otago. In claiming the NPC crown for the first time in seven seasons the team scored 67 tries. It registered successive victories of 84–10 and 82–10 against Northland and Wellington and averaged 60 points a game throughout the final six weeks.

Laney finished with 15 tries, equalling the NPC record set 14 years earlier by Auckland's Terry Wright. In the semifinal against Taranaki (won 61–12), Chainsaw scored four tries and added a dropped goal as well. In the final against Waikato, he scored a further two tries.

If he was ever going to wow the All Black selectors, this was it. But there was no end-of-season tour in 1998 and when the World Cup training squad was named the following season, his name was missing. 'I aimed as high as I could,' says Laney, 'and first division was my lot. I remember the delight everyone felt when Tony Brown made it in 1999. His car was decorated for his return. It would have been marvellous to have experienced that, but I wasn't going to hang myself through missing out. Rugby's only a game, after all.'

Laney believes that his playing 'the odd dud game' counted against him. 'It was probably a concentration thing. Rugby's all about preparation and if you allow yourself to be distracted in the build-up to a match, you can be found out, especially in New Zealand.'

Laney initially looked at a move to the UK late in 1999 after the Bath club had expressed an interest, but after a heart-to-heart with Tony Gilbert he signed for Otago for another two years. By the time the 2001 season had finished, he was ready to go. His agent, Warren Alcock, had put the call out and both Bath and Edinburgh had come forward with offers. Because of his ancestry, it was a no-contest.

Once the All Blacks had departed Edinburgh and a degree of normality had returned to the Laneys, Brendan and Miranda decided it was time to explore their new city. In company with Todd Blackadder, another signing by Edinburgh, they drove around the old city, three Kiwis in a car, complete with map, noting all the significant landmarks.

After experiencing his first white Christmas in the snow-covered border town of Galashiels, Laney was back into international action, a regular in the Scottish team for the Six Nations Championship.

Although Scotland performed disappointingly, Laney made his mark, and after starting the competition as the team's third-ranked goalkicker, he was assigned the duty for the game against Italy, responding with a 24-point performance. McChainsaw was back in business.

For the record

Player
- South Canterbury, 1991–1994 (41 games)
- Otago, 1995–2001 (82 games)
- Highlanders, 1997–2001 (44 games)
- Edinburgh, 2001–2002 (20 games)
- Scotland, 2001–2002 (8 games)

WALES

Beyond New Zealand, Wales is probably the only country where rugby is not only the national sport but an all-consuming passion. The Welsh adore the game, which, in their country, unites all classes. The WRU was formed in 1881, the country winning its first international championship (against England, Scotland and Ireland) in 1893. It has since gone on to claim the title 33 times, a record second only to England's. Wales had to survive massive defections to league when the game was amateur but with the advent of professionalism it has gone into the import business itself. Wales hasn't beaten the All Blacks since 1953 but reigned supreme in the Five Nations in the 1960s, an era when it produced dazzling backs like Barry John, Gareth Edwards, JPR Williams and Gerald Davies.

Founded
1881
IRB
1886
Clubs
372
Players
52,500 men, 740 women
Rugby Nomad
Graham Henry

Graham Henry

It was all looking so rosy for coach Graham Henry at the three-quarter point of the long-awaited Lions tour of Australia in 2001. 'The Redeemer' to a legion of Welsh rugby fans, he was on target to become the most celebrated rugby coach in the world.

After a crushing victory over the Queensland Reds, his team had dealt most emphatically to the world champion Wallabies in the opening test at Brisbane and had been equally dominant for 40 minutes in the second test at Melbourne.

Then, starting with an intercept try to Joe Roff, it all went horribly wrong. A succession of crippling injuries, a defiant, determined opposition and rebellious behaviour by a couple of his players not only resulted in the series being lost but meant the crusade finished on a disappointing and controversial note.

The series went right to the wire, with the teams locked together at 23-all late in the decider in Sydney before the deadly accurate boot of Matthew Burke proved the decisive factor.

In the final weeks of the tour, much of the focus had regrettably been deflected away from the onfield events through comments made by two English members of the team, scrumhalf Matt Dawson and utility back Austin Healey.

Dawson wrote critically of the team's coaching methods, claiming the players were overtrained and alleging the early weeks were a 'harsh regime' and a 'boot camp', while Healey attacked new Australian test lock Justin Harrison in his *Guardian* column, branding him a 'plod' and a 'plank', in the process providing coach Rod Macqueen with rich motivational material.

It was subsequently revealed that a ghost writer was responsible for Healey's column, largely without the player's input. Though this was acknowledged in a Lions committee hearing, Henry, upon his return to the UK, still wrote of Dawson and Healey that they had 'betrayed their mates for 30 pieces of silver'.

Now reinstated at the Auckland Rugby Union as a technical adviser, Henry prefers not to dwell on the negative aspects of the Lions tour, instead expressing pride in the Lions' players for their massive effort under challenging circumstances.

He reveals now, and it was something kept under wraps at the time,

Bob Howitt and Graham Henry celebrate the launch of The X Factor.

that four days out from the crucial third test in Sydney, the Lions were reduced to 10 fit players.

'We had an unbelievably unlucky run with injuries,' says Henry. 'Right from the start, key players fell by the wayside.

'Lawrence Dallaglio, who would have been so vital to us, dropped out first. Then Dan Luger, our number-one wing, went home, and in rapid succession we lost important individuals like Will Greenwood, Mike Catt and Richard Hill.'

Henry doesn't blame the injuries for his team's failure to claim the series. 'With one test in the bag, we had opportunities to play Australia out of the series in the opening 40 minutes at Melbourne,' he says, 'but we butchered several prime try-scoring chances. If we'd cashed them in, the Wallabies would never have come back, even with Joe Roff's interception.'

Henry says he personally gave his team little chance of victory in the third test, given that they were 'held together with willpower and tape. I was so proud of my players that they performed as heroically as they did. There was a very thin line between victory and defeat.'

Of all the rugby nomads featured in this book, none achieved more, after departing New Zealand, than Henry. And being offered the coaching role of the British Lions was the ultimate.

He vividly recalls fielding a call on 8 June 2000 from Donal Lenihan, who had been appointed manager of the Lions. He has no trouble remembering the date, because it was his birthday.

'When Donal offered me the position of coach, I nearly fell off the phone,' says Henry. 'There had been some speculation to that effect in the media, but I'd disregarded it. It was a long shot that a foreigner would be offered the position, given that Britain is the bastion of conservatism. I couldn't ever imagine an Aussie or a Pom being appointed to coach the All Blacks, so for a New Zealander to be given the coaching role with the Lions was a huge honour and a privilege.'

Henry says the planning and preparation for the tour, which, intriguingly, opened with a game in Perth on Henry's next birthday, exactly 12 months on, was handled meticulously and couldn't have been improved upon.

While Henry declines to comment specifically on Dawson's much-publicised complaints, he says he worked the players hard in the UK before departure and again during the first week in Perth.

'I didn't spare anyone in those early sessions,' says Henry. 'That's when we really dug it in. But in the lead-up to the major matches, we kept training sessions to a minimum.'

Henry says that trying to provide equal opportunities for 37 players on a tour of Australia is an impossibility. 'It's a tricky country to tour, because outside of the internationals there are so few matches of substance; probably only four, in fact, New South Wales Waratahs, Queensland Reds, Australia A and ACT Brumbies.

'Trying to shape a test XV from a squad of 37 with so few meaningful games becomes a real challenge, compounded in our case by the horrendous run of injuries. Some players didn't feel they got the opportunity to express their talents against the best opponents, and I can appreciate that. I didn't possess a magic wand. It's easy to look in from the outside and be negative but we prepared the way we believed would give us the best opportunity of winning the series against the world champions. And we came agonisingly close to achieving that.'

The series couldn't have been closer. The Wallabies and the Lions scored seven tries each and it was only the goalkicking of Matthew Burke, who landed 11 penalty goals at Melbourne and Sydney to Jonny Wilkinson's six, that made the difference.

Henry didn't return to the UK for almost three weeks after the tour ended. It had nothing to do with avoiding the media. He'd planned it that way. 'It had been a hell of a demanding year,' he says, 'almost 12 months without a break, and I took the opportunity to catch up with my parents in Christchurch and to take some time out.

'Besides, I believe the Lions' management went out of their way to accommodate the media before and during the tour. People in New Zealand perhaps might not understand what's involved when I refer to the media in relation to a Lions' tour. At the first press conference after my appointment as coach, there were 150 media people in attendance.

'Back in Auckland, when I was coaching the Blues, I was used to dealing with maybe 15 journalists, most of whom I knew, whereas in the UK, every television channel, radio station and newspaper, and there were literally hundreds of them, seemed to be represented. And they were all looking for their own angles.'

Although some, most notably England manager Clive Woodward, had criticised Henry's appointment, he was, in terms of his credentials, the obvious choice to lead the Lions on their daunting down-under assignment.

Matt Dawson, a critic of the Lions' training regime, receives a less than enthusiastic handshake from coach Graham Henry after the final test in Sydney.

No coach in the UK, certainly none of those associated with the English, Irish, Scottish or Welsh teams, knew Australian conditions and the Australian players better than Henry. And none boasted records that could compare with his.

Henry had claimed four straight NPC titles with Auckland and successive Super 12 crowns with the Blues, narrowly missing a hat trick when the Crusaders edged his team out in a nail-biter in 1998. That was before he restored pride to Welsh rugby.

Having achieved pretty much everything as a rugby coach in New Zealand short of taking on the All Blacks, Henry was ready to make the step up to international level. So he was receptive when the Welsh came calling in 1998, especially as there was a fellow called John Hart blocking his path to the All Black summit.

Wales sought out Henry because, as Terry Cobner, the union's coaching co-ordinator, explained, they wanted the best rugby coach in the world. Only New Zealand and South Africa compare with Wales as nations where rugby is not only the national game but an obsession with the vast majority of the population.

But while the All Blacks and the Springboks have continued to prosper, with only occasional blips on their graph, the Welsh, by 1998, were bleeding something terrible. The glory days of the 1960s were but a memory as the national team took battering after battering.

In the 12 months before Henry was recruited, the Red Dragons conceded 51 points to France (in Cardiff, what's more), 60 points to England and, most distressingly of all, 96 points to South Africa. Any team can give up a half-century of points on a luckless afternoon, but only a team in total disarray allows the opposition to rack up 96.

The swiftness with which Henry transformed the Welsh team startled everyone. First up was a decidedly unlucky 20–28 loss to the Springboks, the opponent that had shredded Welsh pride the previous year. That was followed by a rousing victory over the Pumas, who are always a challenge with their powerhouse pack.

Although Henry's men then stumbled against Scotland and Ireland at the start of the Five Nations Championship, they came home singing ragtime, outpointing France in a dazzling tryfest in Paris before rolling Woodward's English team, in an upset of monumental proportions, at Wembley.

Nothing fortifies the Welsh nation more than a rugby victory over

England. That it came in the most dramatic of circumstances, with Neil Jenkins providing a wide-angle conversion to Scott Gibbs's last-gasp try, to deny England Five Nations as well as Grand-Slam glory, sent Wales into raptures.

The *South Wales Argus* declared that Wales was talking about nothing else. 'The last-gasp rugby victory over England has restored pride in our national game. It was quite simply an unbelievable day, producing a victory over the old enemy. Can there have been a better day in recent Welsh sporting history?'

Henry had already been hailed as the saviour of Welsh rugby. After the Paris and Wembley triumphs, he became the most celebrated individual in the land.

Scrumhalf Rob Howley, one of Wales's favourite sons, was unstinting in his praise. 'Graham has turned around Welsh rugby by himself,' he said, 'which I didn't think was possible. He's got vision and foresight and he's given players like Neil Jenkins, Craig Quinnell and Chris Wyatt the confidence to become world-class performers.'

Titles of 'Redeemer' and 'Messiah' didn't sit easily with the former Kelston Boys' High School headmaster, who had already taken moves to insulate himself from the excessively passionate locals by relocating himself seven miles outside Cardiff in a house appropriately named The Coach House.

He preferred to keep himself out of the limelight as much as possible and being based on the outskirts of Cardiff aided this. He had found there was a vast difference between being a high-profile coach in Wales and in New Zealand.

Back in Auckland, he could happily walk through the local supermarket with only the occasional acknowledgement. But he found Cardiff positively claustrophobic.

'It seems to be a very insecure thing,' he said at the time. 'Either a new dawn is breaking or it's all doom and gloom. New Zealanders have a far more low-key approach, which I prefer.'

Henry's wife, Raewyn, refused to allow him to accompany her to the local supermarket. 'It's not worth it,' she says. 'It's too disruptive. They treat him like some sort of pop star, all wanting his autograph and to talk to him. I can't get over all this adulation. I keep saying to him, "You're only a bloody rugby coach!"'

The Welsh nation's love affair with coach Henry had one huge, tangible benefit. They bought his autobiography, launched in 1999, in massive numbers. Worldwide, the book sold 42,500 copies, of which 29,000 were in Wales alone, making it one of the biggest-selling rugby books of all time. For one glorious week, *The X Factor*, written in collaboration with Bob Howitt, topped the UK best-selling chart.

Inspired by Henry's 'X factor', Wales scaled fresh heights in 1999, winning two tests against the Pumas in Buenos Aires, a feat never previously achieved by any UK nation, before toppling the Springboks in the brand-new Millennium Stadium in Cardiff.

'Others saw it differently, but I regarded that as the best performance during my term with Wales,' says Henry. 'Considering the Boks had put 96 points on Wales in Pretoria, it was quite a turnaround.

'As a New Zealander who grew up believing the Springboks were the most awesome opponent in the world, they have always been the yardstick by which other teams could measure themselves. The first test I ever saw was the All Blacks against the Springboks at Lancaster Park in 1956.

'The Springboks came to Cardiff in '99 as world champions, having never lost to Wales. It was quite an achievement to beat them.'

Wales went into the fourth Rugby World Cup on the back of 10 straight international victories, which, given the team's results prior to Henry hitting town, was almost unbelievable.

However, the Red Dragons came back to earth during the tournament, as Henry predicted they undoubtedly would. 'We will be a more serious challenger in 2003,' he told the media, 'but the home advantage this time has to be worth something.'

Notwithstanding a loss to Samoa, Wales emerged top of its pool, which put it on a quarterfinal collision course with Rod Macqueen's Wallabies, the tournament favourites who would carry on to take out the Webb Ellis Trophy.

'We gave a competent display,' says Henry, 'but they were classier. If you were to pick 15 players from the two sides, Wales would struggle to get many in. Mind you, we weren't helped by Hawkeye (referee Colin Hawke), who had a shocker. It's one of the frustrations I experienced while coaching Wales, a belief that referees go into big matches with preconceived ideas about the result and operate accordingly. It used to frustrate the hell out of me. The 50-50 decisions always seemed to go to the team that was meant to win the game.'

As a New Zealander, Henry never quite adapted to the Welsh attitude to the game. 'The game there is very tribal,' he says. 'Village-ism might be the right word. People have a greater affiliation with the local area and the local club than with the rugby scene as a whole. It's not conducive to the bigger picture.

'They have struggled to implement professionalism. I visited one sixth-division club and was astonished to find their players were on a win bonus of £50 per player. Every victory was costing the club £2,200. If the team had embarked on a lengthy winning streak, the club would have finished up bankrupt!'

The longer Henry coached in Wales, the more envious he became of New Zealand with its vast player resources. 'All Black selectors could pick three international squads of 26 players each and they'd all be hugely competitive. In Wales, I had a basic squad of about 30 players, after which the standard fell away alarmingly.'

While the Welsh were competitive in the 2000 and 2001 Six Nations Championships, drubbings from England and continuing losses to arch-rival Ireland meant they were never serious contenders for the major crown.

When the Red Dragons then sustained successive losses to the Wallabies and the high-flying Pumas in Cardiff in November 2001 in the wake of the Lions tour of Australia, it was obvious that Henry's star had begun to dim.

With the support of the Welsh RFU, he had recruited champion Canterbury coach Steve Hansen as his assistant, but they completed just one assignment together, in February 2002, at Lansdowne Road in Dublin. The result was a disastrous 54–10 loss to Ireland, only the second time in Henry's entire coaching career that one of his teams had conceded 50 points (the first being the Auckland Blues' 51–13 loss to the Queensland Reds in 1996). It was an outcome that dismayed everyone, Henry as much as the Welsh fans.

In the days immediately following the Dublin débâcle, Henry took stock of his career. In what he describes as the hardest decision of his life, he chose to terminate his contract with the Welsh RFU, after first establishing that Hansen was prepared to step into the breach.

'I sat down with officials of the Welsh union and we agreed the terms upon which the contract would be terminated. I must say, they were bloody marvellous about it. They subsequently phoned me and asked if I would reconsider, but I assured them I had given the issue a huge amount of thought and my decision was final. We parted on good terms.'

Henry says that, in hindsight, he realises the five-year contract he originally committed to was excessive. 'Five years is too long to coach an international team, I now realise. Having said that, coaching Wales was an incredible experience and something I would do all over again, given similar circumstances. I've come away with many fond memories and also a few scars, which is par for the course when you're coaching at that level.

'I could never have imagined what the experience would be like when I signed the contract with Wales back in 1998.'

Suddenly without a team to coach, Henry departed Wales quickly, partly to escape the media pack but also because he felt he needed time to reflect on all that had happened. He flew to Christchurch to 'chill out' with his parents.

Not unexpectedly, he made contact with the Auckland RFU while in New Zealand, advising them that if they happened to be looking for a coach, he was now a free agent and available.

It didn't take the ARU long to offer him a position as a technical adviser, to assist Auckland coaches Wayne Pivac and Grant Fox and to work with the province's promising young footballers.

Interestingly, since Henry's departure four years earlier, Auckland, the dominant force in New Zealand rugby throughout the 1990s, had largely struggled in the NPC while the Blues, Super 12 finalists three times under Henry, had plummeted to the rank of also-rans.

For the record

Coach
• Auckland, 1992–1998
• Auckland Blues, 1996–1998
• Wales, 1998–2001

IRELAND

Rugby holds a special place among the Irish, not least because the national team has always embraced Northern Ireland, even when the country has been in a state of virtual civil war. Dublin University's Trinity College is the world's second oldest rugby club, having been formed in 1854. Ireland has produced many outstanding leaders: captains like Karl Mullen, Ronnie Dawson, Tom Kiernan and Willie John McBride. Although Ireland has won the Five (now Six) Nations championship only six times in 119 years, it is always a doughty opponent, never easily overcome. At four World Cup tournaments, the Irish have yet to reach the semifinals. Ireland has never beaten New Zealand, but in 1978 Munster completed a famous victory over the All Blacks at Limerick.

Founded
1874
IRB
1886
Clubs
205
Players
64,500 men, 500 women
Rugby Nomads
Brent Pope, Noel McQuilkin, Kurt McQuilkin,
Warren Gatland

Brent Pope

He's known as 'the Mexted of Ireland', co-host of one of Ireland's top TV sports shows as well as a best-selling children's author. Former Otago loose forward Brent Pope offers his reflections on life in Ireland.

THE GREEN GREEN GRASS OF HOME

The year was 1991 and Otago rugby, under the astute coaching of the legendary 'Silver Fox', Laurie Mains, had finally scaled its Everest, winning the National Championship first division title that had eluded it for so long. Party plans in scarfie town were in full swing, with Speight's Brewery about to be relieved of much of its famous product.

Then, late one night, I received a telephone call from Ireland, offering me an opportunity to ply my trade with the St Mary's rugby team, a Dublin club steeped in Irish rugby folklore and prolific at churning out Irish internationals and British Lions. Unfortunately, it meant I would have to miss the end-of-season celebrations. The Irish season had already started a month earlier: I had to commit there and then or the offer was gone.

With a few All Black trials under my belt and over 80 games for my beloved blue and golds, I felt that at the ripe old age of 29 any boyhood dreams I had of wearing the famous black jersey were fading fast.

Legends such as Buck Shelford and Zinzan Brooke were the All Black incumbents and there was a bunch of fine young predatory loose forwards just itching to jump the queue. Two of those up-and-comers, Jamie Joseph and Arran Pene, were becoming increasingly impatient at gathering splinters on the Otago bench, especially for this old warhorse.

I have always regretted missing those Dunedin celebrations, the cheers around the Octagon and the ticker-tape parade. I had been around Otago rugby for nearly a decade and it would have been like a family occasion for me. But looking back, if I had turned down that offer, I may have never ended up here in Ireland. As one door closed another opened.

However, not donning the All Black jersey, even once, will haunt me till my dying day. My hope is that young players will realise just what it means to fulfil their dreams and pull on the silver fern. My only consolation is that I am in the exalted company of a host of brilliant players who, over the years, have fallen at the final hurdle.

So, alas, I bade farewell to all my friends in Otago, relinquished my degree in commerce and, with a knapsack on my back, set off for 'Dublin fair city'.

On the other side of the world I moved into digs with three other messy Kiwi rugby types: my old Otago University mate Kevin Putt, Waikato loose forward Stu Gemmell and, to my delight, my old Otago captain, Richard (Dick) Knight. What a wonderful year we had, enjoying the laid-back nature of the Irish, and the dark stuff in bucket-loads. As the Irish say, 'The craic was mighty.'

Like most Kiwi travellers, I had originally intended staying abroad for just six months, eager to get back and force Laurie — then, of course, the main honcho with the All Blacks — to give me a run with the big boys.

But Murphy's Law still finds me here, nearly 11 years on, greying drastically on top, and fattening on bottom and wondering where all the bloody years went.

During my first years in Ireland my professional career as a property valuer in New Zealand had been replaced by a job with Comans, a drinks' company, for whom I delivered numerous barrels of Guinness to some of the most famous, and infamous, inner-city pubs in Dublin.

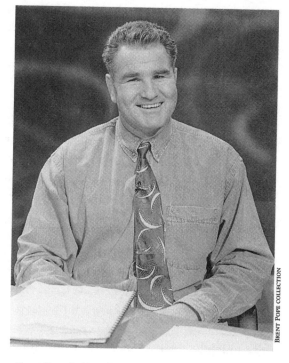

Brent Pope in his role as co-host of a popular TV sports show in Ireland.

Perched high in the trucks I had a first-hand view of downtown Dublin and spent my early mornings loading and unloading pallets of booze while keeping a watchful eye on the young deviants who always wanted to relieve the truck of a few freebies. I loved that job, and after years of study, and stuffy collar-and-tie employment, it was great to be out in the fresh air, mucking in and mixing it with the locals. I'll never forget those early days in Dublin, where everything was fresh and exciting, including, of course, the colleens.

I was fascinated to learn about the different accents, the class system and the stories of hardships and emigration that many Irish families had endured over the years. Every Irishman has a story, a yarn or a ballad to sing. Wonderful stuff.

And while I slogged away at my early-morning job, my old Otago team-mate, Richard Knight, had an equally exhausting job as a mattress tester. Quite often on arriving home, tired and testy, I was greeted by the fetching sight of Richard's ever-expanding backside occupying the couch as he filled me in with the latest from all the TV soaps. It was wonderful to have such a good friend with me in my new country but the hospitable Irish soon made us both feel that we had been there for life.

When I arrived in Dublin the Irish game was completely amateur; after a game — win, lose or draw — any semblance of professionalism on the field went out the door, as cigarettes lit up and the beer began to flow. Teams that were lucky enough to win titles at any level went on week-long benders, while the rugby clubrooms were the centre of all social events.

Irish legends, such as Moss Keane, talked of their pre-match warm-ups, which consisted of switching car heaters onto full and downing pints of Guinness — to gain iron, and often a splitting headache.

The rugby itself was very physical, not nearly as expansive as the New Zealand game but certainly as rugged and committed. Years of hard living, a background in Gaelic games and an uncanny knack in the boxing ring had hardened the Irish, especially in Limerick, where rugby was embraced by the working classes.

In Leinster, the game still remained essentially upper class with very much a 'what school you went to' system. Consequently, the 'mighty men of Munster' (Limerick) just loved sinking their teeth into the so-called Dublin softies, especially on home soil, where one particular ground, aptly nicknamed the Killing Fields, awaited the nervous Leinster bank clerks.

Some of the Limerick teams produced a very hardy type of rugby specimen indeed. When Brent Anderson, the ex-Waikato and All Black lock, arrived in Limerick to play for Garryowen in 1991, he was quickly reminded of the passion that lay in Ireland's rugby capital. One night in a local Limerick bar, a beer mat was skidded along the bar in front of him. Written on it were the words of an opposition club and what they were going to do to him in the next local derby match, and, as they say in those parts, 'it wearn't pretty'.

Limerick has always been the true home of Irish rugby and they constantly remind any Kiwi rugby supporter about the day the great Munster team beat Mourie's Grand Slam All Blacks. In fact, they went as far as to write an award-winning play about it. Mourie and his men will never be forgiven by any Kiwi drinkers in the rugby-mad city.

Ulster, too, has played a vital part in the Irish game and produced some legendary Irish players such as Jackie Kyle, Mike Gibson and Willie John McBride.

In the early 1990s, tension in the North was running high. For an Ashburton-born country bumpkin travelling across the border for games, the border inspections, guns and armoured cars were always nerve-wracking, especially when the bus broke down in the dark, as it often did. Like anything, however, you grow used to it and today, fingers crossed, things are a lot more peaceful in Northern Ireland.

On that front, I was very grateful for my Kiwi accent one day in the early 1990s. I was working for a Dublin packaging company at the time and was asked to travel to Derry to pick up some supplies. Driving the boss's new company car and making good time, I decided to park near the Derry city centre and drop in for a little pub lunch at a nearby bar.

On leaving the pub I saw a collection of armoured cars and a growing contingent of heavily armed police. I wondered what all the commotion was about and then realised that the army was sandbagging the company car prior to blowing it up.

Unbeknown to me, a few years earlier an unoccupied car parked near the centre had exploded, taking out half the inner city. Of course, the fact that I had not seen a massive sign prohibiting parking in the area, combined with my Dublin vehicle registration plates, meant that

I had to put on my best Kiwi twang to get my poor boss's car back in one piece. Needless to say the boys were not too happy when I arrived back at work after being escorted across the border without my supplies.

In Ireland, Kiwis are still regarded as being a little tight-fisted when it comes to buying a drink, but in reality it is just the difference in drink culture. In Ireland you do not just buy a beer for yourself or for you and your friend, but for nearly everyone who is in your company, with rounds often extending to every man, woman and hanger-on in sight. The problem with this system is that you are only as good a drinker as the quickest drinker in the round. Often you are left with numerous pints from different rounds from partly to mostly full as a new drink arrives with nearly every sip.

To say that you don't want a drink in Ireland is often simply laughed off, or completely disregarded, as the Irish answer will surely be, 'Sure you'll have just a small one for the road.' You often wonder why you bothered to say no in the first place.

The language barrier was another thing I had to quickly overcome. Ireland is an amazing place in that, unlike New Zealand, every county, parish, and virtually every street has a different accent. Irish people can almost tell what side of the road they are from through their different pronunciations.

Originally, I couldn't understand the Irish, nor them me, so most of those early conversations, especially in the culchie [country] areas, were confined to simple nodding and smiling at the appropriate times. Of course you were always paranoid that they were calling you a 'bleedin' eejit' or a 'gobshite' and you were agreeing with them.

I also soon came to realise that 'ya man' was not in fact my man, in a sexual sense, but just a general description of somebody, as in 'You see ya man over there, with ya woman?' To add confusion, 'ya el one' is often the term used to describe an elderly person, so a typical bar conversation could go, 'Ya see ya man over there with ya el one? Well, he used to go out with ya woman . . .'

A much misunderstood Irish word is 'craic'. In Ireland it means the fun, the banter, as in 'The craic was mighty', but can you imagine telling an American or a Kiwi to go to a certain bar because 'the craic's great'?

The Irish will often finish a sentence with the phrase 'Sure, you know yourself', which is baffling. It can also be startling for a New Zealand rugby supporter, en route to Landsdowne Road on match day, to notice the bus stops along the way: Stillorgan, Ballsbridge or Ringsend . . .

I love Ireland. It is so similar to New Zealand in many ways: the people are friendly and the countryside is lush and green, just like home. It is more of a drink-based culture than New Zealand, but then that is what the Irish are loved for, their ability to enjoy themselves in any company.

It is in the spit-on-the-floor pubs in the country where you will find the true Irish, black pint in hand, beside the roaring fire, enjoying traditional music and having the craic.

Ireland has a fascinating history and you can read or listen for hours as the Irish talk about their family heritage. Dublin itself, especially over the last 10 years, has become very cosmopolitan and is now little different from other modern European cities. Inner-city suburbs with tales of large Catholic families, hardship and emigration have been replaced by yuppie flats and trendy apartments. House prices have become outrageous, with an average Dublin three-bedroom dwelling setting you back about $NZ700,000.

I am still involved in rugby and delighted to be doing something I love, writing for several European rugby magazines and co-hosting Ireland's most popular rugby programme on RTE television.

I am lucky enough to have coached teams to win all three divisions in the Irish game, unlucky enough to have been sent off during Ireland's biggest-ever club final, in 1993, and happy to have witnessed the emergence of Ireland as a genuine rugby nation, with bona fide world rugby stars such as Keith Wood and Brian O'Driscoll. So I cannot complain.

I now have dual nationality and I am proud to be considered both Kiwi and Irish. My mother's heritage is Irish anyway, but I will always be a New Zealander at heart.

I miss watching Otago play each week, the great outdoors, the view coming into Queenstown, the Bay of Islands' beaches, the Avon in Christchurch, the harbour in Auckland, the wind in Wellington, my old friends from Otago and my family in Ashburton. I miss Marmite, summer barbies, decent fish and chips, roast lamb dinners, Dave Dobbyn and the sun.

But sure, as the Irish say, 'It's all swings and roundabouts, sure you know yourself.'

For the record

Player
• Otago, 1985–1991 (83 games)
• St Mary's, Ireland, 1991–1994 (62 games)

Player-coach
• Clontarf, Ireland, 1994–1996 (55 games)

Noel McQuilkin

Noel McQuilkin is back in Te Kuiti, absorbed in his King Country heartland and enthusiastic about the talent that lies out there in the NPC second and third divisions.

'I love those guys because they're amateurs. They don't want anything, they just want to play rugby.'

But the 2002 New Zealand Divisional coach says he has a very soft spot for Ireland and its marvellous people, and fond memories of his coaching OE.

McQuilkin was taken on by Dublin club Bective Rangers in the dying days of amateurism and left shortly after the advent of the professional era. Given the contribution that professional overseas coaches in general, and Warren Gatland in particular, have made to Ireland's raised profile in recent years it seems odd that McQuilkin should now be encouraging the Irish to aspire to take over coaching at all levels of rugby. He describes it as a case of Irish horses for courses.

'The first thing to realise is that you can't go over there as a New Zealand coach and try to impose New Zealand styles of play on Irish teams. It's not going to work.

'I make no bones about the fact that I found it hard to come to grips with their inconsistency: one day my team would play like All Blacks and the next they'd play like primary-school kids.'

Still dressed in their business suits, his Dublin players would arrive from work for training sessions, which could run for up to three hours. McQuilkin immediately cut that traditional training time down to slightly over an hour with the emphasis on quality. A grid that had previously been repeated all night was replaced by a series of grids which ran for a minute or two.

The players were delighted with the new regime.

'They'd be the most enthusiastic guys I've ever coached and fellows with a hurling background had the best skills,' he recalls.

'They used to get themselves really worked up before a game, run out on the field, do a forward roll, leap around and do bugger-all afterwards. I'd think, *If only you could get that energy and transfer it to the game.*'

There was one element that was out of McQuilkin's control for training sessions: the weather. He deplored the lack of indoor facilities in a

*The father and son pairing who made their mark in Ireland,
Noel and Kurt McQuilkin.*

country notorious for its rainfall and resorted to using nearby racing stables for a couple of sessions. That didn't work, so he took the players back to ploughing around in the mud and badly chopped-up surfaces at the club.

He shakes his head as he recalls that on one occasion the Rangers ground was simply too muddy to train on. 'However, there was an astroturf tennis court alongside so we hopped over there and ran through a few training moves. Then someone from the tennis club saw us, there was a screaming row and we got kicked off. I wasn't to know that the tennis and rugby clubs at Bective hate each other!

'Some pitches can have six teams training on them at any one time and you're up to your ankles in mud. Ireland's an agricultural country — you'd think someone would invent something like a double hay barn and throw some sawdust around for training. I'm surprised that overseas coaches haven't insisted on it.'

He was given a lesson in Irish mud and the feelings of other regions of Ireland towards Dubliners ('They're the Aucklanders of Ireland') when Rangers travelled to Sligo, in the far northwest of Ireland, for a competition game.

'It was a hell of a trip,' says McQuilkin. 'We'd rung ahead and been told the field was "foine" but when we got there it looked like the cows had been through.

146

'There were holes full of water on the playing area, a huge roller on the side of the field which they refused to use and some guy wandering around with a pitchfork.

'We were later told they thought the rougher the field, the better their chances.

'The ref said, "What do you think?" and I answered, "We can't play on that. If you want us to play, you'll be responsible for the injuries we receive," so we had to go home and come back the following weekend.

'Dublin teams are nicknamed D4s after a smart zone in Dublin and if the rest of the country can cock around a D4 side they'll do it and laugh themselves silly afterwards.'

The Irish do not deserve some of the New Zealanders they get, says McQuilkin, who feels strongly about Kiwis who come to Ireland with invented pedigrees.

'They claim to have done this and done that but in reality they've done nothing. They bluff their way into a rugby club, get found out and New Zealand gets a bad name as a consequence.

'One day in Dublin my son, Kurt, and Brent Pope met a guy in the street who was wearing an Otago jersey. He was big-noting away so they asked him, "Oh, do you know Stu Forster?" "Yeah, know Stu very well." "Do you know Brent Pope?" "Popey? I used to drink with him!" So Brent says, "Well, you're talking to him now." The guy split so fast it wasn't funny.'

For the record

Coach
- King Country, 1989–1992, 1999–2000
- Bective Rangers, Dublin, 1992–1996
- New Zealand Divisional Team, 2001–2002

Kurt McQuilkin

In 1996 three Te Kuiti rugby men, John Mitchell, Murray Kidd and Kurt McQuilkin, had a laugh as they walked off Lansdowne Road after an Irish international match.

In McQuilkin's words: 'Here we were, the old King Country trio transplanted to Ireland. Murray Kidd and John Mitchell as the Ireland coaches and me wearing my first international jersey. It was classic.'

Unlike other New Zealanders who aimed to further their rugby fortunes in Ireland, Kurt McQuilkin's entry into Irish rugby came about quite by chance, through his parents, Noel and Josie McQuilkin.

Late in 1992 Kurt decided he would fly to Dublin to spend Christmas with his father and mother, who had recently arrived there to live. The senior McQuilkins had left New Zealand a month earlier, following Noel's appointment as head coach of the city's Bective Rangers RFC. During that holiday break there was much talk of their new lives on the other side of the world, but also a mood of pleasurable reflection as they chatted on the New Zealand season just past, when King Country, under Noel's coaching, had been promoted to the NPC first division for the first time.

Kurt had played in that victorious King Country team, on release from his County Durham club in England, and decided over Christmas that he would stay on in Dublin for a while. He had the perfect excuse, anyway — he was recovering from a knee injury which was keeping him out of action for his English team.

McQuilkin never left. The former King Country and Northland first-five/centre decided that he would stay on to play club rugby for Bective Rangers under his dad's coaching and enjoy the social life of Dublin.

And then it got serious. McQuilkin was a prolific goalkicker and a reliable and versatile inside back; his abilities were soon noticed by local selectors as they monitored Bective Rangers' progress in the domestic competition.

First, McQuilkin was selected for Leinster, the home province of Dublin (later his boot would help it win the 1995–1996 Irish interprovincial Grand Slam), becoming its captain three years later. Then higher honours beckoned. He had met the three-year residential qualification at the end of 1995, and just one month later, in January 1996, playing at inside centre, McQuilkin was awarded his first cap for Ireland in its test match against the United States. He later spoke of the mood of elation he felt on hearing his name called out.

'For me, it was an unbelievable sequence of events. The Irish had taken me to their hearts and I'd taken on their lifestyle. I was happy, too, that I sensed little, if any, hostility towards me as an outsider being selected to play for them. I got on fine with my team-mates because some were friends from Leinster and I'd played against the Munster boys and the Connacht lads over the previous three years and knew them all reasonably well.

'It was strange to be preparing for an international in Dublin with a team coached by Murray Kidd, whom I had known so well in my Te Kuiti days. Murray was trying — with some difficulty — to introduce new techniques to the side and John Mitchell, another mate of mine from the King Country, was taking the forwards, so he was putting his style of things on that.'

The first New Zealander to play a full international for Ireland, McQuilkin went on to win five caps for his adopted country and take his commitment to Ireland a stage further by marrying an Irish girl, Barbara O'Sullivan, in 1999.

Since 1996 McQuilkin has been employed by the Irish Rugby Union and is now an elite player development officer whose responsibilities involve the supervision of Leinster's technical and fitness programmes, along with the nurturing of young talent.

McQuilkin says his role is in its infancy, created in 2001 after Irish Rugby Union officials realised that players with potential had to be better identified than they had in the hit-and-miss system of the past.

'In Leinster, rugby has traditionally been considered a middle- to upper-class game, with the Irish feeder base coming from a relatively narrow band of schools. Now we are targeting mainstream youngsters at state schools, where hurling and Gaelic football are played. We want those players because they are considered elite athletes and both Gaelic football and hurling require good hand–eye co-ordination.'

McQuilkin says his aim, and that of the Irish RFU, is to do as well as New Zealand does in this department. There is a push to have youth development officers in all clubs and care taken to keep feeder schools 'in the frame'. He says that the drive for young players is experiencing some success due partly to the high profile Irish rugby is enjoying at present.

'There is increased game coverage on television and charismatic players like Ireland's captain Keith Wood and Brian O'Driscoll have become cult figures here.'

But Ireland could have done without the negative worldwide publicity it received from an amazed rugby fraternity at the end of 2001 when Ireland's ruling committee parted ways with its most successful international coach to date, Warren Gatland of New Zealand.

McQuilkin said that mood of disbelief was shared in many quarters of Irish rugby.

'I suppose that traditionally you could describe the Irish as the Fijians of Europe — you don't know what the heck they're going to do next. On their day the Irish have always been able to beat anyone, but they are far more consistent than they were and Gatland had a hell of a lot to do with that new attitude.

'There was a lot of feeling within the Irish team when he got dropped by the Irish Rugby Union. Everyone was gobsmacked. The players loved him and he got a good team spirit going.'

Gatland's second to last international as Ireland's coach came against New Zealand in November 2001, when the home side led the All Blacks for much of the game. McQuilkin believes Ireland should have won that match.

'They were ahead, thought *Jesus, we're beating the All Blacks*, got a fright and blew it. Ireland had also just beaten England so it was a great way for Gatty to go out.'

McQuilkin is part of a team committed to keep the pressure on for spreading rugby's playing base at school level.

He says that currently rugby is the fourth-ranked sport in Ireland. Gaelic football and hurling are number one and two in popularity, followed by soccer and then rugby.

'There's still a strong feeling that both soccer and rugby are English games imported to Ireland, so there's some historical animosity. However, it's interesting to reflect that rugby is the only sport where teams have always been selected on an all-Ireland basis.'

Rugby may be running fourth, but attendances at school championship finals greatly exceed anything comparable in New Zealand. For example, in both 2000 and 2001 the Leinster Schools final at Lansdowne Road attracted 22,000 cheering fans. (A comparable New Zealand competition, the schools' end-of-season 'Top Four', would be lucky to attract a quarter of that number when played as a stand-alone fixture.)

Unlike in some of the more lucrative European rugby destinations, McQuilkin warns that players who have got Ireland in their sights will not get rich playing there. 'But the odds are that you will have a very good time. The standard rate for an overseas player at provincial level is about £30,000 ($NZ100,000) plus a flat and possibly a car, so that's OK. Also, you'll be playing for a club which might only see you for five or six games a season, and they will throw in another £5,000 or so.'

New Zealand players also need to realise that only one overseas player can be selected to play for the All Ireland League (AIL) games, although the number is increased to two or three at provincial level.

'The Irish tax regime is punitive at 48 per cent, but there are ways in which foreign players can get around it,' he says with a smile. 'Coming to Ireland for rugby is a lifestyle choice. And you often play better when you're away because you can relax. There's no pressure on you here. You just go out and do what you enjoy.'

For the record

Player
- King Country, 1985–1988, 1992 (54 games)
- North Auckland, 1988–1991 (33 games)
- Leinster, 1993–1996 (40 games)
- Ireland, 1996 (5 games)

Warren Gatland

When the local phoned in to the team hotel the morning following the All Blacks' game against Connacht at Galway in 1989, the player he wanted to speak to was Waikato prop Graham Purvis. Purvis had been socialising with members of the Galwegians club the night before and as he was rushing off to join his colleagues on the team bus they had urged him to 'Come and play here.' The caller was serious. 'Remember what we said last night? We need a prop-cum-coach at our club, someone like you.'

'But I'm committed to play in France,' Purvis told him. 'They're expecting me. I can't pull out now, but here, have a chat with my room-mate, he's a front rower, too.'

Suddenly, Warren Gatland found himself in earnest conversation with someone he'd never met, who believed he was a prop and who was inviting him to return to Galway — a place that was a mystery to him because, throughout the All Blacks' stay the town had been shrouded in fog. From that unlikely introduction would flourish a relationship that, 10 years on, would see Gatland coaching Ireland at the fourth Rugby World Cup.

Just 26 when he made that first visit to Galway, in the role of back-up hooker to Sean Fitzpatrick (which would be his lot in international rugby), Gatland became one of the original rugby nomads, happily pursuing his favourite sport in two countries on opposite sides of the world for many years.

This arrangement allowed Gatland to operate effectively year round as a rugby player without complication until 1992, when, in the first season of NPC play-offs, he suddenly found himself double booked. The Waikato team of which he had been a critical component for seven seasons had pulled off a massive upset by defeating previously invincible Auckland at Eden Park, to set up a grand final against Otago in Hamilton.

Gatland had warned the Waikato coach, Kevin Greene, that in the unlikely event of Waikato qualifying for the final, he would be unavailable, the reason being that to be eligible to play in Connacht again, he had to personally register in Dublin by 1 October. And that was four days before the NPC final.

The Waikato management held an emergency meeting to discuss

the situation. 'No problem,' they said to Gatland. 'You can fly to Dublin, register and be back here by the weekend.'

Gatland gulped. He didn't want to let either team down. So on the Monday evening, he settled down aboard an Air New Zealand flight to London, arriving at Heathrow 25 hours later. After a three-hour wait, he picked up a connecting flight to Dublin, where he made his way to the Lansdowne Road offices of the Irish Rugby Union to commit himself to another season of club rugby in Connacht.

The next morning he drove across Ireland to Galway, where he attended the Galwegians club's Wednesday-night training session. There was time for one relaxing evening in Galway before he began retracing his steps — a drive back to Dublin and a flight to Heathrow before embarking on another 25-hour Air New Zealand journey, all the way back to Auckland.

Gatland wasn't sure whether he'd be double jet-lagged or, in light of the swift return to his natural time zone, not jet-lagged at all when he took the field at Rugby Park in Hamilton on the Sunday afternoon. What he did know was that he'd be damnably tired, and when his head started spinning about 10 minutes from full time, he indicated to the reserves bench that a replacement was needed.

Like Fitzpatrick, Gatland demonstrated amazing durability throughout his career and in establishing a new Waikato record of 140 appearances over nine seasons, he hardly ever missed a game or exited the field before the final whistle. But given his marathon travel effort in the shake-down to the 1992 final, a 70-minute effort was more than acceptable to his colleagues. And besides, in the euphoria of Waikato taking out its first NPC championship by the overwhelming margin of 40 points to 5, almost no one noticed Gatland's early departure.

His celebrations were muted, partly because of his tiredness but mostly because he had only 28 hours to get himself packed and off to the airport for his second journey through to the UK in a week. Connacht beckoned.

'It's not something I would want to do again, three flights like that in a week,' says Gatland, 'but it was worth the effort. When I first played for Waikato, we were in the second division, so to be part of a championship-winning team was pretty special.'

Although Gatland would specialise as a hooker for Waikato, the All Blacks and the Galwegians club in Ireland, all his early rugby was as a No 8. It was from the back of the scrum that he represented Waikato schools and captained the Northern Regional schools' team to a notable victory over Australia.

After leaving school, Gatland assessed his career prospects as a rugby player. He aspired to play at the highest level but reasoned he was neither tall enough to make it as a No 8 nor fast enough to get there as an openside flanker. 'I felt as a loose forward I would have survived at club level and possibly broken into rep rugby. But that would have been my lot. So I decided to become a hooker, where I knew my experience as a No 8 would be a valuable asset.'

And a hooker he became, breaking into the Waikato rep team after two seasons on the fringe and, in 1986, packing down in the front row between Graham Purvis and Richard Loe. They would all become All Blacks. That year, they helped Waikato reclaim first-division status.

Waikato was performing to a mediocre standard, and Gatland understood why after attending an All Black trial where he mixed with Auckland's finest players, most of whom were All Blacks. 'Auckland was setting the standards back then,' says Gatland, 'and I was blown away at how far behind we obviously were.

'When I went back to Waikato, I said that unless there were major improvements in our structure and calls, and in our smartness on the pitch, we would continue to lag behind. I knew we had a promising young group of players and if we stuck together we'd make our mark.'

Gatland was fortunate that in 1989 Glenn Ross took over as coach. He encouraged input from his players and Gatland was one who responded. Initially, Ross wanted Gatland as his captain, but Gatland declined. 'I wanted to concentrate on my role as hooker,' he says. 'I asked Glenn if he'd considered John Mitchell. He thought about it and decided to offer him the leadership.

'It worked out brilliantly. John was an inspirational player and a natural leader, most influential in terms of decision-making. One of his greatest strengths was that he encouraged input from others and was never threatened by it.'

In 1988, Gatland broke into the All Blacks. There was a front-row vacancy following Andy Dalton's retirement and, impressed with the Waikato hooker's ball skills and mobility, Alex Wyllie and his fellow selectors introduced him for the tour of Australia, where he fulfilled the role of understudy to Fitzpatrick.

While Gatland was naturally thrilled to pull on the black jersey, after three years and four overseas tours, he remained understudy to the indestructible Fitzy. Not that it bothered him. 'I was so proud to be there,' he says. 'Although I didn't get to play a test, I never stopped feeling special and privileged at being an All Black. I knew there were countless others who would have given an arm to be where I was.

'My missing test selection was a Catch 22 situation. During my involvement, the team went 50 matches without defeat. For me to break into the top line-up, they needed to play poorly and lose, and I didn't want that. A winning team is a happy team. Alternatively, it required Fitzy to get injured, and I certainly didn't want that to happen. So I accepted my lot and derived enormous satisfaction from touring Australia, Canada, Wales, Ireland, France and Argentina.'

Although he only got to warm the reserves benches at most of the famous test venues, Gatland did get to represent his country in such exotic destinations as Perth, Singleton, Canberra, Townsville, Gosford, Melbourne, Vancouver, Swansea, Newport, Dublin, Galway, Narbonne, Bayonne, La Rochelle, Cordoba, Buenos Aires and Mar del Plata. He vividly remembers his international debut, at Perry Lakes Stadium in Perth. Although the All Blacks won by 60 points, for Gatland the occasion was one huge disappointment. The reason? 'Grizz Wyllie ran the crap out of us! It was a trait of his, to run his players into the ground before matches he knew the team would win. I was really looking forward to my debut, but in the event, I had nothing left in the tank. I wanted to give 100 per cent, but my legs were tired and heavy.'

In addition to the 17 matches he played for his country from 1988 to 1991, Gatland stripped for 14 tests, spending some 18 hours on the All Blacks reserves bench, ever ready for action but knowing that the man in the No 2 jersey, Fitzpatrick (who didn't aspire to the captaincy until after Gatland had been discarded) possessed iron-man qualities. For Gatland, the biggest disappointment was being dropped for the Bledisloe Cup series against the Wallabies in 1991 after touring Argentina and subsequently missing selection for the World Cup (in which New Zealand bombed out at the semifinal stage). Gatland's replacement, Graham Dowd, didn't see one minute of action at the tournament.

There was a major shake-up in personnel when Laurie Mains

succeeded John Hart as national coach in 1992 and Gatland found himself back in the mix, being selected to oppose Fitzpatrick in the final trial at McLean Park, Napier.

Although Gatland's Saracens team caused a major boilover by defeating the shadow test XV, with Gatland producing one his finest performances, he remained on the outer. At 28, his All Black career was at an end, the selectors preferring Dowd as understudy to Fitzpatrick.

Unwanted he may have been at international level, but Gatland had plenty to offer still at representative level, going on to make a further 54 appearances for Waikato and sharing in not only the team's historic NPC triumph in 1992 but the lifting of the Ranfurly Shield from Auckland the following season.

Given that Auckland had held the famous 'log' since 1985 and had withstood 61 defences (the previous record being 25), that represented quite an achievement by the Mooloo men.

In addition to all that, there was a glorious 38–10 victory over the 1993 British Lions. They were halcyon days for Waikato rugby. Gatland was enjoying his rugby to such an extent he decided to make himself available for Waikato again in 1995, the year in which John Boe succeeded Greene as coach.

He'd done an extensive amount of off-season training, but having accepted an invitation to attend the wedding of former team-mate Richard Jerram, both he and Matthew Cooper were unable to take part in a Friday evening fitness test, organised by the new management. In the *Waikato Times* on the Monday, Boe expressed satisfaction with the testing but said he was disappointed Gatland and Cooper hadn't attended.

'That conveyed the impression I didn't care,' says Gatland. 'I'd notified the management I couldn't be there, so I wasn't impressed with that attitude. I told them they could stuff their team, and retired. At least I went out on my terms.'

As Gatland the player exited, Gatland the coach entered. He was immediately snapped up by his club, Taupiri, and before long Willie Hetaraka, a friend, invited him to assist with the Thames Valley NPC team, which was languishing in the third division. Together, they worked the oracle, Thames Valley qualifying top before smashing Poverty Bay 47–8 in the final to win promotion to second division.

Gatland intended following a similar programme in 1996, until he received a phone call from Ireland. The coach of the Connacht representative team had resigned and they were offering him the post. 'I was mulling it over when they advised me the team was going on a pre-season trip to Sweden. That clinched it! It's one of the great things about rugby, you get the opportunity to visit diverse and interesting countries.'

Gatland had been teaching at St Paul's Collegiate in Hamilton and was apprehensive about breaking the news to the principal, Steve Cole, who happened to be the son-in-law of former All Black John Graham. 'Steve was brilliant,' says Gatland. 'He just said, "Go for it."'

And with that, Gatland was off to Ireland, this time permanently. He and his wife, Trudi, had developed a strong affinity with the people of Galway. During his third season with Galwegians, Trudi had given birth to their first child, Shauna, a spina bifida baby who lived for only four months. It was a traumatic time for the Gatlands and Warren says he will never forget the support he and his wife received. 'It cost them a lot of money,' he says. 'I'll never forget what they did for us, which was why I was so delighted to be returning to help with Connacht.'

To say Connacht represented a challenge to Gatland would be a monumental understatement, for the men from the west had been the perennial whipping boys of Irish rugby. But by introducing basic New Zealand precepts, Gatland soon had them competitive, to the extent that in the 1997–98 northern season, they qualified for the European Cup.

While interviewing Gatland, a prominent Irish rugby correspondent proffered the opinion that, in a pool featuring Nice, Begles-Bordeaux and Northampton, the possibility existed that Connacht might go through without a solitary win.

'I promise you,' Gatland told the reporter, 'we will win a game. I'm not nominating which one, but we will have a win, don't worry.' Well, Connacht didn't have a win. It had lots of wins. It beat a Northampton side bursting with British Lions, home and away, it downed Begles-Bordeaux, home and away, and it won at home against Nice. The solitary loss, through a last-minute penalty try in controversial circumstances, was away to Nice.

All of which installed Connacht top of its group, qualifying it for the quarterfinals. Gatland's men were the toast of Ireland, no other side from that country having previously won on French soil. Gatland recalls that the Connacht players developed a fantastic team ethos. 'Because we kept winning matches we were expected to lose, the celebrations became heartier and heartier. The guys would often party through until 6 a.m., then run the grog out at a 10 a.m. Sunday training session and start the build-up for the next challenge. You couldn't put a value on the fun we had. We even introduced a team song. It was a special time.'

In the quarterfinals, Connacht drew Agen, a team with a massive pack, including such celebrated international players as Abdel Benazzi and Philippe Benetton. Connacht led 12–6 at halftime but then blew a two-man overlap and the opportunity to go ahead 19–6. Agen scored at the other end, instead, and went on to win 40–34.

Gatland says that although Connacht missed out on the big prize, the team achieved a major breakthrough for Irish rugby. 'There existed an aura about French teams. They were seen as big and powerful and virtually unbeatable on their home grounds. It was obvious many Irish teams had lost before they'd even taken the field, so we became a catalyst for all Irish teams. "If Connacht can do it, so can we."'

Gatland was at a wedding in Galway when Pat Whelan, the Irish manager, phoned him to announce that Brian Ashton, the national coach, was under stress and was about to quit his position, partway through the Five Nations Championship. Was he prepared to take over?

'I said I was delighted to accept,' says Gatland, 'but only on the condition that I had an input into selection.'

That was acceptable to the Irish Rugby Union and, with bewildering speed, Gatland found himself coach of Ireland. His first assignment was a daunting one: a Paris meeting against a French team that had just put 50 points on Scotland at Murrayfield.

Gatland was mindful of media predictions that Ireland could be heading for a record heavy loss. Well, the pessimists had forecast doom and gloom for Connacht and been proven wrong. He would have to see if he couldn't silence them again.

'I would have preferred a longer preparation time, obviously,' says Gatland, 'but that wasn't possible. We assembled on the Monday, flew to Paris on the Thursday and were up against a highly charged French team on the Saturday.

'I changed the team's defensive pattern but, tactically, there wasn't time to adjust much else. Instead, I concentrated on bringing them closer together as a team. I set up a fax line and, through the Irish Rugby Union, encouraged the rugby fans to send messages of good-will to their team. In the event, 5000 faxes came through, which we plastered around the walls of the team room. They provided inspiration and let the players know their nation was behind them. In asking them for a hundred per cent effort, I said all I wanted was that they could look at themselves in a mirror after the game and know they'd given their best.'

After 75 minutes of torrid action, Ireland led 16–13. The unthinkable had become the achievable. But France scored a late try, assisted by a knock-on the referee missed, to claim the game 18–16. France went on to win the championship, undefeated.

Ireland subsequently lost to Wales and England, finishing with the wooden spoon. It wasn't the result Gatland wanted, but there were enough positives for him to look ahead with optimism. 'There were,' he says, 'a number of things to be addressed before the next season rolled around. For a start, the players weren't fit enough for international rugby. And then it was a case of prioritising issues. Fitness was number one, followed by scrums and lineouts and, very importantly, the mental approach.

'I was the eighth or ninth coach Ireland had had in the 1990s, so understandably the players were seriously lacking in confidence. They were afraid to have an opinion, always feeling threatened. This attitude was manifesting itself on the field. They were more concerned about getting through 80 minutes without making a mistake than in attempting anything. That was the first thing I sought to change. I encouraged them to take chances, assuring them they wouldn't be dropped on the basis of a few mistakes.'

Ireland improved its standing in the 1999 Five Nations Championship but came unstuck in the World Cup, losing first to Australia in pool play and then, disastrously, to Argentina in a repechage match that cost it a home quarterfinal against France.

Irish rugby fans were plunged into despair and Gatland's position as coach was in jeopardy. 'It was an experience I wouldn't want to go through again,' he says. 'Through it all I learnt a lot about myself. It was, I can assure you, character building.' Gatland survived and over the next two seasons built Ireland into a formidable international team, one which beat France in Paris (for the first time in 27 years) and again at home, destroyed England's Grand Slam hopes with an epic victory in Dublin and continued its recent domination over Wales.

Such was Ireland's form, they went into the clash against John Mitchell's All Blacks in November 2001 favoured to win, but after leading 21–7 early in the second half, capitulated, going down 40–29.

Although Gatland was contracted to the end of the 2001–2002 season, he encouraged a review six months out. Given that Ireland had enjoyed its best sequence of international results in 15 years, he anticipated a favourable result.

He was dead wrong on that. The committee thanked him for what he had done, said they felt he had taken the team as far as he could and bade him farewell.

'I was pretty bitter at the time,' says Gatland, 'because I believe the team had developed well and we were getting results. I personally came out with a reasonable financial deal but my dismissal caused a massive uproar. I don't think the IRFU anticipated the public reaction.' The union chose as its new coach Eddie O'Sullivan, who had been Gatland's assistant.

Disillusioned, Gatland returned to New Zealand for a five-week break and was surprised at the offers that rolled in, from NPC unions and from UK clubs. In the end, he linked up with the Wasps club in London and had only been involved a short while when Nigel Melville, Wasps director of rugby, announced a move to Gloucester, leaving him in charge. As 2002 unfolded, Gatland was relishing the fresh challenge.

For the record

Player
• Waikato, 1986–1994 (140 games)
• New Zealand, 1988–1991 (17 games)

Coach
• Thames Valley, 1995
• Connacht, 1996–1998
• Ireland, 1998–2002
• London Wasps, 2002

FRANCE

The essence of French rugby can be found in the towns and cities in the southwest of the country. Although Paris hosts internationals and its clubs occasionally claim the national championship, the game flourishes in the southern regions. The French love the physicality of rugby, which, when blended with their natural Gallic flair, produces a volatile concoction capable of overwhelming any team. Among the first to challenge rugby's amateur principles, France was thrown out of the Five Nations Championship in the 1930s but later restored. France has gone on to win many Five Nations titles and has twice reached the final of the World Cup, in 1987 and 1999.

Founded

1920

IRB

1978

Clubs

1720

Players

237,000 men, 4100 women

Rugby Nomads

Tabai Matson, Scott Palmer, Graham Purvis

Tabai Matson

A number of coaches and players interviewed for this book have, like Tabai Matson, plied their rugby trade in several countries. In each instance there has been one country with which they have identified and loved above others. For Matson that country is France.

The affinity can be traced back to 1995, when Matson was drafted into the All Black team in France while working there as a representative for Coca-Cola. The ultimate goal had arrived unexpectedly through another player's injury as well as being in the right place at the right time, and so began his French connection.

In 1996 Matson went with the All Blacks to South Africa nursing an injured calf. He had hoped it would come right on tour but it refused to heal and the injury-prone Canterbury centre, who made just two appearances on tour, at Port Elizabeth and Potchefstroom, said he later regretted he had not ruled himself out of contention.

'Looking back, I probably shouldn't have gone, but I was a young guy hoping my leg would come right and who could resist an All Black tour?'

He was 23 and hoped he had years ahead of him at the top, but the New Zealand coach had other ideas, says Matson. 'John Hart was the All Black coach and, reading his comments on injured players in his biography, I knew that as long as he was there I wasn't going further. I didn't stand a chance.

'I thought he would be the All Black coach for years and so I concentrated my energies on doing my best for Canterbury and the Crusaders and then looking offshore for the future.'

The red and blacks had a brilliant year in 1998, with the Crusaders and Canterbury winning both Super 12 and NPC first-division titles. Matson, as centre, operated in the country's slickest backline, along with Andrew Mehrtens and Mark Mayerhofler (a combination of surnames which prompted one of New Zealand's leading rugby writers to liken them to a Viennese stockbroking firm). Then came an offer at the end of the season for Matson to spend two years at the Brive club in France. Matson's wife was enthusiastic and, he later said, it became one of the best decisions he had ever made in his life.

His introduction to the Brive club was an eye-opener; Matson was amazed to see the team coach stagger off the field with a torn shirt and a bleeding nose. He asked Gregor Townsend, the former Scottish and Lions five-eighth, what was going on. 'The coach is a nutter,' explained Townsend. 'He motivates his players before a match by shouting at them, abusing and punching them. But today Rambo [Brive's imposing blindside flanker] whacked him back. The two of them went at it, smacking the hell out of each other. The coach loved it.'

Brive won.

Coming from Crusaders territory, where Matson believed they knew everything there was to know about rugby, he was surprised to discover how much he learned about the game while playing in France. Including passion.

Both he and his Kiwi team-mate, former Auckland prop Kevin Nepia, lacked passion, the French told them. 'You can't play rugby without it.'

Kissing and hugging his fellow players after games took some getting used to, Matson admitted, especially having come from such a staunch, 'men are men' environment. 'It was strange — and scary at first — having to shake everybody's hand every day, half the team kissing each other every morning and players putting their arms around you when they spoke. But after a while it became natural and it was quite pleasant having team-mates showing genuine emotions. And what emotions! I have vivid memories of our coach having to physically pull our open and blindside flankers apart as they demonstrated their emotions for each other.'

Mid-week training took the form of a highly competitive match between the club's A and B teams, and was another shock for Matson. Injuries came thick and fast: one player did his shoulder, another his medial ligaments. So fierce were the Wednesday night training sessions that they attracted a number of spectators keen to watch the usurpers take on the top dogs.

The major difference for Matson, though, was in the players' and spectators' attitudes to home and away matches.

'For a home turnout you can get up to 50,000 at an important local game. The church bells are ringing, the players are crying . . . Brive only lost one game at home while I was there. Then you play an away game before huge crowds in another town, their church bells are ringing and that team is crying . . .

'They just don't seem to care about winning away games, it's the home ones that count, and if a team wins two games away they're straight into the semifinals of the competition. You wonder how the French are so successful.'

Ironically, after his early days of being sidelined through injury, Matson has had only one major injury since leaving New Zealand and that came after he was selected to play for Fiji (Matson was born there and has a Fijian mother) in the 1999 World Cup. In the build-up in France, where Fiji was based, he was laid out two days before the cup competition started and was sent back to Brive to recuperate. There's unfinished business on that front: Matson would like to have another crack at the World Cup in 2003 and says he will throw his hat into the ring for Fijian selection.

Nowadays, Matson lives with his family in Japan under contract to the Yamaha corporate team but dreams that one day he can return to France and coach in a little village there. 'My wife and I love the place and I'd like to get our kids speaking in French.'

He says he gets annoyed with ongoing media criticism of the player-drain from New Zealand. 'That's a no-brainer. Of course you go out and experience the world. If I had stayed in Christchurch, where would I be today? It's such a fickle business now with coaches changing all the time. One coach might want you, the next might not.

'I believe we produce the best rugby players in the world. Maybe there are only a hundred or so of Super 12 calibre, and this explosion of our rugby talent around the world is excellent, especially for our top club players, who are highly regarded in countries like Japan.'

For the record

Player
- Canterbury, 1994–1997 (58 games)
- New Zealand, 1995–1996 (5 games)
- Canterbury Crusaders, 1996–1997 (12 games)
- Fiji, 1999 (5 games)

Scott Palmer

The year was 1997 and prop Scott Palmer was a new boy at Begles-Bordeaux, a club which had last won the national championship in 1991 when they boasted a front row feared throughout France: Serge Simon, Vincent Moscato and Philippe Gimbert. The trio had also formed the French front row and had later been dubbed 'the Beasts of Begles', their notoriety enhanced when Moscato was ordered off in the England international in 1992.

Six years on, France's coach and a former Begles captain, Bernard Laporte, reunited that formidable front row to play for his Stade Francais side against their old club. It was to be the first time they had returned as a front-row unit to Bordeaux, where they had made their names, and interest in the contest was intense.

The media build-up in the week leading up to the match was content to focus on the two teams' powerhouses, the front rows: the old Beasts of Begles versus the new-look Begles pack. The day arrived. Such was the tension that five minutes after play was due to start Stade Francais and Begles-Bordeaux players remained locked in a stand-off, jogging up and down on the spot in the players' tunnel with neither captain prepared to lose face by leading his team out first.

Under pressure from the referee and a roaring crowd, Begles captain Olivier Brouzet took the home side out, incurring the disapproval of his team for backing down and allowing Stade Francais captain Mascato to gain the psychological advantage.

'We were on the back foot to start with,' recalled Palmer. 'In the first scrum of the game I was eye-gouged. I couldn't see a thing, one of my eyelids was bleeding and I thought, *Hell, this is going to be a long day.* In the second scrum the same thing happened (after the game someone told me I looked as if I'd been playing against a cat because my whole face was covered in scratches) and I knew that if it wasn't sorted then, it would follow me around. I had to do something; deal with it.

'There was a bit of a scrap on the sideline and to this day people have said the punch was thrown from behind. I'd like to think he saw it coming . . .'

Led by its new pack, Begles-Bordeaux won. The beasts were no more.

Scott Palmer is restrained by Begles-Bordeaux team-mate
Thomas Ossard as he lays into an Agen prop.

After the game Serge Simon, whom Palmer had packed down against, kept his sunglasses on until the sun had gone down and they had to be forcibly removed.

'He was a great guy off the field,' Palmer discovered. 'He came up to me and said it was the best black eye he'd had in eight years!'

Front rows in France were violent places at times, Palmer learned, with locks coming through from the second row and hitting the front rowers in the face. There was not a lot that could be done to avoid it. 'When you play in France you've got to realise that violence is a big part of French rugby; it's just part of the environment.

'With teams like Begles-Bordeaux you have these huge strong packs around you, so you don't see many problems at all on the paddock because they are sorted out so quickly. We had a call, "Feu, feu" ["Fire, fire"], in which the front row would split apart and guys would come through the middle and smack whoever they could in the face and then try to drop them. From there the whole scrum would erupt in a huge fight.'

He learned it was more fun to be a prop in France than in New Zealand. It was macho and it was cult, with the French putting great emphasis on their packs and front rows. At warm-ups before major matches, it was the front row that led the team and this carried through to the game.

Begles-Bordeaux had its fair share of characters, including hooker Marc de Rougemont, a former French international.

'He had a steel plate inserted into his forehead following a motorbike accident and one of his favourite after-match tricks was to line up ice cubes on the bar — the most I saw him do was 20 — and smash them with his forehead,' says Palmer. 'I've seen him knock himself out on the bar once because of the solid wood underneath.

'We'd spend half the night with this trick. I got roped into it too with the other French front rowers, who thought it was great fun. You'd go into a bar and there would be four or five guys standing around with bleeding heads and crushed ice all over the place.'

Begles-Bordeaux was followed by a year with Aurillac, a small club at the bottom of the first division, and then, in 2001 Palmer was contracted to a famous old first-division club, Bourgoin Jallieu, which boasted many past and present internationals in its ranks, including Stefan Glas and the legendary Marc Cecillon, France's long-standing No 8/lock and town hero.

Palmer arrived with a big reputation. The former North Harbour and Auckland tighthead prop, in his fourth year in France, was one of the country's highest-paid overseas players. He had helped hold off the Beasts of Begles in a famed encounter and been selected by a French magazine for its playing XV of those not in the current national team.

However, no one in Bourgoin Jallieu, including Palmer himself, could have anticipated his off-field introduction to town. The team was jubilant. It had beaten Toulouse in a pre-season tournament, a rare achievement against the champion French club. Palmer had propped opposite Toulouse and France international Christian Califano, and although Califano had got the better of the encounter, Palmer whole-heartedly embraced the post-match euphoria with his new team-mates.

It all started with a few beers at a local Irish bar owned by Dave Morgan, the former Otago prop who had been selected for the Blues Super 12 team in 2000 (but didn't play because of a serious hamstring injury). Towards the pub's closing time at midnight Palmer decided he would head back to where the players were still celebrating, in the *salle* — a large white sponsor's tent alongside the function hall at the ground. He returned with a French girl he had met at the Irish bar; she had worked at one of the beer tents sited around the ground that afternoon. From that point on, things became rather messy.

Palmer picks up the tale: 'I was pretty drunk by this time. Somehow or other I got up on the stage and took over the drums, the band scattered, I did some singing and ended up falling over the microphone and smashing it. To make matters worse, I was stark naked and doing on stage what is commonly called "The Dance of the Flaming Arseholes" — an ancient dance that most rugby players know — which involves hanging some toilet paper out of your backside. Someone lights the paper at the other end and the aim is to scull a pint before the flames reach their destination.

'It wasn't long after that, when I'd got my clothes back on, that a French guy in my team started throwing chairs at me . . .' As ever, the fight was triggered by the fatal combination of drink and a pretty woman. Both men were drunk and both wanted the girl.

Palmer's version of events is that he decided to walk away from the situation, saying that with the language barrier it was going to be just too difficult to sort out. The girl, however, indicated that she wanted to remain with the New Zealander.

'This French guy proceeded to jump on the stage and throw chairs at us across what was pretty much a crowded room, so I was running around dodging them and then he hopped down off the stage, came up to me and a bit of an altercation started.

'Everyone cleared out of the *salle* and it was down to the two of us fighting. The sponsors had run, the girl had disappeared and the Frenchman was going crazy. I landed a lucky punch and stopped him.

'He was knocked out cold and stretchered out by the local fire brigade, which had arrived on the scene in response to a mobile call from one of the sponsors, who had panicked when he saw the flames coming out of my backside.'

The fight continued in the car park. The French player's friend, a large French Polynesian, took up cudgels on his mate's behalf and, although dazed, Palmer was astonished to find himself still standing. That was until Marc Cecillon decided that no Kiwi was going to have the better of a Frenchman, spun Palmer around, hooked him with a magnificent left to the face and dropped him to the ground.

At 3 a.m., 'with quite a lot of people still around, including the 12-

strong fire brigade crew and a couple of ambulances that had arrived', a shirtless and bloodied Palmer was bundled into the team manager's car and driven home.

The call came early next morning. Palmer was to appear before the president of the rugby club to explain his behaviour: not only the fight, but also the broken microphone, his nudity and the dance in the sponsor's tent. He was allowed an interpreter, he was told.

Palmer opted for Morgan, who was also permitted to defend him. The two men held an anxious conference at the Irish pub prior to meeting the president, says Palmer. 'We decided our only defence would be that "The Dance of the Flaming Arseholes" was considered to be the equivalent of the haka and it was our native right "when and where" to perform this old New Zealand tradition, much like performing the haka.'

A stony-faced club president was unimpressed. Palmer was fined the equivalent of $NZ3,000 and suspended from play, along with the Frenchman he had fought, for eight days.

The question then was how would the French react upon his return to the club? Palmer admitted he was nervous about the reception he would get, in particular from Cecillon, and opted to keep a low profile for several weeks after the incident.

It was difficult, he admitted. The atmosphere in the club was icy at first, but Palmer said he was relieved to find there was a consensus that he had not been in the wrong as far as the fight went.

'It was probably because I was regarded as a Begles player and a rank outsider. I was later told the incident was the talk of the town; apparently they hadn't had such an interesting start to the season in 10 years.'

He never saw the girl again and the player he laid out is today one of his great mates. Cecillon greeted Palmer the next time they met — and thereafter — with an embrace and smacking kiss on each cheek. The club later opened its heart to Palmer and he, in turn, loved playing there.

Palmer was tempted to stay on. He had an outstanding reputation in France and was relishing the lifestyle. His salary had trebled in three years, and his contract package included an apartment, a car and return air fares to New Zealand. But, after four years away, Palmer knew he had reached a point where his career had to come first. There were postgraduate papers to finish off for his Master of Business Studies. It was time to hang up his boots there, leave his onfield and off-field antics behind and settle into life as a sober businessman, half a world away from the violence and passion of the French rugby field.

In 2002 Palmer was drafted back into Auckland's NPC team and says he is enjoying being back at home and working in his new professional career. There are, too, fond memories of France, its rugby, magnificent food, wine and lovely women.

'People believe that the French are arrogant. That's so untrue. The French are great people and once you establish yourself in a town and meet the locals, they look after you. First, though, you have to prove yourself, but maybe not in quite the way I did at Bourgoin Jallieu.

'There are some things I'll never forget. Eric Rush had come up to talk to my club, Aurillac, in 1999 and was staying at my place. The French are normally very well behaved when they drink, unlike many New Zealand teams, whose after-match behaviour is often a shambles by comparison. But this night someone had got pretty drunk and was causing trouble, so one of the players decided to drop him and it was quite a big fight.

'The president came up to me and asked me to tell Eric that he was sorry he had witnessed this fight and hoped that he wasn't shocked. They were not happy that such a thing had happened while Rushy had been in the club. The president was apologetic and wanted me to explain that this sort of thing didn't usually happen in France.

'I reassured him that Eric had probably seen the odd punch or two thrown in his time. I'd actually looked over at Rushy during the fight and saw him enjoying himself immensely.

'And then there was the time I was playing for Aurillac against La Rochelle. I got injured — I had done my knee and was hobbling around. The play had moved to the other side of the field and I heard the crowd of about 6000 heckling and booing me. I couldn't hobble any more so I just sat down in the mud. The crowd's booing got even worse so I took offence to this and decided to give them the fingers.

'I gave them the one-fingered salute and to this day I've never seen so many Coke cans, hot dogs and umbrellas rain down on a player. I just got pelted. At this stage the 60-year-old physio had arrived to tend to my injury and he said in broken English as he got hit on the back of the head with an orange, "Scottee, can you please stop giving the fingers?" That was the last time I ever gave anyone the fingers at a game in France.'

For the record

Player
- North Harbour, 1995–1996 (35 games)
- Begles-Bordeaux, France, 1997–1999 (42 games)
- Auckland, 1999, 2002 (14 games)
- Aurillac, France, 1999–2000 (22 games)
- Bourgoin Jallieu, France, 2000–2001 (26 games)
- Thames Valley, 2001 (8 games)

Graham Purvis

The longest journey for Graham Purvis wasn't from Waikato to All Black, or from Hamilton, New Zealand, to Ussel, France. The big one for the 22-year-old was the decision to leave his mates and his home town of Waihi in pursuit of a rugby dream of becoming an All Black.

To his astonished friends from Waihi College and the Whiritoa Surf Club it was an ambitious pipe-dream. Purvis had played no representative age-grade or even school rugby and had his first game in a Thames Valley Under 21 grade — at the relatively late age of 18.

When a friend's father noted that Purvis was of similar stature to the current All Black props and quizzed him as to the reason why he shouldn't become an All Black, Purvis struggled to find an answer. He had an ally in Waihi senior coach Tom Tubman, who believed he had the build and the ability to make it to the top; he just needed to leave town to get there.

It was a pretty daunting challenge when the odds were considered rationally.

As a prop, Purvis had rivals Steve McDowell and Kevin Boroevich, who were the same age as he and on the brink of All Black selection at a time when he was shifting to Hamilton in a bid to establish his career at a local club.

Purvis asked around and found that Hamilton Old Boys was the one to join. In March 1984 he arrived early at the club's first pre-season training session and was seen jogging around the ground's perimeter as the first players arrived. 'Who's he?' the Old Boys' coach, Bill Kindley, asked, taking in the newcomer's bulky frame and obvious fitness. The first hurdle had been surmounted.

By the end of that season Old Boys had covered itself in glory, winning Waikato's three club trophies — the Has Catley Memorial, the Breweries Shield and the Stag Trophy — and Purvis had been picked for George Simpkin's Waikato team.

While the dream was inching closer, to Purvis success was a journey, not a destination. If he was to continue his progress he would need to cram in as much experience as he could within a relatively short time. He decided to play rugby in France while his competition lay on the beach over summer.

At the end of 1985 the Union Sportif Usselois (USU), which had

Former All Black captain Buck Shelford leads the ex-pat Kiwi team in a haka at Ussel, France. On the extreme left is Graham Purvis.

recently been promoted from France's third division to the second, was happy to take on the 'fairly green' prop from Waikato.

Ussel's only club was looking for forwards and a New Zealander with provincial experience would be ideal. Purvis, along with former Waikato loose forward Wayne Bullot, packed his bags and flew to France for the start of what was to become 11 consecutive winter seasons.

Purvis was pleased to discover that rugby enjoyed a fairly high profile in Ussel, a town of about 25,000 people set in the mountains close to a number of attractive lakes. A hard core of well-placed rugby enthusiasts had managed to establish one of France's four elite 'francais-sportitudes' (lycées or colleges, with rugby academies attached) in town, an, living in a château nearby was a prominent supporter of the game, Jacques Chirac (now President of France), who was Mayor of Paris at the time.

Rugby in France was very different from Purvis's New Zealand experience. 'In my first match our captain, Olivier Loutrat, had his nose broken when an irate touch judge ran onto the field and whacked him with his flag!' says Purvis.

'In my second game, at home, as I was rucking players out the back, my team-mates were kicking them back in. Clearly, an interesting time lay ahead.'

There seemed little interest in exploiting his ball skills and general mobility around the field. 'Gra-arm Purvees' was there to be a prop

173

and that meant scrummaging. Props went from scrum to scrum, and if there wasn't a scrum within the first 10 minutes they were ready to walk off the field, Purvis was amused to see. 'Some teams even kick the ball out on the full from the first kick off so the game can start with a scrum!'

Initially Purvis found himself in Ussel's B team, but forced his way into the top line-up ahead of two local props when it was seen that the second team was performing above itself because its scrum was working so well.

'Because I'd come from New Zealand and had been used to playing in good teams alongside strong props, I hadn't realised just how much a deficient front row would impact on the rest of the team,' reflects Purvis.

'I learned a lot about scrummaging in my first year in France, particularly as New Zealand had flirted — mercifully only for that 1985 season — with a one-metre rule for the NPC competition. So for me, a return to the full-on shove was a wake-up call.'

A clip on the ear dished out in New Zealand was usually enough to send an opponent back in line, but 'give someone a clip around the ear in France and you've got 10 people swarming around you. All of a sudden you're in the middle of a bloody fracas where everyone's kicking and punching. I guess it taught me to respect other people and a lot about the emotional elements of the French way of life.'

It was the amateur rugby era, but everyone in the team was paid in some form or another. A pseudo-professional environment functioned, and for Purvis in that first year, 'payment' — arranged by the club — consisted of a job teaching conversational English at a high school, an apartment and a car.

The next season he returned to a warm reception. He had good friends, his French had improved and he had become a public drawcard for the club. Purvis responded with a couple of strong performances in his first two appearances, a public-relations coup which ensured that crowds would turn up and support the team for the remainder of the season.

He was gaining invaluable experience and a mental hardening that would later enable him to foot it with top-class competition in New Zealand and around the world.

Purvis had learned that most of his orifices would get a regular working over, that winning a tighthead meant a punch on the nose for his hooker, that teams, particularly in the south, wore boxes to stop things getting tangled up in other people's hands and that referees were an endangered species if the home team lost.

He learned and appreciated that there was a lot of emotion in the dressing room before and after games and that tears would flow freely whether *les Usselois* won or lost.

Off field it was back to a familiar happy routine. There were team meals together after games and, following training on Thursday or Friday nights, a basic three-course meal at Chez Denise. Each player would put in 20 francs (about $NZ5), the club would pay the rest and, now and then, a splinter group would go on to bigger and better things at the Château de la Borde, a nightclub in an old castle on the outskirts of town.

Purvis was comfortably blending into the way of life and was glad to be back in France. After all, who could knock a nation that enjoyed good food, good wine and good rugby?

'A lot of my mix-and-mingle French classes took place in the bars and cafés after training,' he laughs. 'I remember one guy, Bruno Chadebech, whose brother Pierre played for France, saying to me, "I do not have a large vocabulary in English, but when I am drunk it arrives to me very quickly", and I think it was the same for my French in those early days.'

The major rugby sponsors were Pastis 51 and Ricard, who made versions of the popular aniseed-flavoured aperitif. Beer was considered a thirst quencher, to be drunk straight after a match, before going on to pre-dinner Pastis served in small spirit glasses.

The problem was that like other New Zealanders in France, Purvis was accustomed to continuing as he'd started. 'I was still going pretty hard on the beer, they start serving up the Pastis, I carry on consuming at the same volume. They slow down at this stage, but the Kiwi just goes on drinking at the same pace.

'There were a few trapped days after rugby in those early years. It's a bit like coming off the field and getting straight into the whisky.'

It was a challenge returning to New Zealand, where he had to prove himself to make it back into the Waikato squad and to overcome the disadvantage of his opposition getting valuable pre-season exposure in Barbarian-style games.

His first major challenge came in 1987, when he found that a recent All Black prop, Brian McGrattan, had moved into the province from Wellington. As Richard Loe was away with the All Black World Cup squad, McGrattan and Purvis shared a couple of games before Loe returned.

During that week the three props trained together, uneasily aware that one of them was about to be eliminated. Waikato's coach, Duncan Dysart, called the squad together halfway through the final training session to name the team for the coming Saturday and gave the nod to Loe and Purvis. Purvis watched as McGrattan stormed off the field and went home. He knew McGrattan had been wounded psychologically — and he says it was a huge boost to his morale.

'That was when I thought, hey, I really rated Scott Crichton and McGrattan as Wellington's All Black props when I was starting to play rugby. Now I must be getting to that same level.'

Back in Ussel there was also plenty to celebrate. In the 1987–1988 season USU was promoted to the first division, due in part to the impact of their New Zealand prop; as Purvis was upping his performance, so was the team.

Purvis had arrived back just in time to participate in the last of the qualifying rounds of play the following season when Ussel caused an upset by beating France's champion club, Biarritz, and then losing narrowly, 21–20, to Grenoble — another top first-division side.

'We were like the Eketahuna of French rugby and to beat Biarritz with Serge Blanco, Jean Condom and Pascal Ondarts playing, was a huge coup for our club,' says Purvis. 'To share in that joy was one of the deep memories.'

An unexpected visit from Ron Preston, a first-five from the Bay of Plenty, led to Ussel's big rugby event of that winter season. Preston was passing through the town and called into a local café which doubled up as the USU clubrooms.

'Look, Purvees.' The lady in the café pointed excitedly to the club's latest fundraiser — pieces of a jigsaw puzzle of Purvis's face — when she realized she was talking to a New Zealander. A phone call, a meeting in the bar between the two Kiwis, and three days later Preston resumed his trip to Toulouse. That was the spur Purvis needed to put together a French-Kiwi team to play a French invitation team at Ussel.

He got on the phone and arranged sponsorship through a supermarket chain, Le Clerc. With their help and that of the Ussel treasurer, 'Fee Fee' (local tax department chief Daniel Delpy), he wrote to the French Rugby Federation and obtained the names of all New Zealand players registered in every club. Then he wrote to the clubs and asked them to pass on the information to their New Zealand players. The response from the guys was great.

The match was staged on a Thursday night to avoid a clash with championship games. A number of leading French players, including Jean-Pierre Garuet, Thierry Picard and Serge Blanco, were there to watch, and as the All Black captain, Wayne Shelford (playing off-season for Toulouse's second-division team, TOEC) led his troops in the haka there was a roar of appreciation from the large French crowd. The match was keenly contested and the Kiwis just scraped home the winners.

After the game, the guitars came out and the beer flowed in the changing rooms as the New Zealanders, who had leapt at the chance of getting together again, celebrated into the night. A special set of jerseys had been made for the occasion and Purvis says he told his team-mates to keep theirs as a souvenir of the game.

'Buck Shelford said, "Oh no, I can't be bothered. If you want to, sell it or raffle it." So we decided to auction it off in pieces. We got to the formal after-match dinner and auctioned off the sleeves, $100 for each of the cut-off sleeves, and then we got about $400 for the body of the jersey. We told them to make the cheque out to the Château de la Borde. We went straight from there and plonked it on the bar of the nightclub. The rest of the evening was oblivion.'

In that third year, Purvis started to realize what other players in France and his team were earning from rugby, and so was able to negotiate a better deal for himself. But, because he knew that without Ussel and his off-season play he would never achieve his goal, he was in a weak position.

'I wasn't about to hold a knife to their throats because I so much wanted to keep going back to Ussel to make it succeed. I could see the gains happening. I had learned so much; my scrummaging in particular had advanced and I just so desperately wanted to be an All Black.'

A year later he achieved his dream. In 1989 Purvis was selected for the All Blacks, to tour Ireland and Wales.

However, there was still a commitment to honour with his club in

Ussel. At the end of the All Blacks' tour he returned to finish off his fifth and final season with the USU. He had remained loyal to the club and said he had no inclination, at any stage, to switch to higher-profiled first-division clubs in the area, such as Brive or Clermont-Ferrand.

'My rugby ambitions lay in New Zealand, not France. By going back I earned a lot of respect and developed strong friendships and relationships with the players. Many of them see foreigners in a sort of shady light, taking the place of one of their French mates. I would notice a bit of coldness to the overseas guys who'd just come into the club for a short period, yet they were quite friendly to me.'

He had delighted in his club's achievement in consolidating its place in the first division, and for their part the people of Ussel were very proud that their adopted home-town boy and friend 'Purvees' was now an All Black.

A memorable highlight of his relationship with Ussel was to come several months later, in October 1990, when he was chosen for the All Blacks' tour of France. Returning to France with the All Blacks meant Purvis was able to offer a valuable insight for the team in to French lifestyle and rugby philosophy. Everyone is given an off-field role in an All Blacks tour party and on this tour Purvis was allocated the key position of 'translator'.

His fluency in French proved to be indispensable to the team's manager, John Sturgeon, whose tolerance of their French hosts' convenient lack of English when it suited them had been declining since the day the All Blacks had arrived in the country.

After months of negotiating the tour schedule, the mayor of Toulon wanted to change the match kick-off time to suit his business schedule. Incorporating several of his finest West Coast adjectives Sturgeon instructed Purvis. 'Tell these pricks we don't care if the f—ing Queen's coming, the game starts on time.' The body language and tone of Sturgeon's voice was enough; it was clear that the French understood his meaning. The match started on time.

But, in just his second appearance on tour, against the French Barbarians at Agen, Purvis limped off the field with a torn calf muscle. He was invalided out of the game and, he thought, the tour. Under normal circumstances he would have returned to New Zealand, but Sturgeon insisted that Purvis remain on tour to assist him in the day-to-day tasks of team affairs and he gladly obliged.

'Injuries must rate as the most disheartening thing about rugby,' says Purvis. 'So much training, preparation, devotion and commitment for months, years, and it can vaporise in a split second. Those feelings are compounded tenfold when it happens while wearing an All Black jersey.'

Olo Brown took Purvis's place in the All Blacks for the final midweek match of the tour. A couple of years later, in 1992, it was Brown who would be preferred when Richard Loe was invalided out of the second test against Ireland, and then Brown who would withdraw from the one-off Samoan test in Auckland later that year to give Purvis his one match for the All Blacks on home soil. An interesting series of 'tag propping'.

The second-division French club he'd come to, five seasons earlier, had done him proud. Purvis had come from humble beginnings in Waihi to test matches and six tours with the All Blacks, via seven club championships with Hamilton Old Boys, second- and first-division NPC titles with Waikato and winning the Ranfurly Shield twice off Auckland.

And it was his Ussel call 'En bas' ('Go down') which was used by Waikato's front row to take the win, 27–21, against Auckland in the 1992 NPC semifinal. The country's two All Black front rows — Auckland's test trio of McDowell, Fitzpatrick and Brown against the more experienced combination of Loe, Gatland and Purvis — packed down for a second-half scrum, with Auckland desperately defending its goal line.

Gatland, an astute thinker of the game, chose the moves before every scrum and called 'en bas'. Down went Richard Loe. The collapsed scrum was reset, referee Dave Bishop moved around to Loe's side and, as Auckland's halfback, Jason Hewett, presented the ball to feed the scrum, Purvis, unseen by Bishop, palmed it back on the Waikato side for halfback Simon Crabb to race over and score before the opposition realised what was going on.

'Unfair,' the stunned Aucklanders claimed as television replays clearly showed 'the hand of God' at work, but a decade on, Purvis is unrepentant. 'Auckland were the biggest cheats in the country, and everyone else in New Zealand went "Yeehaa" when we got one back on them.' (The next week Waikato went on to win its first-ever first-division NPC title, defeating Otago 40–5.)

For Purvis, and many other players, winning the Ranfurly Shield and NPC are often more satisfying than being singled out for national recognition or personal achievements.

'The Waikato team of my era developed an amazing sense of togetherness. Along with the enormous pride and excitement of being named an All Black there was always a tinge of sadness as other deserving players in the team missed out. Winning things as a team produced the irreplaceable *we dunnit* feeling, something that will bond that group of players for ever.'

Asked if he believes he could have become an All Black without his time in Ussel, Purvis shakes his head. 'No, I don't think I would have had the experience; I don't think I could have. As a cultural rounding it was bloody marvellous. When I first went to France, Marque Vue or Chardon was about my exposure to wine. Certainly white wine was the limit. By the time I came back here, I wouldn't think of having a meal without a glass of wine. And the food was great, though I did draw the line at donkey sausages!

'I have some great mates in Ussel who I still keep in touch with, like my old captain, Loulou (Olivier Loutrat), who came out to New Zealand for the 1987 World Cup and connected so well with the New Zealanders he called his dog Kiwi. They're such neat people — very hospitable, generous and loving.

'I just can't imagine having any more fun than I've had out of rugby.'

For the record

Player
- Waikato, 1984–1993, 1997 (147 games)
- Ussel, France, 1985–1990 (110 games)
- New Zealand, 1989–1993 (28 games, 2 tests)
- Highfield, Ireland, 1994–1996

ITALY

It was a monumental breakthrough for Italy to be welcomed into the expanded Six Nations Championship in 2000 to play annually alongside heavyweights England, Ireland, Scotland, Wales and France. Although Italy has taken out the wooden spoon three times, the experience can only benefit its game. Unlike France, where the game's strength is in the south, in Italy it's in the north, with clubs like Rovigo, Padua and Treviso. The game was first played in Italy in 1910, with the FIR being formed 18 years later. Italy's two most recent national coaches have been New Zealanders, Brad Johnstone and John Kirwan.

Founded
1928
IRB
1987
Clubs
505
Players
36,000 men, 490 women
Rugby Nomads
John Kirwan, Richard Turner, Grant Kelly

John Kirwan

When Auckland's senior coach, John Hart, plucked 18-year-old John Kirwan out of third-grade obscurity with the Marist club to play for his champion side in 1983, he launched one of the most illustrious careers in All Black history.

Nineteen years on, as Italy's new coach, John Kirwan took an even bigger punt with another unknown 18-year-old, Sergio Parisse, selecting the teenage No 8 for Italy's one-off test against the All Blacks at Hamilton in June 2002.

Will Parisse become another Kirwan? Who knows, but Kirwan's decision was as typically fearless as any slashing run made during his marvellous 10-year, 96-game, 63-test record for the All Blacks. As a player 'JK' was known for his passionate commitment to Auckland and New Zealand. Today that same professional and personal commitment belongs to Italy.

Kirwan's links with Italy began when he went to Treviso in 1986 for a six-month contract with the Benetton club. He was 21 and already established as an All Black star, but the Benetton connection was to shape his life and open his eyes to a culture far removed from his early years in Auckland.

He returned the following year on holiday, after becoming a stand-out player of the 1987 inaugural Rugby World Cup, where his dazzling try-scoring run from within his own 22 against Italy, in the tournament's opening match at Eden Park, ranks as one of his finest ever.

For the next four years Kirwan returned to play his off-season rugby for Benetton, being joined there by Canterbury and New Zealand winger Craig Green after the conclusion of the 1987 World Cup. The two of them took a flat together adjoining Benetton's smart new sporting complex, with free access to its gymnasium, weight room and tennis courts. Life was brilliant for the two All Black wingers. Both loved the food and the country, both would later marry Italian girls from Treviso and the duo would be instrumental in steering Benetton to the Italian championship title in 1989.

This was a momentous year for Kirwan, with great personal highs and lows. The Benetton win at the end of the long European season delayed his return to New Zealand until late May 1989, which caused him to miss the All Black trials and come in for some media criticism over his 'Italian sojourns'. Then on 18 October 1989, during the All Blacks' tour of Wales and Ireland, he suffered a crippling injury, snapping his achilles tendon in the match against Pontypool. He was rushed to hospital, where he underwent surgery that evening, later rejoining the All Black team on crutches. It was an even more serious injury than the one he had suffered to his shoulder in 1984, but Kirwan won the admiration of his team-mates and coaches with his determination to fight back, which subsequently saw him return to full recovery.

Fiorella Tomasi also came into Kirwan's life in 1989 and they were married in November 1991 at the conclusion of the second World Cup in Britain, Ireland and France.

In September 2001, seven years after his All Black career had come to an end, John Kirwan again returned to Italy — via a playing stint with the NEC corporate team in Japan and two seasons with the Auckland-based Blues Super 12 team as manager and assistant coach — in his new role as assistant coach to the Italian rugby team.

With him went Fiorella and their three children, Francesca, Niko (named after Michael 'Niko' Jones) and Luca. Kirwan says that when he took the decision to make coaching his career, he was open-minded about where it would lead him.

'My home is where Fiorella and the children are. When you choose to live this sort of life you live wherever your contract is, and so it is very important for me to have my family around me wherever I go. It's hard leaving Mum and Dad and the family here, but it's the same for Fiorella leaving her family there.

'I don't feel homesick any more. I pretty much dream in Italian these days and I don't have to translate, which is good, but I still need to improve and so I've started reading in Italian because I leave out bits which I should know. I need to better understand the subtleties of the language.'

His return to Italy was triggered by a Blues board and NZRFU decision not to reappoint him to its coaching panel at the end of his one-year Super 12 contract in 2001. Kirwan was popular as the Blues' manager in 2000 under Blues and former Otago coach Gordon Hunter and, following Hunter's resignation through ill health, he was approached to put his name forward as assistant coach to Frank Oliver.

Kirwan was recommended by a panel which included Peter Thorburn, Bruce Robertson and his mentor, former All Black coach

John Hart, who later considered Kirwan did an outstanding job in his first major coaching role.

'I saw, at first hand, his excellent contribution to the 2001 Blues team. With Frank, John was having to work in partnership with a coach who is excellent technically, but one of the old school. The two were incompatible. Some of these old-school coaches are very good, but they haven't gone with the technology development and analysis which, it's generally recognised, the game now needs. John is of the new breed.'

At the end of the 2001 Super 12 competition, in which the Blues finished eleventh of the 12 teams, Kirwan was dropped, along with Oliver, a decision which Hart has slammed.

'There was no assessment of his future, or contribution as a coach, given that he went in at short notice and was new to coaching. He didn't even make the final interview slot despite staying back here for six weeks at the end of the season, waiting for the interview process to take place.'

Hart said that Kirwan was poorly treated by the Blues' board and the NZRFU, who failed to appreciate the qualities and work ethic he brings to coaching.

'He could have made an outstanding contribution as a coach in New Zealand. I think there was a lack of honesty in the process of communicating with him. You can't blame Peter Sloane [the Blues' 2002 coach] because the decision was taken out of his hands, but I think they made a very bad decision, which is New Zealand's loss and Italy's gain.'

Kirwan said he learned much from his two years' involvement with the Blues, but concedes he made some mistakes.

'I was not being myself and was probably trying too hard — as a young professional coach I was on a learning curve too. But you can learn more from losing than winning and although the Blues weren't doing well in 2001, I never lost my enthusiasm for the team or the job. I loved every minute of it, but I would have liked longer to have been given the chance to settle into my role with the Blues,' he says.

'We're very impatient in New Zealand. Coaches don't seem to be given time to lay the foundations, which can take at least a couple of seasons to put in place. We look for immediate success but I believe that sometimes you've got to be prepared to put in the long haul to get those results.'

Italian rugby men can be impatient too, as dumped Italian coach Brad Johnstone would testify after being sacked in April 2002 for failing to deliver the goods with Italy's national team, which finished bottom of the Six Nations pile for the third consecutive year. The new coach would be John Kirwan, the Italian Rugby Federation announced, after he had spent just seven months as assistant coach working under Johnstone.

At the time of the announcement a bitter Johnstone, who had been appointed to the role in January 2000, was quoted as saying that the Italian Rugby Federation had not informed him of his dismissal and he indicated that Kirwan had been working to replace him.

Not so, said Giacomo Mazzocchi, director of communications with the Italian Rugby Federation and the press attaché for the 2002 Italian tour of New Zealand. 'It certainly did not come from any initiative of John's. His appointment as the Italian coach through to the end of the 2003 World Cup has been driven by public opinion, the players themselves and the Federation.

'Brad Johnstone didn't fit into our psyche. He wanted to stay on his own, maybe he was also a shy person, I don't know. He didn't get himself involved with the Italian lifestyle more than was necessary and you can't do that in Italy if you want to create the bond between the players and the coach,' says Mazzocchi.

'I see it being like a stream of water flowing back and forth . . . you cannot stay at your own table and eat on your own. We tried — personally I tried very much — with Brad to help him understand that he could trust the Italians a little bit more and have more confidence in us. But we felt he saw it mainly as a job: *I am here for the time being, tomorrow I will not be here*, and with that attitude you don't fit in with the ambience of Italy.'

Mazzocchi is enthusiastic about the qualities that Kirwan brings to the role, explaining that he is seen as a great All Black hero in Italy, has shown his commitment by playing in Italian championships over a long period, speaks Italian fluently, and has an Italian wife and an affinity with his adopted countrymen. He has his family home in Treviso, Mazzocchi adds, and he is widely known, even by non-rugby Italians, which is a good promotion for the game in his country.

'It is a very good situation to have John at the helm of Italian rugby. The best thing with him is that within a very short time he has freed the minds of the players and given them a new confidence in them-selves.'

The choice had originally been to invite John Hart to coach Italy and, late in 2001, discussions were held with the Italian Rugby Federation. Hart says, 'The idea I was prepared to support was having JK and Zinny [ex-All Black Zinzan Brooke] doing the coaching with me providing mentoring and management backup. The NZRFU was prepared to support such an initiative but, in the end, budget constraints and politics meant that the plan didn't proceed.'

Kirwan hadn't nursed any particular ambition to be Italy's national coach, but having been offered the challenge said he wasn't about to turn it down.

'I wanted to be a head coach and probably it's come around a bit earlier than I thought it would. That's seemed to be the way of my life. In fact, I was pretty much surprised when I got the offer because I thought I was off to the Montferrand club in France.'

However, the decision didn't leave him much time for reflection. Less than a month after his appointment Kirwan and Italy's national team, the Azzurri, were in Palmerston North preparing to meet Manawatu for the first game of their three-match New Zealand tour.

At Kirwan's side was his even newer assistant, former All Black and 2001 Southland Stags coach Leicester Rutledge, who had spent just five days with the squad at a training camp in Rome before the tour had started.

A 'rather surprised' Rutledge had been offered the job as Italy's assistant coach after Kirwan had watched the Southlander's ability in moulding the New Zealand Under 19 forward pack at the world champs in Treviso a month earlier.

Kirwan said he was hugely impressed by Rutledge's work in the scrums, lineouts and rucks, the three specific areas he wanted to target for the improvement of Italy's team.

'I was looking for a particular type of person who obviously had forward skills and could keep an eye on that side of the team, but was also an educator. Leicester's great; within a very short time he'd made a big impact on the guys, he's up with modern forward play and he's just got so much experience,' says Kirwan.

'I think it's important that the talent in Italy is properly coached. A lot of the players are not quite formed by the time they get to us, so we need the educators, the people who can improve their technical ability when they come to us. You need a special type of New Zealander to take on an Italian team and I think Leicester was ready for the challenge.'

The Azzurri were presented with Kirwan's first goal on arrival in New Zealand. Their aim was to win two of their three games and compete in the third, against the All Blacks. First-up Manawatu was rolled 37–13, and in the second match, against the New Zealand Divisional XV, the dream stayed alive until — with time up on the clock — Divisional fullback Tim Manawatu crashed over in the corner to score a try and make the final result a 35-all draw.

The tour ended a single point from his target, but later Kirwan expressed overall satisfaction with the performance of his young team, which lost its third match, 64–10, to the All Blacks. Given his way, Kirwan declared, he would expose the Azzurri to as much top competition as possible to ensure they were physically able to compete at international level.

'I had four guys who had never played senior rugby prior to this tour, and one of them was player of the night against Manawatu: Sergio Parisse, who I took out of the Italian Under 19 side, really kicked on well, and a couple of others also improved markedly, including our test replacement halfback, Juan Manuel Queirolo, who outplayed Byron Kelleher.

'We have got the youngest captain Italy's ever had in 21-year-old lock Marco Bortolami, who has played just 11 tests and was our tryscorer in the New Zealand test. I looked a bit outside the square for this tour and I'm pleased with what emerged. There is talent in Italian rugby, but it has to be hunted out and developed.'

Kirwan feels he understands the Italian culture and has no problem with the 'home and away' mentality towards winning matches, which so maddens Australasians playing in France and Italy.

'You just need to understand it and work within it. I'm happy as long as you get the win away from home, rather than lose. The size of the win is not that important and anyway the "home and away" thing is declining because of the way the game's gone global. Our guys who've spent time playing overseas bring back a different attitude.'

Likewise, under Kirwan the Italians will continue to enjoy their traditional Friday nights at restaurants and nightclubs — they don't have a drink problem but they will stay out late, he explains, and extra sleep time will be put in the following afternoon, to recover in time for Sunday's match.

'I don't think it's necessarily wrong what they do. I believe that, as a foreigner, I must give them the things that I believe are good from our culture but not disturb theirs in the process. My job is to grow Italian rugby and I believe this is the best way of going about it.'

The Italians need to start playing a style of football that suits them and brings out their distinctive personality. (Under a new ruling, no more imports are allowed into the Azzurri from 2002, but those with bona fide Italian passports, such as South African-born fullback Gert Peens, can continue to be selected.) That style will be closer to French rugby than that of New Zealand, believes Kirwan, who has set himself the lofty goal of bringing a global quality to Italian rugby.

In this scheme of things the team would aim to combine the flair and hardness of the All Blacks, the organization of the Australians and the Latin temperament of the French.

Another, and even bigger, call is Kirwan's stated aim in May 2002 that Italy should win the Six Nations competition within six years.

'I believe the Italian Federation must head towards achieving that goal. I don't think I'll be there, but I certainly want to start the ball rolling. The union needs some goals like that so we can all head along the same road.'

Kirwan's objectives for his first year as the national coach are well documented. Two World Cup qualifier wins, against Spain and Romania, a victory over Argentina and the ability to be competitive against Australia comprise the 2002 list. In 2003 the target is to win one game in the Six Nations competition (the last win came 15 matches ago, when Italy recorded an upset win against Scotland), moving towards that elusive goal of winning the Six Nations in 2008.

It will be hard to achieve, he concedes, but it is possible.

'Normally coaches in Italy tend to hide their objectives from the public. I've taken a different approach by telling everyone what I want to achieve and I'm prepared to live and die by that. We need to develop a bit of belief in ourselves and I'm not interested in any player who doesn't want to be successful at the highest level.'

Kirwan has set a target team for the 2002–2003 Six Nations season, with an extended group of 75 players — five for each position — plus a group of 35 people who can come in and out of this group.

He believes that disappointment in Italy's performance at the Six Nations competition has arisen because Italian expectations have been inflated by the Azzurri's promotion into what was previously the Five Nations Championship.

'Critics fail to appreciate that the team is competing against five other nations with longer track records in rugby and a far greater player depth to call on. Things may have looked rosy when Italy competed against teams like Spain and Romania, justifying the decision to add Italy to the Five Nations competition, but, contrary to some opinion, Italian rugby has not collapsed, rather it is having to adjust to the higher level at which it is expected to compete.'

There are some healthy signs for the future, he said, such as the promotion of rugby in Italian schools, the emergence of second- and third-generation players, bringing an established culture to the game, and the introduction of the Super 10, which has heightened competition on the domestic scene.

'In 2002 we had five teams competing for four spots, and Benetton, for the first time in a long time, failed to make the finals. So that's a very positive sign that the net is widening,' says Kirwan.

Kirwan has found his feet. He is more confident in his coaching role and has additional experience under his belt. Things are improving, but he says words now have to be backed with action and results.

In his distinguished career Kirwan has battled and overcome setbacks including injury and depression. Italy is the new battle, and if the prince of wingers can become the saviour of Italian rugby that really will be something the rugby world can celebrate.

For the record

Player
- Auckland, 1983–1994 (141 games)
- New Zealand, 1984–1994 (96 games, 63 tests)
- Benetton, Italy, 1986–1990
- NEC Japan, 1996–1998

Coach
- Blues, 2000–2001 (assistant)
- Italy, 2002

Richard Turner

Shakespeare spoke of a tide in the affairs of men, which, if taken at the flood, led to fame and fortune. Former All Black Richard Turner had more fame in New Zealand than in Italy, and the fortune he amassed in two years of playing for Amatori Milan wouldn't have dented the pocket of the club's owner. But there was a favourable tide, and it would lead the former North Harbour captain to a lasting love affair with the country and its lifestyle.

Success came early for Turner when, in 1985, as a 17-year-old pupil at Napier Boys' High School, he was selected to represent Hawke's Bay at senior provincial level. The big No 8 had two seasons for the Magpies and in his second, at 18, he became New Zealand's youngest-ever first-class captain. His future looked set with the Bay. And then he decided he'd come up to Auckland and stay with friends for a couple of weeks.

Those two weeks stretched out to 10 years as Turner took to Auckland life like a duck to water and opted to stay on. He worked for a time at *Rugby News* and joined North Harbour, where he was selected for the New Zealand Colts, the New Zealand Development Team and the All Blacks. (In his debut test at the 1992 All Blacks' centennial match in Christchurch, Turner had the distinction of being the first All Black to score a five-point try.)

North Harbour was good to him and he returned the favour, serving it well in his seven years there, the last four as captain.

At the age of 28 he decided it was time for a change. In October 1996, when the NPC season ended, Turner flew to Italy to take up a contract at Amatori Milan, a club that was owned by its more famous soccer arm, AC Milan.

Unusually, Turner's contract was not with the club. He was to be paid by Christchurch-born businessman Michael Watt, who ran a communications company (CSI) based in Ireland. CSI had a sponsorship relationship with the long-established Italian club and was looking to get a foot in the door to TV coverage rights for Italian rugby. As part of that package, the company employed Turner as a player to help lift the profile of Amatori Milan and put him on the CSI payroll.

It was a top deal in anyone's rugby language. Turner was paid in sterling, £80,000-plus (approximately $NZ275,000) a year net, while

Amatori Milan picked up the tab for his accommodation, car and playing kit. In Milan, the fashion centre of Italy, that meant style. The 'No 1' kits issued were smart suits and long trench coats, and even the casual training gear oozed class.

'So the whole deal was pretty good, by contrast with my Super 12 and North Harbour package of around $85,000, which was taxed,' says Turner. 'When I left New Zealand I had non-resident tax status so I set up a bank account and away I went.'

He was interested to see on his arrival that soccer and rugby co-existed easily. Amatori Milan's office occupied a small area within the expansive premises of AC Milan and both clubs were substantially funded by the same person, wealthy media mogul Silvio Berlusconi, who would later become the President of Italy.

Turner would probably be the first to acknowledge that he was never one of nature's great trainers, but says he struggled in his first season to get used to the Italians' casual approach. He also missed the intensity of New Zealand rugby and was surprised to find that even his usual pre-match butterflies in the stomach had disappeared.

Amatori needed to practise harder, he told his team-mates. They agreed. What should they do to step up their playing commitment?

Turner suggested they should look at training one more day each week. 'Oh no,' they replied. 'We'd have to ask the president for more money.'

Training sessions were held twice-weekly, on Wednesday and Friday evenings, starting at seven, to cater for players who held down jobs during the day. Sunday was match day so Turner initially declined offers to wine and dine on Friday nights after training.

It was the usual custom when training finished to go out to a restaurant until one in the morning, before heading to a nightclub to party on until the small hours.

'This is a Friday night before a Sunday game! When I originally went there I'd decline saying, "No, we've got a game on Sunday", and the reaction was, "Well, everyone else is doing it. What's *your* problem?" Then they'd sleep all day Saturday and be ready to play on Sunday.'

Italians were enthusiastic socialisers, but they seldom went to drinking extremes. It was not the done thing to be seen intoxicated, Turner noted. In this, the contrast between New Zealand and Italy and the two countries' traffic police was graphically brought home to Turner when he slammed his AC Milan-red Mazda sports car into a brick wall at five one morning after a long night out.

The car, emblazoned with club logos, was a write-off and as Turner clambered out with barely a scratch on his body, he braced himself for the inevitable police interrogation on his level of alcohol consumption.

'I'd been at a nightclub, but I hadn't had an excessive amount of drink, perhaps four or five glasses over a long period,' he says. 'The reason for that was that we had been put in a VIP drinking area where a drink cost the equivalent of $NZ50 regardless of what you had. I was told the rationale was that if you were considered a VIP you should be able to afford to pay through the nose for your drinks!'

Turner had left the nightclub and driven back to his apartment through heavy rain. Near his home, he had hit a puddle and the car had spun out of control, smashing into the wall. When the police arrived on the scene he was amazed to find he wasn't breath-tested or even asked if he had been drinking.

'In New Zealand that would be the first question!' he laughs. 'A couple of days later I got a call to go to the police station to make a statement. I was really shitting myself, and I called up one of my mates, Pietro, and asked him what I should do. Did I need him as an interpreter to help me? Pietro assured me it was OK and they just wanted a statement.'

They did. Never once was alcohol mentioned — proof, Turner says, of the Italians' mature drinking habits.

The players were paid generously by the club and for some of the 43-strong squad this was money for jam, as the names of Sunday's 23- or 24-man playing squad were announced each Friday after training.

'There were guys there who I never saw play a competition game but they all got paid,' recalls Turner. 'A really good friend of mine, Mario Rovelli, used to tell people, when asked what he did, "I'm a professional skier."'

'"Oh, really?"'

'"Yes, I get paid to ski."'

'Mario would come to training every Friday night. He'd have his skis and ski gear in the car and then they'd name the team. He was never selected, so he'd get in the car and drive up into the mountains, which were about an hour away, and ski all weekend. He probably played one-and-a-half games of rugby the whole time I was there!'

Turner's first Christmas in Italy was as unforgettable as it was un-expected. He was at a loose end. His Italian friends had invited him to join their families for the day, but he had declined, saying he would catch up with them at the team doctor's Christmas-night party, a leg-endary event by all accounts.

On Christmas Eve, Turner made a spur-of-the-moment decision to jump on a train and attend midnight mass at St Peter's, in Rome. There wasn't a religious bone in his body and this would be just the second time in his life he had been to church, apart from attending the usual weddings and funeral ceremonies.

Surely the Pope blessed everyone from the balcony on Christmas Eve, he asked an Italian as he watched queues of people lining up to go inside the magnificent old basilica? No, Turner was told, tickets were essential to witness the Pope conducting midnight mass inside St Peter's.

He had come from Milan for this and was not about to be foiled in his quest. He tacked himself onto the end of a queue and shuffled past the first line of ticket collectors to enter the church.

'All the seats were numbered, which meant another lot of tickets. A lady in front of me gave the guard a handful of tickets and in they went, so I tucked in at the back. The guard said, "Where are you going?" I said, "I'm with them." "Well hurry up, hurry up."

'I ended up just 20 feet away from the big man when he came out for midnight mass,' says Turner. 'It was an amazing experience. I was so blown away by it all I hopped into a phone box afterwards and rang all my friends in New Zealand. "You're not going to believe what I just did . . ."'

That was unforgettable, and so was the doctor's party back in Mi-lan, where the champagne flowed throughout the night.

Amatori had reached the national club finals at the end of Turner's first season and in soccer-mad Milan the club's proud officials decided that publicity was needed to expose the successful rugby arm of AC Milan. The club's PR machine organised a promotion whereby Amatori's leading players, Italian internationals Marcello and Massimo Cuttita and Richard Turner, could be photographed by the media alongside the superstars of AC Milan.

The day arrived and the three Amatori players were introduced first to the president, then the coach, and ushered into the best seats of the grandstand to watch AC Milan play. The home team won, much to the jubilation of the fans, and the Amatori trio were taken into the locker room to meet their AC club-mates.

Turner describes it as a thrilling experience. 'I felt like a little school-boy getting my photo taken alongside these soccer stars! It was really cool too, because the AC boys were generous in their praise, pointing to us and telling the reporters and photographers present that "These guys are in the final", so we felt pretty good about that.'

Sadly, Amatori Milan lost the match to its old rival, Benetton Treviso, a team it had beaten twice during the season, and although Amatori's placing qualified it for Europe's Heineken Cup competition, the club was plunged into financial crisis almost immediately.

The good times had come to an end for Amatori Milan.

Turner's belief is that Berlusconi, who was a keen rugby supporter, came under pressure from his family to withdraw his funding after the team's loss to Treviso, in favour of local charities that would at-tract better publicity for his political ambitions.

'That is what we were told. But whatever the reason, the result was that they pulled out and so we had no sponsors, no money, nothing. Later a bank came through with some money so we could get to the Heineken Cup.'

Two of Amatori's players were sold to France, which helped finance the team for Europe's top club tournament that was played against the 1997–1998 champion clubs of France (Toulouse), England (Leicester) and Ireland (Leinster).

Along with other New Zealanders playing in Europe, Turner found the deeply ingrained 'home and away' mentality maddening, particu-larly when it came to a competition as important as the Heineken Trophy.

'We ran close to Toulouse and Leicester and thumped Leinster at home, then lost miserably to them all when we played away. It was the same during the season. It was nothing for Milan to win 88–10 at home then go away and scrape a 45–33 win or something like that. Because we were a strong team, visitors would come to us and virtu-ally throw in the towel. When you're playing away on their home ground, they're all fired up and so you struggle.'

(Italian rugby is played on a round-robin basis where the 'home and away' ruling applies for both quarterfinal and semifinal rounds, while, perversely, the final is a sudden-death game staged on a neutral ground.)

In the following season, lacking both money and several leading players, Amatori was knocked out in the quarterfinals of the club championship. 'That was the tragedy, and so the president shut the door on the club,' says Turner. 'Milan had 70 years of tradition and the guys were upset. It's a bit like Auckland being sold up and the key thrown away.'

Amatori merged with Calvisano, a club an hour away from Milan. Michael Watt bailed out of his sponsorship and Turner took up a contract in Japan. It was all pretty sad, reflected Turner, who says he would like to have stayed on in Italy, a country with which he felt such an affinity.

'I loved the lifestyle, the beautiful, well-dressed women, the food and the wine. I wasn't a big red wine drinker until I went there but Italy changed all that — I especially liked the chiantis.

'One of the boys in our team had a bar at Breschia, about 100 kilometres from Milan, and I can vividly remember soaking up the atmosphere in his place one night, drinking red wine and thinking, "Yeah, I should have done this a long time ago." Generally speaking, I love the Italians; I think they've got a really good balance to their living.

'The whole time I was in Italy I never once heard the excuse "I can't do that because I've got to work tomorrow." It was "OK I'll do it, then I'll worry about waking up in the morning and going to do my job." Those were their priorities in life. It was family, then social life, then work.

'Work wasn't the be all and end all of life. I found that fabulous. I am so glad that I had the Italian experience. It's probably trivial, but one of the really cool things was that you were anonymous — I was looking at everyone else!'

Shortly after Turner's return to New Zealand from Japan in 2002 he was taken fishing on Auckland's Waitemata Harbour. It was a beautiful late-summer afternoon; to his left there lay a 38-ft cruiser and to his right a 10-ft dinghy. His boat, he says, fitted somewhere in the middle, with the fishing equally accessible to all three craft. It was good to be back.

'I loved my time in Italy, but I also love what New Zealand has to offer. I think it should be compulsory for all New Zealanders to leave the country for a while, so that they can appreciate what's at home.'

For the record

Player
- Hawke's Bay, 1985–1988 (20 games)
- New Zealand Colts, 1989
- North Harbour, 1989–1996 (86 games)
- New Zealand Development Team, 1990
- New Zealand, 1992 (2 games, 2 tests)
- Amatori Milan, 1997–1998 (40 games)
- World, Japan, 1999–2002 (35 games)

Grant Kelly

Grant 'Ned' Kelly is one of the tallest players New Zealand has ever produced, but that lofty 6 ft 7 in (2 m) frame was no asset to the rangy kid from Tokoroa when he was young. He was told he was too big to play rugby. If he wanted to take up the game he'd have to wait until he reached the under-18 level at which age-grade restrictions no longer applied.

Encouraged by his father, Roy, Kelly joined the Tokoroa Old Boys' club after leaving school and by the end of his first season, in 1986, local rugby spotters were circling the name of the young forestry worker as someone to watch in the future.

His height had not hindered his athleticism and, despite the late start, Kelly took to the game effortlessly, playing either at lock or at No 8.

Waikato Colts followed, and in his breakthrough season of 1992 Kelly had his first All Black trial, played for Waikato in the CANZ (Canada, Otago, Waikato and North Auckland) series, toured with the New Zealand Maori team and represented his new province, Canterbury.

The decision to move south was taken on the advice of Maori coach and noted Cantabrian and All Black, Bill Bush, who spoke to Kelly on the Maori tour about his future, suggesting he come down and play his rugby for Canterbury.

'Waikato was well supplied with tall timber at that time,' explains Kelly. 'I was competing for a starting line-up slot against two well-established Waikato reps in Richard Jerram and Mike Russell, as well as two guys who had already made the All Blacks, Steve Gordon and 'Buck' [Brent] Anderson.

'I didn't want to spend my career sitting on the bench and that decision, instigated by Bill, paid off. When I went south in the middle of 1992 I was put straight into the Canterbury starting line-up and, for the most part, I remained there for the next five years.'

He experienced life with Team Canterbury in the NPC and the Crusaders in the Super 12, represented New Zealand Maori until 1997 and had a further three All Black trials, in which he was pitted against the incumbent All Black locking combination of Robin Brooke and Ian Jones. It didn't matter to Kelly that he failed to make the All Blacks.

'A career high for me was being selected for the All Black trials and just mixing as an equal with players I had so looked up to. It was an awesome environment. And I was happy being with Canterbury. It was an interesting team and era to play in and I experienced some of the best moments of my rugby career there,' he reflects.

'Two Ranfurly Shield matches — the first in 1994, when Canterbury took the shield off my old province, Waikato, and the second in 1995, when Canterbury's de-

Grant Kelly wins lineout ball for his Scottish club, Galashiels.

fence held out Otago in a desperate finish that forced Otago's captain, David Latta, to concede the penalty on full-time — were real stand-outs. I also rather enjoyed being credited with a couple of tries on the match stats after another game, when my number was accidently transposed on the programme with another guy's!'

A tour high came for Kelly when Canterbury played Queensland at Ballymore. 'I was up against John Eales and after the game he came up to me and complimented me on my lineouts and how well I had played. Then Rod Macqueen, the Queensland coach, came up and congratulated me on the lineout ball I'd won,' says Kelly. 'I was rapt by their comments. It felt just great to be moving in the same circles and competing with some of the best in the world.

'Then 1997 brought changes for me. I lost my position in the Canterbury squad and I had a great opportunity offshore with the lucrative Japanese market open to me — only to be halted by my [non-paying] NZRFU contract!'

Kelly was entering the twilight of his playing career and wanted to play overseas. Unfortunately for him, even with legal help he was unable to obtain a release from the NZRFU and was still bound to his non-paying contract.

He was given a choice of unions to go to and decided he would head north to the King Country RFU as it was closer to his family. For the next two seasons Kelly represented King Country, while playing his club rugby for Taupo Sports and eagerly awaiting the expiry date of his NZRFU contract.

There were discussions with some Americans in Los Angeles in 1998 who were looking for some tall timber but, said Kelly, 'there was no cigar'. Then in 1999 an advertisement in *Rugby News* caught his eye.

Kalamunda RFC, on the outskirts of Perth in Western Australia, was looking for players, and Kelly decided that Perth seemed a good place to be based in preparation for a northern-hemisphere move. Arriving in time for the club's 25th anniversary celebrations, Kelly's eyes were opened wide by the number of drunken ex-pats chundering up their champagne breakfast and sleeping under the gum trees.

'Being a bit of a teetotaller I thought, *What the f— have I come to here?* But the president, "Shaddy", a hard, bald prop — along with a few other members who were one-eyed Cantabrians at heart — didn't seem to be too bad so I grunted on and helped my new team finish fourth on the points table. Everyone was happy with that and, of course, drank more in those celebrations! Well, I guess it did get pretty warm over there . . .'

At the end of the season Kelly took up an invitation to go to the 1999 World Cup and then join the Scottish Borders team, Galashiels, better known as Gala RFC. The famous old club (formed in 1875) was coached by former Scotland international Jim Hay. Along with Kelly, the team's imports included Scott Paterson, an ex-Taranaki fullback, and P.J. Solomon, an ex-league player from Warrington in England.

'I admired the Scots — they weren't very big players but they had a bit of mongrel. They were a staunch bunch and the rivalry between their little towns was fierce,' says Kelly. 'They had a local comradeship second to none and both players and supporters backed their clubs with one hundred per cent passion.'

However, the weather was a killer. Kelly nearly froze in the cold and devised his own pre-training and match preparations to keep his feet warm. First, on went his socks, followed by several of the local Co-op supermarket's plastic shopping bags and then his boots, to stop his feet being frozen into immobility. The twice-weekly match structure was also a challenge.

'The old achilles tendons reminded me that these bloody Scots play a very long and hard season.'

Grant returned to Perth in 2000 for his second year with Kalamunda as the club's player/forwards coach. It was a highly successful season and, for the first time in a decade, Kalamunda went through to the finals of the Perth competition. That success extended through to the junior grades and Kelly bowed out on a high note, at a club he had so enjoyed, to leave for his next rugby stint overseas at Rugby Livorno in Italy.

'Where's the coach?' Kelly asked.

'*Tu sei lui!*' ('You're him!') they replied.

'*Scusa? Cosa? Va f—!*' ('Excuse me? What? F— off!') he later learned to say.

'I soon found out I was IT. There was no coach, no trainer, no manager and they expected me to be the lot — yeehaa — and the season was already under way with four games lost plus one default!'

This was going to be some challenge. Kelly had a total of 18 players to select a team from and his knowledge of Italian, in those early days, was minimal.

A former winger from Treviso who spoke reasonable English helped him out, but dealing with a race as passionate as the Italians provided some testing moments for the team's new coach. At an early training session, Kelly was disconcerted when he suggested to a prop that he should try another way of executing a move and it resulted in tears from the 35-year-old Italian strongman.

'He was my rock in the scrum,' Kelly laughs, 'and these weren't the only tears to be shed on or off the field. It staggered me that some of the players' mothers wouldn't let their boys come to training if it was too cold or if their gear wasn't ironed! However, it did teach me that I had to be far more sensitive when dealing with the Latin temperament. But as sensitive as these boys were, they had a major problem with discipline. In one game we had about six sin-bins and only in the first 20 minutes of the game did we have a full team on the pitch. *Mamma mia!*'

Shortly after his arrival, Kelly was drafted into an Invitation team comprising South Africans, Britons, Australians and New Zealanders to meet an Italian side as part of its Six Nations preparation. The Italians had spent three weeks in training while the Invitation side, which

Kilted Kiwis. **Above:** *Brendan Laney, who burst into test rugby in Edinburgh in 2001, receives his first cap from the SRU president, Graham Young.* **Right:** *John Leslie directing operations for Scotland at Murrayfield.*

The Gatland family on holiday in France, 2002. From left: Gabrielle, Trudi, Warren and Bryn.

Richard Turner surveys the wreckage of his AC Milan car.

*Graham Purvis testing the
temperature at Ussel in France.*

*Scott Palmer on the catwalk with
a French model at the 1999
Bordeaux Trade Show.*

John Kirwan, back in Auckland in May 2002 as coach of Italy.

Grant Kelly and friends at a Sunday barbecue at Kalamunda, Perth.

Brad Meurant, left, enjoying an 'awesome' day out in the mountains during his brief coaching stint in Georgia.

George Simpkin getting the message through to the 2002 Chinese national team.

Warren Gatland directing operations as coach of Ireland.

The 1996 Spanish national team that beat Russia 52–6. Bryce Bevin is on the extreme left of the back row.

*Balie Swart, the new coach of
the Nelson Bays NPC team.*

*Steve Devine, the Aussie who's found his place in
New Zealand rugby.*

*The tallest member of the 1990 King Country team was 19-year-old Martin Johnson.
That's him, fourth from the right in the back row.*

GETTY

Christian Califano on the burst for France.

PHIL KINGSLEY-JONES COLLECTION

Phil Kingsley-Jones with his famous protege, Jonah Lomu.

had Kiwi Mac McCallion as its forwards coach, came together for its only training session at 9.30 a.m. on the morning of the match.

'Brad Johnstone, the Italian team's coach, came up to me before the game and said, "Take it easy on my boys." Of course, he was only having a joke, I think! It was an uncompromising contest and we went down by 12 points, which I thought was an awesome effort for a group of guys who had just got together on the day.

'It was a great feeling though, passing the ball to an Aussie or a South African and knowing that he'd instinctively know what to do. I could only dream about such skills emerging from my new team, Livorno!'

Livorno was not a Treviso, Calvisano, Parma or Roma. It languished in the first division and Kelly set himself the realistic goal of clawing back the team's regular losses, on average by 50-point margins, to opposing teams. The gap did close up and the losses averaged 12 to 15 points by the second round.

Some of Livorno's forwards were nearly 40 years old, but they were desperately needed to keep the team's numbers up against opposing teams, who could have fully professional 30-man squads which trained and worked out every day.

'I admired the older players, some of whom were awesome. They were loyal to the end and I think it restored the guys' confidence that we managed to get those losses down to 15 points on average by the end of the 2001 season,' says Kelly. 'The team realised it was possible to close the gap and when you get that confidence, you're not far off forcing the odd win.'

Rugby was clearly not Livorno's passion, Kelly discovered, as the team's hundred or so regular supporters turned up to cheer on Livorno — while less than 500 m down the road the soccer ground could attract more than 20,000 people for a local derby.

On those occasions there was no shortage of atmosphere as the opposition soccer team arrived off the train to a flurry of police motorcades, flag waving and a parade through town to the ground, flanked by riot police.

Kelly also took on the coaching for some of Rugby Livorno's junior grades and had an uplifting 'Kiwi experience' when the father of two of the boys in one of his teams invited him out for a sail the following Saturday.

'I said OK and turned up at the harbour, unaware that there was anything special going on. There were all these yachts and flags — it was a regatta — and it transpired that my host's boat was called *Barracuda* and was owned by the Italian Naval Academy syndicate.

'*Barracuda* was the former *Steinlager II*, which had been captained by Sir Peter Blake. As we sailed back to the wharf they insisted I do the haka. It must have been quite a sight — a 6 ft 7 in Maori leaping up and down on the deck. Certainly the Italians looking on appeared transfixed! Later my host took me on *Barracuda* as his personal grinder for three days of racing off the Italian coast. It was just awesome and this could very well be my next sport!'

Rugby aside, Kelly describes the Italian people as the warmest and most welcoming people he has met on his travels and their country a wonderful place to visit. He had grown to love Italy, and tears were shed all round — even by the Kiwi — when he left at his contract's end early in 2002.

'*Arrivederci Italia! E grazie!*'

Mid-2002 found Grant Kelly upskilling his coaching certification with Sports Canterbury and taking on the NPC assistant coach role in Buller.

The journey goes on . . .

For the record

Player
- New Zealand Maori, 1992–1997
- Canterbury, 1992–1997 (53 games)
- Waikato, 1992 CANZ series (9 games)
- Kalamunda, Perth 2000–2001 (50 games)
- Galashiels, Scotland 2001 (36 games)
- Livorno, Italy, 2001–2002 (20 games)

Coach
- Buller, 2002 (assistant)

OFF THE
BEATEN TRACK

SPAIN

Rugby has made modest progress in Spain, where the game is modelled on the French style, but received a boost when the national team qualified for the 1999 World Cup, where it lost to Uruguay 15–27, South Africa 3–47 and Scotland 0–48, managing not to score a try. The game is played almost exclusively in Madrid and Barcelona and has relied heavily on the contribution of ex-pats from South Africa, the UK and New Zealand. New Zealand Maori toured there in 1982 but the All Blacks have not yet found a place for Spain on their schedule. Rugby runs a distant third in public popularity behind soccer and bullfighting.

Founded
1923
IRB
1988
Clubs
212
Players
13,000 men, 1500 women
Rugby Nomad
Bryce Bevin

Bryce Bevin

It is said that during our lifetime the gods allocate us 15 minutes in the sunlight. The Spanish national rugby team was given 80 on 15 April 1996, when it thumped Russia 52–6 to record Spain's first-ever victory in the two teams' 80-year playing history.

It was a glorious birthday present for Spain's coach, New Zealander Bryce Bevin, who had nervously paced the sideline until the result lay beyond all doubt. 'We absolutely murdered them. What a thrill.'

In 1992 Bevin, an Auckland lawyer, was head coach for University seniors and happy to be back home after two brief coaching stints in England and Scotland. And then came the call.

Judge Ian Barker had recently returned from an academic exchange in Spain. While there, he had met a member of the Spanish Rugby Federation, an academic at the University of Madrid, and promised him that he would find a New Zealand coach to foster the game in his country. Initially Bevin declined the offer, but then, intrigued by the challenge, decided to accept.

As the country's first international coach he was to live in Spain for six years and grow to adore the place while lifting the profile of the game to heights undreamed of by the Spanish Rugby Federation.

Rugby had started as a university game at Barcelona in 1923 and was for the following seven decades the fiercely guarded domain of a handful of devotees drawn from the city's professional, middle and upper classes. They possessed a sincere and residual passion for rugby, as with kindred spirits in other countries that similarly enjoyed a totally amateur status.

But times were changing. Neighbouring France had long excelled at the highest level and Portugal was also coming through. By the early 1990s, with the inevitable advent of professionalism, it was time to get real and bring in an expert from the place the Spaniards regarded as the acme of rugby — New Zealand.

Bevin had one aim on arrival. He was there to spread the message beyond the metropolitan centres of Madrid and Barcelona to towns and villages throughout the country. It was a commitment on a religious scale and, he believed, it was fortunate that he was a bachelor at the time. 'It would have been very hard for a family over there. I travelled around the country for five or six days every week. Starting in

Madrid each Monday I would climb on a plane or into a car and move around the provinces for the rest of the week.'

He learned to speak the language fluently, which he attributes to a solid grounding in Latin and French when he was a schoolboy at Sacred Heart College in Auckland. 'That helped so much when I was learning Spanish. I also spoke French, which I learned when playing for the Romans Club [home also to Sean Fitzpatrick and Philippe Saint Andre] in France.'

Bryce Bevin in formal mode.

Bevin targeted provincial schools and clubs and within a comparatively short time the results were beginning to show. A wide base of Spaniards were committing themselves to the game.

He found it sobering to learn that Spanish rugby was supported 100 per cent by the government, with its infrastructure funded by the Ministry of Sport.

'I suppose there is a good comparison between rugby in Spain and soccer in New Zealand, though I believe the level of rugby is better in Spain than soccer is here. But would the New Zealand Government ever be prevailed upon to support soccer a hundred per cent? I doubt it.'

And 'when in Spain . . .' the difference in time scale also took some getting used to. 'In Spain they play internationals at midday because it gets too hot by mid-afternoon. Kick-off is typically on a Sunday at 11.30 a.m., which to us is very odd.

'But you must consider the Spanish lifestyle. Each Sunday families go to church, then eat lunch together and promenade, so a late-morning kick-off is the only time you can expect a good attendance at games.'

Local Madrid matches would attract about 5000 people to the Campo Centrale, a tree-lined amphitheatre ringed by grass banks, which Bevin says is the nicest international ground he has ever seen.

The Spaniards possess courage, agility and speed and, under Bevin's tutelage, have developed a better grasp of skills. In 1997 his team qualified for the Rugby World Sevens in Hong Kong and two years later, for the first time ever, the Spanish national team qualified for the 1999 Rugby World Cup in Wales. One decade on since Bevin's arrival it is not too grandiose to claim that there has been a revolution in Spanish rugby, with 200 teams now scattered throughout the country's 17 provinces, many of them with professional players in their ranks.

Bevin's initial contract ended in 1997, but in 1999 he was invited back as coach of Moraleja Alcobendas Rugby Union (MARU) after the club's coach had been sacked. Bevin took the club from the second division to the first division.

This year, 2002, MARU is the top club in Spain. Not bad at all, says Bevin.

'I think guys who have travelled play rugby far better for the experience. I would scoff at those New Zealand players who don't benefit by it, like the young fool who caused a punch-up in Argentina, the player who sat in his hotel room in Barcelona playing cards all day "because there was nothing to do" and the first-five who returned from France after three months moaning that it was terrible because no one spoke English.

'Idiots. Fortunately they're the exception. I was blessed to go to Spain and I was not alone in feeling that. Many others have revelled in the experience, including one Tongan player I know who has a Spanish wife and now speaks better Spanish than the Spaniards!'

Among other favourite memories: 'I was invited to go down to Las Palmas, the capital of the Canary Islands, as they were starting up a local rugby union and making a bid to enter the Spanish competition. They invited me to open the club and cut the ribbon. After much dancing, eating and drinking — as you do at Spanish gatherings — I finally crawled into bed in the small hours.

'Next morning, with hardly any sleep, the coach and 100 players were all assembled at the training ground raring to go. It was a dusty, stony place in the mountains above the city. They went full tackle on this gravelly pumice pitch for a couple of hours, dust in their eyes, scraping their bodies on the ground, blood everywhere and no complaints. Just full-on enthusiasm.

'When I look at some of the prima donnas in New Zealand I think, *Come to the Canary Islands and I'll show you people who have a real passion for the game.*'

Jaime Gutierez, a Spanish rugby international, had this to say about

Bevin: 'Throughout my international career we have had coaches from France, Spain and New Zealand and if you take a look at the records, Spanish rugby has a before and an after since Bevin was in charge. He is, with no doubt, the best coach we have ever had in Spain and the only one to give himself 24 hours a day for our rugby without selfish interests.'

For the record

Player
• New Zealand Universities, 1979–1986 (8 games)
• Manawatu, 1981–1982 (5 games)
• Auckland, 1983–1984 (5 games)

Coach
• Auckland University Seniors, 1990–1992
• Spain, 1993–1997

ROMANIA

Romania has one special claim to rugby fame that New Zealand cannot match — it has competed in rugby at the Olympic Games. In the 1924 Games in Paris, three nations entered: France, the USA and Romania. France and the USA fought out the final (the USA winning 17–3) after Romania had lost its two matches 3–61 and 0–37. Although the Romanian Rugby Federation was formed in 1914, it wasn't until the 1950s that the national team began to play matches against major rugby nations such as France. In 1975, Romania toured New Zealand, drawing its 'test' with New Zealand Juniors 10-all. Although Romania has participated in all four World Cups, the 1989 revolution, when the Ceaucescu regime was toppled, left the country virtually bankrupt, and rugby has suffered accordingly.

Founded
1914
IRB
1984
Clubs
74
Players
5590 men, 60 women
Rugby Nomad
Ross Cooper

Ross Cooper

Sport is a lot about taking your opportunities. No one appreciates that better than Ross Cooper, who, in fairly rapid succession, bounded from being an almost unknown club coach in the Thames Valley to the exalted posts of New Zealand selector and assistant coach of the All Blacks.

Along the way, he experienced his share of euphoria and frustration and was always prepared to expect the unexpected. Which is how he came to be the co-coach of Romania at the 1991 World Cup, in the UK. His participation at the World Cup owes a lot to a chance phone call he received in 1984.

Having retired as a player the previous season after 44 appearances as a lock and No 8 for Thames Valley, he was finding his way as a coach with the Valley Colts. A phone call he received one Sunday morning was to enquire if he could possibly take the lineouts at an NZRFU-organised coaching seminar in Paeroa because Andy Haden hadn't turned up. A little reluctantly, because he didn't consider himself sufficiently qualified at the time, Cooper agreed to help out and duly dispensed instruction on lineouts, under the general supervision of former All Black Ralph Caulton.

Caulton was obviously impressed with the talents of the Waihi schoolteacher because a week later Cooper received a call from Laurie O'Reilly, an NZRFU resource coach, inviting him to Lincoln College to organise the lineouts for the New Zealand Under 17 team.

The weekend proved a revelation for Cooper, for assisting Grizz Wyllie with Canterbury at the time, and also called in to help with the Under 17s, was Jim Blair. He had introduced revolutionary new training grids, which would later be picked up by Auckland but at that time were virtually unrecognised outside Canterbury.

'This man introduced me and others to these grids, which I thought were incredible,' says Cooper. 'I brought them back to the Thames Valley, where they were enthusiastically adopted by my club, Paeroa West, which went on to win the championship that year.'

Over the next few seasons Cooper progressed from Thames Valley Colts coach to senior representative team manager to senior rep coach, taking the Valley 'Swamp Foxes' from the third division into the second division in 1988.

The same year he was appointed coach of the New Zealand Under

17 team, guiding them undefeated through a five-match tour of Australia, including a 17–10 victory in the test match at Brisbane. In 1989, while still coaching Thames Valley, he assisted Earle Kirton in preparing Mike Brewer's team against the shadow test line-up in the All Black trial in Hamilton.

With individuals like Va'aiga Tuigamala, Frano Botica and skipper Mike Brewer playing out of their skins, Kirton and Cooper's team came close to pulling off a major upset, eventually losing 25–31, the shadow test side having to fall back on Grant Fox's impeccable goalkicking to remain in front.

By the time of the Romanian tour of New Zealand in 1990, Cooper had been appointed coach of the national Under 19 team, so, given his burgeoning status, it wasn't altogether surprising he was the man the NZRFU turned to when the Romanians requested the services of a technical adviser to accompany them throughout their eight-match tour. Cooper joined the tourists in Wanganui and immediately struck up a rapport with coach Petre Ianusievici, an impressive individual who spoke five languages.

'He was a delightful person, but it quickly became apparent his coaching methods were seriously outdated,' says Cooper. 'They had brought one ball with them, which the flyhalf kicked every time it was passed to him, and their training didn't involve much more than running around the field. Their game plan was basic, to say the least.'

Referring to the tragedies of their recent past, one Romanian journalist said, 'An enslaved nation could never play free-flowing, adventurous rugby. Forty-five years of communist rule mutilated the soul of Romanian rugby.'

But they'd come to learn, and Ross Cooper was only too delighted to help.

'They couldn't believe our country when they first arrived,' says Cooper. 'The lush green grass, the plentiful supplies of bread, milk and meat. They were used to queuing for life's most basic commodities.'

Coach Ianusievici told Cooper that he wanted his team to play 'expansive and exciting' rugby like the New Zealanders. Cooper understood the sentiment but knew that making the conversion would be a tortuous and lengthy process.

'They were big on talking when they arrived and short on action,' says Cooper. 'So I started with the forwards, upping their intensity and commitment, then moved on to the backline. All their flair had been suppressed but as the tour progressed, we got them playing more enterprisingly.'

Before they kicked off in Wanganui they set two goals: one, to beat a first-division team, and two, to win more matches than their predecessors in 1975. With the 1975 side having won four of its eight games, five victories was the target.

Soon after their arrival the players were hosted in Wellington by the local Romanian fraternity. 'It was an incredible occasion,' says Cooper. 'All these old people who had defected from Romania were there. Most of them had never seen a younger generation of their countrymen. They were overwhelmed at the sight of these great, hulking young men.'

The tourists opened with victories over Wanganui and Horowhenua before stumbling against Wairarapa-Bush. It was while the team was in Masterton that Cooper realised the players still retained their passports. What customarily happens with New Zealand rugby teams is that, for security purposes, as soon as the team arrives at its destination the manager takes responsibility for all passports, usually storing them in hotel safes. Cooper advised manager Viorel Morariu that this was a wise course of action.

Now it so happened that in Masterton the hooker, Christian Stan, had given a particularly poor performance and that evening, when manager Morariu demanded his passport, Stan went ballistic. 'He thought he was being forced to sacrifice his passport because he'd let the team down,' says Cooper. 'He refused to part with it, shouting that it was an infringement of his democratic rights. I had to intervene and assure him it was purely for security reasons, nothing else. He accepted my assurances — finally!'

The victory over a first-division union was achieved in Napier at Hawke's Bay's expense. Cooper watched proudly from the grandstand as the backs worked a double miss move and winger Catalin Sasu, given the overlap, ran around the fullback and planted the ball behind the goalposts.

'I couldn't believe it,' says Cooper. 'They would never have scored that try three weeks earlier.'

That evening, the tourists having achieved the first of their goals, Cooper decided to introduce them to a typical New Zealand court session. The call was Big Drink Tonight, Big Training Tomorrow. However, Cooper and NZRFU liaison officer Don Shuker appreciated that while manager Morariu (who was also the president of the Romanian Rugby Union) was around, the players could never relax.

'His presence would have had a severe dampening effect on any court session,' says Cooper, 'but fortunately the Hawke's Bay officials agreed to entertain Morariu separately. After that, the players relaxed and had a great night. There was lots of Steinlager, singing and even dancing in the team room.

'The Big Training took place the next day in Taupo, where I introduced them to a traditional Kiwi gut-buster. Big Drink, Big Training, became the call for every game thereafter!'

Unusual things happened during the team's stay in Taumarunui. First, the local laundry burnt down and the players lost all their training gear. The sirens of the local fire service racing to the blaze unnerved the tourists, Cooper noted. 'It brought flashbacks of the revolution.' Then in the match, which Romania won 28–6, King Country's veteran loose forward Glynn Meads was ordered off, which created an intriguing situation. King Country's chairman was Meads' famous father, Colin, while the NZRFU judicial representative at the game just happened to be Pinetree's great mate Kel Tremain.

'It wasn't a huge surprise,' says Cooper, 'when it was announced that no further punishment was deemed necessary for Glynn!'

Counties became a second division-one scalp for Romania, which scored a handsome 30–17 victory at the expense of Andy Dalton's team. When Cooper realised Dalton had put a specialist lock in the No 6 jersey, he advised the tourists to probe the blindside, tactics which paid a handsome dividend.

From Pukekohe the Romanians moved to the seaside resort of Whangamata, on the Coromandel coast, to prepare for the game against Thames Valley. 'The mix of crashing surf and native bush just blew them away,' says Cooper. 'They thought Whangamata was just heaven.' It was on match day at Paeroa that manager Morariu approached Cooper and invited him to work with the team at the World Cup. Romania had been drawn to play all its matches in France. Cooper was overwhelmed. He asked if it was all right to make it public. Morariu cautioned against that, saying the appointment still had to be ratified by the Romanian Rugby Federation. 'Well, can I tell my wife, then?' asked Cooper.

'Certainly,' said Morariu.

Cooper went up to his wife, Judith, who was in the grandstand, and whispered the good news in her ear. However, before he could advise her that it was still secret, she exclaimed loudly, 'You're going to the World Cup? Wonderful!'

'Suddenly, everyone knew!' said Cooper.

By the time the Romanians arrived in Auckland for the tour finale against a powerful New Zealand XV (coached by John Hart and Peter Sloane), they had achieved their pre-tour objectives. They'd beaten two first-division sides and, with five victories from seven outings, had managed a superior record to the 1975 team. They were now into bonus territory.

The New Zealand XV, captained from No 8 by Buck Shelford and including such accomplished individuals as Eion Crossan, who scored 32 points, Eroni Clarke, Mark Carter, Robin Brooke, Olo Brown and 'Bull' Allen, roared away to a 60–10 advantage with less than 20 minutes remaining. That's when coach Ianusievici ordered the team to resort to its traditional powerhouse forward approach. 'We are determined to introduce the New Zealand style into Romanian rugby,' he said afterwards, 'but out there today we had to resort to the tactics we were familiar with.' The result was a barnstorming finish by the Romanians that yielded four tries in a dozen minutes, the final scoreline of 60–30 allowing them to return home well satisfied with their tour achievements.

Throughout the tour, the Romanians received the daily allowance of approximately $30 approved by the IRB. Cooper says he never saw one player spend as much as a dollar throughout the entire tour. 'They saved every cent that was paid to them and took it all home.'

The NZRFU approved Cooper's appointment as Romania's co-coach for the World Cup and in late August he set out for Bucharest. It would be an assignment with countless challenges.

The first World Cup coaching school was at Constantia, on the Black Sea. Cooper's hotel bathroom had no shower and the bath lacked a bath plug. This was not an insurmountable problem, his fellow coach, Ianusievici, assured him. 'Just do as we Romanians do,' he instructed Cooper, 'and put your heel in the plug hole.'

Ianusievici had diligently translated Cooper's skill drills from English into Slav, with all the appropriate diagrams, and was faithfully photocopying them for all the squad members. The problem was, after four copies, he ran out of paper. 'It was so sad,' says Cooper. 'He'd done all the work, but there was no copy paper left in Constantia, it seemed — certainly none the rugby union had access to.'

Cooper ignored the missing bath plug, the fact his hotel room was missing most of its light bulbs and the less than appetising breakfast fare of green salami and goat's cheese and worked diligently to have the Romanians primed for the World Cup.

'It was a culture shock, I assure you,' says Cooper, 'but New Zealanders are pretty resourceful and just get on with things. I resolved never to take anything for granted again after my experiences there.'

Cooper had the privilege of being the first ever Westerner to hold any coaching position in Romanian rugby. Such an appointment would not have been possible before the revolution, when Soviets or East Germans were the only options from outside Romania.

Notwithstanding the challenges, Cooper thoroughly enjoyed working with the Romanians. 'They were great guys,' he says. 'And I had a wonderful rapport with Petre, the coach, and Haralambie Dumitras, the captain.' The weekend of the team's departure for the World Cup coincided with an uprising by the country's miners, who had been disenfranchised. They were marching on Bucharest to present their case.

With a military escort, the rugby team made it to the airport about 12 hours before the miners reached the city. The following day there were major riots.

'It was a relief to be out of the place,' says Cooper, 'although the Tarom Airlines flight to Paris was just as hair-raising. There were no seats allocated. You just tried to find one that wasn't broken and still had a seat belt intact!'

The Romanians were never going to win their opening pool match, against France at Beziers, although with less than 20 minutes to play and a scoreline of 12–3, an upset did seem possible. In the finish, the French got home 30–3.

The next match, against Canada at Toulouse, was the one the Romanians needed to win if they were to advance to the quarterfinals, where, intriguingly, they would have taken on the All Blacks.

The game was eminently winnable but the Canadians came out on top, 19–11, although the teams scored two tries each. Cooper recalls that the same winger, Sasu, who'd scored against Hawke's Bay, was once again put into the clear, but this time, with the goalline beckoning, he dropped the ball.

In their final encounter, against Fiji at Brive, there was immense satisfaction when the Romanians registered their first World Cup victory. Although they scored three tries to none, they only just sneaked in, 17–15, the Fijians hanging in through their drop-kicking expertise, landing four.

'Although Petre's men had to disperse straight after the pool play, there was general satisfaction with their performances,' says Cooper. 'They were hugely competitive in all their matches, and a couple of their big men, skipper Haralambie Dumitras, who played for Pau in France, and Constantin Cojocariu, won high praise.'

After emotional farewells, the Romanians, apart from the odd individual who was playing in France, headed back to Bucharest while Cooper headed home to New Zealand.

He's never been back to Romania, but following the All Blacks' tour of the UK in 1997, by which time Cooper had risen to the rank of assistant coach to John Hart with the All Blacks, he made his way through to Frankfurt, where he assisted at a coaching school organised by his friend Petre Ianusievici.

'Petre was one of countless rugby personalities who had defected from Romania,' says Cooper. 'By 1997, he was involved in the coaching of the German national team.'

Cooper despairs of Romanian rugby ever flourishing again. The state funds sports like gymnastics and soccer, but rugby, which ranks at the bottom of the pile, receives nothing.

While Cooper was earning honorary Romanian status in 1991, Counties endured a shocking season, at the conclusion of which it was relegated to the second division. Andy Dalton was sacked as coach and the position advertised.

Cooper applied, won the appointment and went on to enjoy three hugely productive seasons with the Pukekohe-based union. In 1992, he got Counties into the second-division final, where it stumbled against Taranaki in a match played in gale-force winds in New Plymouth.

There were no such setbacks the following year. Cooper had the team humming. They put 60 points on Manawatu, 67 on Nelson Bays, a whopping 103 on Poverty Bay and 53 on Southland. In the semifinal,

Cooper's men beat South Canterbury 33–18 and in the final they hammered Bay of Plenty 38–10 to regain their first-division status.

The team Cooper guided to fifth in the premier grade in 1994 included a 19-year-old Jonah Lomu fresh out of Wesley College, Joeli Vidiri, Errol Brain and a player who would eventually play, and star, for France — Tony Marsh.

Mac McCallion took over Counties in 1995 as Cooper stepped up to become a national selector with Laurie Mains and Earle Kirton and to coach the New Zealand Colts to success at the southern-hemisphere tournament in Buenos Aires.

For the next two years he and Gordon Hunter assisted Hart in coaching the All Blacks. Since 1998 he has been a resource coach with the NZRFU, working closely with the Japan Rugby Union; indeed, he has an office in the Prince Chichibu Stadium in Tokyo, which he visits six or sevens times a year.

One rugby outpost he called on in 2002, as part of an IRB initiative to globalise the game, was Guam. His brief was to introduce rugby to middle and high schools and to assist the national team. Guam is an American protectorate where, predictably, American football is the preferred winter sport. Even so, Cooper was confident he knew how to win their attention when he addressed a middle school on his first day there.

'All right,' he said, 'who's heard of Jonah Lomu?'

Not one hand went up.

'I knew then my assignment wasn't going to be easy,' says Cooper. 'Some 150,000 people live in Guam, which is the site of a huge American army base. Because rugby doesn't feature on television there, the population have no concept of the game. And because the players aren't allowed to wear helmets and padding, as they do in American football, their schools don't permit tackling,' says Cooper. 'So we had to settle for New Image rugby.'

Notwithstanding all the impediments, Guam does field a national team, comprised mostly of ex-pats from assorted rugby-playing nations, which participates in sevens and tens events, largely in the Asian region.

'The hardest part with the schoolboys,' says Cooper, 'was to stop them passing forward. Yes, it was one of my greater challenges in rugby!'

For the record

Player

• Thames Valley, 1979–1983 (44 games)

Coach

• Thames Valley, 1988–1990
• Romania, 1991
• Counties-Manukau, 1992–1994
• New Zealand Colts, 1995
• New Zealand, 1996–1997 (assistant)

GEORGIA

One of the game's minnows, with just 15 clubs. The Georgians were playing rugby with such enthusiasm they had formed their own governing body even before the birth of the Soviet Federation. Rugby has been played in Georgia since 1930 and, during the Soviet communist era, many Georgian team players were regulars in the USSR teams. The Georgian team is nicknamed the 'Lelos', so called after an ancient Georgian national game (lelo), which is played with an oval ball. Georgia joined the IRB in 1992. The nation's appearance at the 1992 World Sevens finals in Mar del Plata made it the first Georgian team to reach the finals of a world sports tournament. In 2001 Georgia won the European Nations Cup, the Six Nations B competition.

Founded
1964
IRB
1992
Clubs
15
Players
1600 men
Rugby Nomad
Brad Meurant

Brad Meurant

Life can be perplexing for professional sports coaches, as Brad Meurant discovered after a disappointing 1997 rugby season. Three years after being crowned coach of the year by the NZRFU for his dazzling achievements with North Harbour, he suddenly found himself unemployed. At the pit face when rugby overnight abandoned its amateur principles, Meurant, who until then had enthusiastically combined plumbing with rugby coaching, became the founder coach of the Chiefs Super 12 team. In the first season, 1996, he performed worthily enough, the Chiefs finishing sixth, ahead of the Highlanders, the Hurricanes and the Crusaders (who, incredibly, given what was to follow, finished up with the wooden spoon).

Meurant's Men, featuring such quality individuals as Frank Bunce, Glen Osborne, Norm Berryman, Walter Little, Liam Barry, Duane Monkley, Ian Jones and Blair Larsen, suffered two losses in South Africa before embarking on a winning streak against Western Province, the Brumbies, Northern Transvaal and the Highlanders. Their final match was against the Hurricanes in Rotorua. Five points would have secured them a semifinal berth; instead, disappointingly, they suffered a surprise loss, leaving Graham Henry's Blues as the only New Zealand team in the play-offs.

Still, it was an encouraging entry into the Super 12 for the Chiefs (a franchise which initially bound North Harbour, Waikato and Northland together) and everyone looked forward to a bumper season in 1997. It wasn't to be. After a promising start, which produced victories at Palmerston North and Sydney, the team went into a downward spiral, losing six of their final seven matches. They finished a dismal eleventh, ahead only of the Highlanders.

In the new professional environment in which coaches were highly accountable, neither Meurant nor Highlanders coach Glenn Ross was reappointed. They gave way to Ross Cooper and Tony Gilbert. It was a depressing time for Meurant. As frustrated as anyone at the team's string of defeats, he was particularly upset at the vitriolic outbursts that came his way from the media and sections of the public. 'I needed a confidence boost, a lucky break,' he says. 'And it came my way, through the most unexpected of circumstances.'

McConnell Dowell, a New Zealand construction company, was

renewing an oil pipeline from Azerbaijan to the Black Sea along a route that took it through Georgia, where the New Zealanders were intrigued to find rugby was a flourishing sport.

They were encouraged to do their bit for the game and through Ron Williams, the former New Zealand and North Harbour prop who does contract accounting for the company, agreed to sponsor a coach to Georgia. Williams approached Meurant, who decided it was just the diversion and challenge he needed. There was one small problem: he didn't know where Georgia was!

'I hadn't a clue as to its whereabouts, let alone know anything about the country,' says Meurant. 'I had to look it up on the map. Anyway, rugby was my business and, unwanted locally, I was prepared to go anywhere to coach a team. So it was off to Georgia, or, more precisely, Tbilisi, its capital.'

Meurant's first experience of Georgians was on the flight from London. 'They were all big fellows who ate and drank everything in sight. I think they would have had a go at the air hostess if she had stayed still long enough.'

At Tbilisi Airport, Meurant discovered that his new rugby connections had sufficient influence for him to sidestep customs and all the other airport formalities.

Brad Meurant with his Georgian mate Datto, who together prepared the Georgian Under 19 team.

'I was pretty impressed with that,' he says, 'but it was a bit of a shock to discover the Georgian national team already had a coach, Frenchman Claude Saurel, who apparently went spare when he heard I was coming to town. I didn't know anything about him and he knew nothing about me. In the time I was in Georgia, we never once met.

'The Georgian rugby fraternity weren't at all fazed by this apparent complication. They just shrugged and said, "Well, since you're here, we may as well use you. You can prepare the Under 19 team, which is off to the World Cup tournament in France."

'They invited me to help coach the team, which I happily accepted. After all, there didn't seem much else for me to do. I had one month to prepare a bunch of guys, none of whom I had ever met or seen play. I was looking for a fresh rugby challenge and I'd sure found one!'

Back in 1997 the Under 19 World Championship was conducted under the auspices of FIRA (Federation Internationale de Rugby Amateur), before the IRB took over the running of it, at which point the rugby world's super powers, notably New Zealand, Australia and South Africa, became involved.

As he settled into life in Tbilisi, Meurant had an interpreter, a guide and a driver made available to him. The driver, Tonto by name, Meurant quickly identified as a personality extraordinaire. 'He was a pimp, driver, jack-of-all-trades, who drove an old BMW he'd purchased in Germany. He drove me all over the place in that car. Whenever he encountered a one-way street, he'd back down it banging his horn the whole way!

'The roads generally were in shocking condition, being driven on by endless Ladas, most of which exuded a smoky blue haze. Fortunately for the car owners of Tbilisi, no one seemed particularly concerned about the foul emissions.'

On the night of his arrival, Meurant was the special guest at a restaurant where a traditional meal known as Georgian Table was served. About 20 people were in attendance, including Meurant's Kiwi mate from McConnell Dowell.

'We ate a little and talked a little,' says Meurant, 'and then the toasting began. We toasted nearly everyone and everything that is Georgian.

'Tradition dictates that every toast concludes with an "empty vessel". That might be all right for the locals but for a jet-lagged New

Zealander it represented a daunting challenge. After four or five shots of a dubious rose-coloured wine, I began to falter and reverted to sipping rather than, as they say in Georgia, "quaffing".

'Around 11.30 p.m., I made my apologies and headed for home. Before I could collapse into my bed, however, there came a call on my mobile phone. Tonto and his mates had been picked up and were at the police station drunk in charge.

'Concerned, I started making calls to the local rugby officials, who, I hoped, would be able to extricate Tonto from his predicament.' Then came another call on Meurant's mobile.

'Tonto here.'

'What's happening?'

'All OK. We are now on our way home.'

'What? Are the cops taking you home?'

'No. I'm driving and they are giving me a police escort.'

Meurant said he realized then that social life in Tbilisi was going to be a little different from a couple of 'quiets' at the Poe (North Harbour's Poenamo Hotel).

Before the break-up of the Soviet Union, Georgia had supplied a considerable number of players to the Russian national team. They were in demand, Meurant had it explained, because of their size. The Georgians excelled, it seemed, in the loose-forward roles. Relieved to be finally independent, the Georgians are happy to be in control of their own destiny these days.

The coach of the Under 19 team was known to Meurant as Datto, who was the former Soviet Union coach. He had been awarded 50 test caps as a halfback, but was later dismissed as coach because he included too many Georgians in the team.

The other coach brought into assist was Levin, whom Meurant describes as 'like a character from the movies'.

'He towered at about 6 ft 4 in and was an ex-Soviet Union officer with only one eye. The other eye had been shot out in the Afghanistan war, and to add to his exotic appearance he also sported a mouthful of gold teeth.

'He would point to his gold teeth and say "The only good thing from Russia". Rumour had it he would sell off a tooth every time he was short of cash!'

Soccer, wrestling and judo were the top sports in Georgia, with rugby very much a minority sport and desperately short of facilities. 'To use a field for training, we would have to pay the guard on the gate, pay extra to shower and pay again to exit the gate. It was bloody challenging, I tell you!'

Electricity was rationed in Tbilisi, with power available for three hours in the morning and four at night, which made night-time training sessions for Meurant's team virtually impossible.

'At night, you'd be watching television when suddenly the power would go off for the duration of the evening!'

The Georgian national rugby side possessed only two rugby balls, so Meurant considered his team well off with four. But the young side struggled for basic equipment.

Meurant went out to the McConnell Dowell compound looking for cones to use for training. He ended up making do with grinding discs. 'I'm sure it's the only time grinding discs have been used for gridwork skills.' Meurant had taken with him a large number of the miniature ASB rugby balls to distribute to children and was overwhelmed at the delight Georgians of all ages got from them.

Tackle bags were another scarce commodity in Georgia, Meurant's team having available just two hit shields with straps on. He said to Datto, 'Two's not enough. I need eight.'

Datto said he could produce three more, but when were they needed?

'Tomorrow,' said Meurant.

The next morning, three hit shields arrived. Meurant could see immediately that they were not professionally made. 'They were of denim material, obviously stitched together on a domestic sewing machine and stuffed with rubber.

'I later found out that Datto's wife had made them, working all through the night to meet the deadline. They were fine for our needs, although obviously they wouldn't last too many seasons. But they did the job.' Meurant was amazed at how passionate the Georgians were about the game. Typical of this was the night when a group of them piled into Datto's Lada and drove to the home of his sister, who owned a television set. There they watched a Six Nations match — appropriately, for Meurant, Warren Gatland's first as coach of Ireland.

'They were all enthralled with the contest and then we drank vodka.' Meurant found that, as in many developing countries, the Under 19 players of Georgia possessed a good theoretical knowledge of rugby but putting that into practice, particularly where second-, third- and fourth-phase play were concerned, presented difficulties.

'They didn't have the instinctiveness of New Zealanders, South Africans and Australians, which made it hard for them. That side of it was frustrating, but they trained diligently to improve. For these kids, it was an important opportunity to get out of their country to see Europe. And they knew, if they could excel at rugby, there was the opportunity to earn money. So they trained desperately hard to win selection. It was an enormous disappointment to those kids who didn't make the team. For some of the boys in the Under 19 team, it was a start for the future. I see two or three of them on the sevens circuit now, but who knows what they're getting out of it? The IRB allocates those countries £10,000 to £15,000 a year, of which the local mafia are probably milking half.'

One day a swarthy, Arab-looking individual who had been observing some of Meurant's coaching sessions told him he wanted to show the New Zealander 'the old Georgia'.

Meurant explained that he had already seen many of the popular tourist attractions. 'No,' said the local. 'I want to show you the old Georgia,' and reminded Meurant that the ancient capital had been built in 1AD.

'So off we went in this guy's dilapidated truck, after first stopping at the market for wine. That was an experience for a start. In this shed were four cream cans variously filled with red and white wine. On the wall were several old, stained, enamel mugs for sampling. You dipped the mug into a can and tried the wine, pouring the unconsumed liquid back into the can. Once we'd indicated our preferred brew, he grabbed a bottle, plunged it into the can and 'glug, glug, glug' filled it, then took an old rag out of his pocket, ripped a bit off and shoved it into the neck of the bottle as a stopper. I just cracked up.

'As we drove into the mountains, with our old truck continually overheating, we could see these bombed-out sites which he explained were old Georgian churches that the Russians had used as target practice for their tanks before they ventured into Afghanistan. We reached our destination and I was introduced to a friend of my new colleague. He turned out to be Georgia's leading seismologist. It was apparent we were about to undertake some serious tramping. I had on jeans and shoes, entirely inappropriate. The seismologist, of first-five proportions, came out of his office wearing a bandana, leather waistcoat, jodhpurs, long shiny boots and carrying a staff in his hand. He proceeded to leap ahead of us, from rock to rock, across the mountain top, which was right on the border of Azerbaijan.

'I was taken into caves where I saw magnificent old frescoes that had been painted on the walls centuries earlier. Then I was taken behind the caves, where we encountered a number of venerable old monks, who were just standing there. It was a surreal situation. They had hair down to their shoulders, beards to their waists and were wearing dark robes that draped to the ground. I was completely blown away.

'The seismologist then invited us back to his office for lunch. We had shish kebabs with wild mushrooms and wild radishes, washed down with our wine. It ranks as one of the most memorable, indeed awesome, days of my life.'

The Georgian Under 19 team spent four weeks preparing before flying out in a Russian Aeroflot plane which Meurant describes as ready for a place in a museum.

'The overhead lights were taped together with elastoplast, the carpet was torn and people aggressively shoved each other aside to get on board. I managed to secure a seat and watched with intrigue as the heavies from the rugby union, all wearing leather jackets and numerically almost equalling the players, stood at the rear of the plane smoking cheroots.

'The air hostess came rushing down as the pilot positioned the plane for take-off. The rugby officials told her to 'f— off', whereupon she returned to the front of the plane crying. We duly took off with these guys standing all the way to Frankfurt.

'From there, we travelled by train down to Toulouse, then on through Tarbes to our ultimate destination, Bagneres de Bigorre, which lay at the foot of the Pyrenees. It was spring and the place was beautiful.'

FIRA ran the competition in four sections, with Georgia in the B grade. Those in the A grade were accommodated in larger towns and cities like Tarbes and Toulouse, but Meurant was content with his team's hotel. 'We couldn't afford anything else, but the quaint place we stayed in was perfect for our needs.'

Two days before Georgia was due to play its opening encounter, the team's jerseys and boots still hadn't arrived. Someone had slipped up in arranging the gear, through a sponsor from Montpellier.

'Georgia's colours are maroon but what eventually turned up were black-and-white jerseys and black-and-white shorts, plus boots,' says Meurant. 'Throughout our preparation, the boys had trained in sand-shoes or whatever they had. None of them owned rugby boots. So when the boots were allocated 48 hours before the first game, they were, as you can imagine, over the moon. They insisted on training in them, there and then. They all finished up with blisters but simply bandaged over them and ignored the pain.'

Georgia's first game was against Germany, which they won. And then they defeated Spain, which set them up against Portugal in the final, the winner earning promotion to the first division.

Meurant marvelled at the players' resourcefulness and enthusiasm. 'Each morning, their gear would be hanging out over the balconies to dry. They washed it in their hand basins because they could not afford to have it laundered. I wondered how pupils from some of New Zealand's affluent schools would handle such challenging situations. You had to admire the Georgians' commitment.

'It was the only time these boys had ever been out of their country and I didn't have one problem with any of them going on the booze or misbehaving. They were completely dazzled by what they experienced in France. On our off-day we went to watch Ireland play Argentina in one of the first-division semifinals. At the ground, we encountered the Portuguese, who would be our opponents the next day. They were impeccably attired, many with dyed hair. Then we walked in. None of our players' gear matched and the track suits were too small. You could see the Portuguese eyeing us with disdain.

'We used that as our motivation for the final, in which the Georgian boys scored a stunning upset victory against the fancied Portuguese team. The boys had certainly absorbed what I had taught them about pre-match preparation and how to handle three matches in 10 days.

'I had been elated after some of the victories achieved by North Harbour and the Chiefs, but those celebrations were nothing compared to the Georgian reaction at the realisation they had won promotion to the first division. There was lots of hugging and kissing, which comes as a bit of a shock to a New Zealander, especially when the person kissing you looks like a mafia lieutenant! I defied gravity for about 30 seconds as the Georgian players tossed me in the air soon after the final whistle.'

Meurant never returned to Georgia. He was joined in France by his wife, Helen, who, however, did sample a little Georgian hospitality. Anticipating her arrival in Bagneres, Levin presented her with a bunch of hand-picked flowers, delivering them with an exaggerated bow, gold teeth flashing.

A year after the Under 19 tournament, when Meurant was coaching in Cork, in southern Ireland, he went to Lansdowne Road to watch the Georgian national team play Ireland in a World Cup qualifier. It was a grey Irish morning and the first person he bumped into was his old coaching colleague from Tbilisi, Datto.

'After much kissing and hugging, we went off down the road to share breakfast,' says Meurant. 'It was an odd experience. Here I was living and coaching in Ireland, walking arm-in-arm with a Georgian and heading for a rugby game in Dublin that was being refereed by a friend of mine from my days coaching Border in South Africa. Where did my allegiance lie?'

Footnote: In March 2002, Georgia and Russia fought out a 12-all draw in front of 65,000 spectators at Tbilisi, in a qualification match for the 2003 World Cup.

For the record

Coach
• North Harbour, 1992–1994, 1996
• Border, South Africa, 1995
• Waikato Chiefs, 1996–1997
• Dolphin, Cork, Ireland, 1998–1999
• Ricoh, Japan, 2001

CHINA

On the world rugby scale, China scarcely registers, with fewer than 1000 players. But the game is attracting recruits, helped by the IRB's decision to include Shanghai on the international sevens circuit in 2001. The China Rugby Football Association was founded in 1996 and joined the IRB the following year. China received its biggest exposure as a rugby playing nation in 2001 and 2002, when their Sevens team, under coach George Simpkin, entered the IRB Sevens circuit, debuting in Brisbane, and later hosting events in Shanghai and Beijing. China's Olympic Committee, in conjunction with the IOC, is pushing to have rugby sevens in the 2008 summer Olympics in Beijing. In the fifteen-man game, China's first full international was against Singapore in November 1997.

Founded
1996
IRB
1997
Clubs
30
Players
900 men
Rugby Nomad
George Simpkin

George Simpkin

George Simpkin has always had the knack of looking at things from left field. The man who elevated Waikato to first-division status by using the techniques he had employed with the Matamata College First XV, whose shrewd eye turned Fiji into a potent force, who transformed rugby in Hong Kong, who invented the Super 12 kicking tee by inverting a saucer on the kitchen table, who is teaching rugby to the Chinese army and who is running sevens tournaments in Sri Lanka, is one of rugby's visionaries.

Simpkin grew up in straightforward style in Northland and played for Otago University while studying for his Physical Education degree. He went on to play for the Belfast club of Christchurch and thence to coach at Matamata College in the affluent rural heart of Waikato. Once there, it didn't take long for his presence to galvanise the locals. Winston Hooper, in *The Might of Mooloo*, describes him thus:

'Within weeks [of his appointment as coach] Matamata enthusiasts began to make excited noises about their team's performances. It was not so much the wins being obtained, but it was the style displayed in their achievement. There were backs and forwards who had pace, handling, passing and kicking abilities at least the equal of most, and certainly better than some representative players in the early 1970s.

'The word spread quickly through the rugby grapevine: "Watch Matamata College". Later, invitations were made to the shaggy-haired PE teacher to try his hand at something wider than the school arena. He accepted the challenge and within a couple of seasons Waikato had appointed him as its senior coach.'

Was he being too cautious in his step up to divisional coach, or were forces opposed to him determined to keep him on a narrow path? Wherever the truth lies, Waikato failed to break into the first division under Simpkin's stewardship until, in 1980, with his back to the wall, he let loose with his successful Matamata College First XV's highly disciplined backline pattern. In Australian style, he set three inside backs very close — pass, pass, pass — to draw in the defence and open up the space out wide for players to run into.

Waikato responded in spectacular fashion, taking the Ranfurly Shield 7–3 off Auckland at Eden Park in September 1980 and a short time later winning promotion to the first division.

Then in the following year, 1981, a bitterly disappointed Simpkin had the mortification of watching his team pace restlessly around the changing room while protestors battled it out with police on the centre of Rugby Park before Waikato's match against the Springboks was aborted. The traumatic episode took its toll on Simpkin, and although he became a North Island selector in 1984 he turned down an invitation to become an All Black selector, believing it was time to move on.

In May 1985, in his role as a North Island selector, Simpkin prepared to travel to Fiji with All Black selector Bryce Rope on a two-week coaching stint. At the last minute Rope pulled out and Simpkin travelled alone. Not that he minded, he later reflected.

'While I was there the Fiji government offered me a position to set up a Ministry of Sport. I accepted that on 29 June 1985 and have been largely out of New Zealand since.'

As the first major New Zealand coach to take his skills overseas, Simpkin found there was a great deal of interest him, despite a kerfuffle from sectors of the Fijian rugby community who questioned the wisdom of having an overseas coach as technical advisor to the national team.

The Fijian squad was assembled and put through its paces by Simpkin, who took no longer than 24 hours to figure out what was wrong: Fijians were very strong torso-down, but not as strong torso-up, which was why their scrummaging had always been so poor, he explained to anyone interested in listening.

He realised that technically the Fijians were also inferior in scrummaging and set-piece play because they had never been taught to work on these areas, relying instead on their natural athleticism and speed to shine in open or broken play.

Simpkin taught the forwards how to keep their distance, to set their feet and their bodies low from the waist down in scrummaging, to ruck and to win lineout ball; then he placed the entire squad on a radical weight conditioning and training regime.

Simpkin decided he would get the local media on side, according to Sri Krishnamurthi, who was then the sports editor of the *Fiji Times*.

'The first time I ran into George he came down to the paper and said, "I want to have a meeting with you guys," so we went out and had a coffee. He told us what he was looking for and what he expected of the media. Then he said, "Look, I think when you guys

watch a game you don't look specifically at what I'm looking for
in a game."

'He showed us the technicali-
ties of what he wanted in a scrum
and in the set pieces. It was completely new to us, because in Fiji
we'd never got an insight into the
way New Zealand rugby worked
on its technical strategies.

'We were all sitting there
amazed, thinking, *Gee, should he
really be showing us that?*

'Then he said, "Look, if you
don't understand it you won't

George Simpkin, who went from Waikato
to China via Fiji,

know what I'm trying to do with this team." You knew George was a
strange man; he had that preoccupied way of looking almost beyond
you and saying things that were unusual, but we really appreciated
those insights.

'We admired him greatly for what he was trying to do with Fiji.
George pretty much laid the foundations for Fiji which the team has
followed since.'

As Simpkin had limited time to build Fiji into a competitive force
for the upcoming 1987 inaugural World Cup, he concentrated his game
plan around a platform of rucking rugby and quick ball release from
the base of the scrum.

Then, just days before the team was to leave for New Zealand and
the World Cup, Fiji was torn apart by a military coup, instigated by
Colonel Sitiveni Rabuka and his fellow army officers, following the
election of the country's first Indian prime minister.

Simpkin had no hint that there was anything amiss on the day of
the coup when he called to visit some officer friends. 'Most of the
officers were great friends of mine and I was actually in the army camp
with the guys who led the coup when it happened. I could hear a
whole lot of marching going on outside, though. They were bringing
in the reservists and there was a lot of frenzied activity.'

Fiji cut all phone lines to the outside world, and while the Fijian
team continued to train, locked away behind walls at the Suva army

barracks, an anxious NZRFU attempted to find out whether the Fijians would be turning up.

Frustrated local media were also kept in the dark about the team's intentions. Some took direct action, like Krishnamurthi, who went to military headquarters and called over the barracks fence to the players, 'What's going on? Did you know New Zealand's looking at sending some other team to replace you?'

'Yeah, yeah, we're still going,' they replied. 'Ring New Zealand and tell them we're coming.'

Not easy when there were no phone lines.

'Look, if you don't give me a bloody phone line to New Zealand you won't have a Fijian team at the World Cup,' an exasperated Krishnamurthi told the woman at Fintel. A line was opened and a call made to Dean McLachlan at *Rugby News* in Auckland, who passed the message onto the NZRFU. 'The Fijians are coming!'

At the first scrum of its pool game, Fiji was barrelled backwards by the strong Argentine pack and it seemed to be all over. Then Simpkin's rucking techniques and defensive patterns set in and, as the Fijians hit their rucking straps, the Argentinians faltered.

That day in Hamilton, Fiji pulled off the biggest upset of the 1987 World Cup by emphatically defeating one of the tournament's favourites 28–9. Fiji could have caused an even greater sensation in the quarterfinal against France, until, at a crucial stage of the match, flyhalf Severo Koroduadua dropped the ball when heading for a try.

'I'll never forget that moment.' Simpkin shudders at the recollection of the large Fijian sprinting down Eden Park's sideline with a clear line ahead.

But his boys had covered themselves with glory, showing flashes of brilliance while going down 16–31 to the team that would go on to play New Zealand in the final.

Then Simpkin, who had grown so close to the Fijans and who had totally immersed himself in that country's culture and customs, was forced to leave Fiji in November 1988 after a second coup when the New Zealand government withdrew its funding to New Zealanders working on Fijian government-sponsored projects. But the legacy endures, Krishnamurthi says. 'When George left he had put systems into place that were going to work. He had shown each of the provincial unions how to work on very basic set-piece play and he had taught them things they could build on. He laid the foundation that enabled them to develop beyond being a specialist sevens force — and he was a brilliant sevens coach too. Without his influence Fiji would be lost in the wilderness by now.

'You talk about the Johnny Appleseed of rugby — that's what George was. He went there and showed them. It really was the quality of what he did.'

The Hong Kong RFU had offered Simpkin the job of developing rugby beyond its traditional ex-pat enclave. The island's most famous rugby event, the Hong Kong Sevens, had started in 1976 and been highly profitable since its inception, but there were few Chinese playing either version of the game, Simpkin found.

'Hong Kong was settled by entrepreneurs and you find the same qualities in its rugby. A lot of money has been made out of the Hong Kong Sevens, and the local Hong Kong sides were almost solely comprised of ex-pats or imports.

'So I started more rugby clubs to attract locals, but there was a real problem because of Hong Kong's lack of space. There were only 35 grass fields in Hong Kong and only two of those were used for rugby.'

There was ample land just across the border in China and so Simpkin had an idea. From his base in Hong Kong he would introduce rugby to mainland China.

Simpkin approached sponsors and supporters to raise $US300,000 ($NZ600,000) to get started. He planned to take the game to China's three main centres — Shanghai, Beijing and Guangzhou — encouraging local Chinese to become involved with rugby, rather than turning his energies to each city's ex-pat population.

Universities and the Chinese army were also targeted in the plan, and by 2002 Simpkin was well satisfied with the success of his missionary work to date.

'Essentially there are now three centres of note in China; they're all Chinese players, no ex-pats, but because of the huge distances involved, they don't get the opportunity to play much rugby. It's about 16 hours from Beijing to Shanghai and another 22 hours from Shanghai to Guangzhou.

'The army is getting organised with rugby too. There are now 15 new teams in Guandong province and I think there will be hundreds more teams starting all over China in the next few years.'

In 2002 Simpkin travelled to the Guangzhou army base to coach its teams, urging Westerners to discard their cultural prejudices when thinking of rugby in Asia.

'In the past, Chinese concerns centred on feeding its huge population and only now can minority sports like rugby get some official encouragement. However, there are some big men playing in China and their rugby is improving out of sight.

'Most of the players at present come from the Shandong province. Its capital is Qing Dao, which is an old German town and the site of one of the biggest breweries in the world, making Tsingtao beer.'

Simpkin is emphatic that unless it becomes an Olympic sport, rugby will never become mainstream in China. It is not played in schools and there is a limited appeal at university level, but there is no follow-up afterwards because there are no clubs to affiliate with in the cities. In his words, there is no point in having teams when there is no one to play against.

In early 2002 Simpkin brought his sevens team from China for a short tour of Australia and New Zealand, with three of the team playing their first season of rugby and one player, an outside back called Zhiang, impressing all who saw him play.

But if rugby does become an Olympic sport . . .

The Chinese army has magnificent sports facilities and a strong sports structure parallel to that of universities and sports institutes in China. Crack into the sports-stream structure and everything is paid for by the state. Now that is tantalising, admits Simpkin, who believes if the Olympic dream becomes reality, China could become a rugby force of the future. 'Many of these people are not taking up rugby until they are 18 or older. Maybe they've bounced a basketball, but then they take up rugby and they're not too sure what to do with an oval-shaped ball.

'They're very intelligent and they can follow set pieces, they are very good at that. They can practise scrums and lineouts every day, but the timing and passing is difficult, because they don't have anyone to play against.

'Most of the guys playing for the national side have played more games for the national side than they have in the rest of their life put together. They only get a couple of games a year, but having said that they're doing OK.'

China is not the only country that will benefit if rugby becomes an Olympic sport. Simpkin points to the former communist countries of eastern Europe, as well as wealthy European countries like Germany, Sweden and Holland, where huge injections of funds would be provided for an Olympic sport, along with a search for players of the right stature to play the game in those countries.

'Rugby needs the Olympics, because even though rugby is played all around the world, it's only played as a serious sport by a few countries. The IRB is doing a wonderful job now in promoting and developing rugby around the world. Which is not before time, because for more than a hundred years they did absolutely nothing; in fact they stifled rugby. No one was allowed to join the IRB . . .

'Now it's changed dramatically and there's excellent work going on to promote rugby, but still everyone knows who is going to win the qualifying matches in the Rugby World Cup, so there's no competition there.'

Simpkin sees as the next step a thrust to encourage a second tier of teams to reach a stage where they are competitive with countries who play professional rugby.

'I find it astonishing that since the Iron Curtain's been lifted we've suddenly discovered that there's good rugby being played in Georgia,

George Simpkin shares the limelight with his Chinese players.

Kazakhstan and Poland, the Czech Republic and Russia. Had the IRB gone out to them at a time when the state was funding sport, all of those countries would be strong entities now.'

It is paradoxical that this chapter on George Simpkin has concentrated on his track record and opinions on 15-man rugby, when, if asked, most people would say they associate Simpkin's name with the sevens game.

'George has got a great eye for players,' says his close friend, New Zealand rugby commentator and sevens expert Keith Quinn.

'He'll usually say to me at sevens tournaments, "Have a look at this fellow, Keith. There's a good story about him," which he knows will go into the commentary and help broaden people's understanding of the personalities in the Chinese team.

'He's quite a distinctive sight at sevens tournaments. You see George walk out slowly to the halfway mark, with that familiar roll as he walks. Then he speaks about five sentences and it's translated to the players and then another four or five sentences, which are translated to the players, who stand around him in a huddle at halfway.

'George is a legend and he's taken the game to some far-flung corners of the world and everyone has benefited from it.'

Simpkin believes there is huge potential for the sevens game in the East, where Asian players can compete on a par with their Western counterparts.

'In sevens, you don't tackle unless you have to and most of the tackles are from the side, so Asians can compete, whereas with fifteens and tens most of the tackles are from back or front, requiring real strength.

'The sevens branch of rugby has a big future in Asia. Virtually every millionaire in Singapore, Malaysia and Sri Lanka and a large number of hugely wealthy people in Taiwan, went through schools which play rugby, but they're not going to unlock any money for sponsorship unless their team has a chance.'

In 1996 Simpkin was approached by NZRFU board member Rob Fisher, and CEO David Moffett, when they were in Hong Kong. They told him they were concerned about the number of New Zealand players going to Japan and the United Kingdom to play rugby, and asked, with his background, could he think of some way in which the player-drain could be stopped?

Simpkin already had an idea for a sevens circuit and said he would come up with something. He drafted two alternative concepts and flew down to the NZRFU in Wellington late in 1996 with the proposals. One of them was to franchise the Super 12 into Asia.

'I drafted up a scheme whereby the NZRFU would contract NPC players to cities in Asia and I had already found eight cities there who were keen to explore the project. These guys would play in those franchises for an Asian Super 12 series and then they would return to New Zealand to play in the NPC.

'They would make more money doing this, and it would stop some of them from going overseas, because they would be under contract to the NZRFU,' he says.

'My other idea was for a sevens tournament. I had a meeting with Bill Wallace, a director, and Fraser Neill, the business development manager, of the NZRFU. We spent two or three days on this and drafted up a scheme whereby New Zealand, Australia and South Africa would own the sevens circuit, with part ownership going to Fiji, because of their excellence at sevens.'

He is reticent on the outcome of those discussions, but will say that his idea was taken to the IRB commission, which 'grabbed it' while Fraser Neill and Bill Wallace subsequently left the NZRFU and now run the World Series Sevens. The NZRFU's inaction on his proposals still rankles. 'It was a no-brainer as far as New Zealand was concerned. It was an easy way to raise money for a small population and to keep players.'

In 2002 Simpkin has a financial interest in three sevens tournaments around the world: one that's struggling, in Hungary, another in Jerusalem, which started off well until becoming a victim of the renewed Palestinian-Israeli hostilities, and the third, which he describes as thriving, in Sri Lanka.

'I organise and run that one. It's doing well and I believe it will go from strength to strength.'

His craggy face lights up when the words 'Sri Lanka' crop up. He loves the place, has a home there and a financial interest in a factory which makes sportswear items. (His other factory is in Guangzhou, where he manufactures his 'upturned saucer' invention — two heights of kicking tee as used in the Super 12 competition.)

There are some incredible stories about rugby in Sri Lanka, which has a long and proud history in the game, Simpkin explains. Like the club in Sri Lanka's old capital, Kandy. In 2002 the club is still going strong and in its 128th year of existence. It won its first trophy in 1992 — 118 years after its formation in 1874.

Then there's the club up-country, famous for a heated argument in the clubhouse in the 1920s. An enraged Englishman who pulled out a knife and slammed it into the table, taking out a large chunk, was forced by the committee to pay £200 for the damage. Today, the club is still there, the table is still there and the knife gouge is still there.

But Simpkin's favourite yarn concerns the old Havelocks club. As he tells it, when the club was formed there was a government lease in operation which prevented the club from establishing a permanent building on the site. The resourceful committee built a vehicle similar to a Western chuck-wagon and rested it on wide steel wheels. Inside the clubhouse, there was a bar at one end and, dominating the room, a long table with its centre cut out so that the barman could move noiselessly down the middle, serving drinks to the seated committee without disturbing them as they talked.

Then, to meet the terms of the lease, which required the club building to be shifted each year, an annual ceremony was held amid great pomp, at which, in front of plumed-helmeted British administrators of the colony and other invited guests, the Havelocks clubhouse was moved an inch and a half.

In 2002 the Havelocks club is still in existence, as is the old chuck-wagon, which has been retained as a cherished souvenir of the club's colourful colonial history. Simpkin smiles.

For the record

Coach
- Waikato, 1976–1984
- North Island selector, 1984–1985
- Fiji, 1985–1987 (technical advisor)
- Hong Kong, 1992–1997
- China PLA, 1997–1998
- China Sevens, 2000–2002

Consultant
- Sri Lanka RFU

The Basque country

Just five minutes from the Spanish border lies the coastal town of Biarritz, formerly the resort playground of royalty and Europe's wealthy leisured classes. Today Biarritz is the centre of a bustling tourist industry for the Basque country and home to around 30 New Zealand Basques who originally came for the rugby and surf.

Biarritz Olympique — a first-division rugby club bristling with present and past French internationals — has been the main attraction for New Zealanders such as former All Black Mike Clamp who, when their playing days ended, chose to stay on.

It is a tiny chunk of paradise, the New Zealanders claim, a region where French is spoken alongside Basque, a language with no known links to any other, and located just one hour from fabulous skiing in the Pyrenees and a similar time from Paris and London by plane.

Throw in the region's magnificent beaches, golf, snowboarding, pelote basque, wining and dining, hunting, fishing and the weekly festivals of summer and you can begin to understand what these ex-pat Kiwis are on about.

Jeff Bradburn and Sean Spring are two within the group who married Basque girls and consider themselves to be among life's lucky people. In Bradburn's case it all came about through a midnight phone call. Since a childhood spent on the beach at Mt Maunganui, his twin sporting passions have been rugby and surfing and it was while he was living in Sydney, playing rugby for Manly Warringah and surfing during summer, that he was offered a two-year contract as player/coach in Parma, Italy.

Bradburn accepted and when his contract came to an end decided to head to southwestern France, where he could continue to play rugby and pick up his surfboard again. There he met his future wife, Denise, fell in love with her and the Basque country and decided to stay put.

Today, Bradburn (a former Bay of Plenty and Auckland age-group, New Zealand Under 19 and Auckland B rep, and nephew and cousin of the cricketing Bradburns) is the general manager for Europe of the Quiksilver surfing empire — a mix of business and pleasure that he claims was surely forged in heaven.

'Finding this piece of paradise and then meeting up with Harry Hodge, the president of Quiksilver International, and Jeff Hakman, the world surfing champion, has enabled me to carry on with this marvellous lifestyle.' He beams.

Quiksilver now has offices throughout Europe and there's a strong Kiwi connection, with ex-Manawatu rep Peter Skelton as its European operations manager and Mike Clamp running the Quiksilver shop on the main beach in Biarritz.

For the past 20 years Bradburn has also been player, coach and now president of the second-division Bidart Union Club, which has hosted a multitude of Kiwi rugby travellers over the years.

The sublime combination just keeps rolling on, says Bradburn.

'By opportunity and luck I have travelled all over the world with my job and with various rugby tours, surfing and work adventures to Fiji, Tahiti, the Maldives, South Africa and South America.

'Some of the New Zealand players who have come to the Basque area have also worked here temporarily and we have been able to help them out at Quiksilver Europe,' he says. 'Others have made their own lives here, including two former Wellington players: Scott Keith, who is playing professionally for Biarritz Olympique and coaching their Under 18 side, and Chris Tutt.'

Kiwi Basques ready for sporting action at Biarritz.

Jeff Bradburn in full cry in the beach rugby sprint at Biarritz.

Several New Zealanders have been introduced by his good friend and fellow surf-nut Murray Mexted, who honeymooned at 'Chateau Bradburn'.

The name of Bradburn's home is ONGI ETTORI, which means 'Welcome' in the Basque language. It's an apt choice, given the hospitality the Bradburns extend to the many New Zealanders who arrive to savour the romance and conviviality of the region. They have included former All Blacks Grahame Thorne, Wayne Shelford, Craig Green, Sean Fitzpatrick, John Kirwan and kindred surfing spirit Josh Kronfield.

Bradburn's twin passions have extended to the next generation, he notes with pride. Suzie, 15, a student at the International Language School in Bordeaux, shares her father's love of surfing and son Cheyne, 18, is a rugby player of real promise.

Bradburn says he is thrilled that the next generation of New Zealand Basques are now making their mark on the local rugby scene. Cheyne Bradburn and Sean Hegarty (son of ex-Wellington and Biarritz player Brian Hegarty, who so loves the place he writes an annual Basque country guidebook in English) are France and Côte de Basque age-group representatives, Marlon Clamp and Brendon Hegarty are in the junior ranks, while Nathan Skelton and Max Spring are keen starters, but still too young to play.

So could the Basque country produce France's first 'home-grown' international of New Zealand parentage? 'Possibly. That really would be something to celebrate!' Bradburn smiles.

Sean Spring is a business associate of Bradburn, Skelton and Clamp at Quiksilver who came to France in 1991 on a rugby OE. The former Wellington B rep said he was approached by a Basque second-division club (Garazi) through a friend, Rob Moffitt, a former New Zealand Universities and Canterbury player who had spent two seasons with the team.

What was to have been a three-month contract running until the end of the 1991 season has, for Spring, ended up being a continuous love affair with the Basque country.

'The Basques are renowned for their distrust of foreigners, which includes anyone north of Bayonne and east of Mauleon — that is, non-Basques,' says Spring, who was smart enough to learn to count in Basque before learning to count in French and modestly describes himself as somewhat lucky in a Basque card game that resembles poker.

'Add to that a couple of lucky tries to help win games and a healthy appetite for food, wine, singing and the local after-dinner nightcap, and I became accepted as an adopted Basque.'

Basque rugby is 'very interesting', the real characters residing one layer below the professional playing circuit, he says.

'The advent of professionalism has dramatically changed the face of French club rugby, which has gone from 64 teams in the first division down to 16, and they are still thinking of downsizing. This means that there is only one Basque club currently in the first division, Biarritz, and it doesn't contain many Basques,' he says.

(In 2002 Biarritz has two playing New Zealanders, Scott Keith and Legi Matiu. In 2001 the tally was bolstered by the addition of former All Blacks Frano Botica and Glen Osborne).

Professionalism has therefore left untrammelled true Basque rugby in the divisions below, where players emulate the passion of the professionals with their hard, tough attitude to the game. Basques are not generally tall but they are solid and renowned for their uncompromising scrummaging. They are also the inheritors of a proud tradition of battling, says Spring.

He was soon to discover that Basque players are just as uncompromising after a match as during, often going right through the night

The Basque Kiwis, enjoying a get-together.

and lustily singing many of the hundred or so Basque songs everyone seems to know. But his first away game with the team, at a venue four hours' distant, left him gasping at his team-mates' appetites and complete disdain for the accepted norms of match-day eating.

'We got on the bus at six in the morning and I was certain a few of the guys had just come straight from the neighbouring village festival,' he says, laughing. 'Two hours later, at eight, the boys started pulling out sandwiches, which were really entire baguettes filled with ham, omelet, chillies, et cetera. At the back of the bus out came the homemade wine — there must have been a dozen bottles handed around the bus — and then the cheese, which could be smelt before it could be seen.

'This feast lasted for half an hour and then, just two hours later, the bus slows down and we're stopping for lunch!'

A bemused Spring looked on in amazement as one course followed another.

'First up, there were plates of grated carrots, celery and sausage, washed down with a litre of wine for four people. This was followed by ham, boiled eggs, and a request to the waitress to "top up the wine carafe, thanks".

'Then we faced the main course of steak and mashed potatoes, with more wine, followed by cheese, yoghurt, fruit and coffee. One hour later we're running around the playing field,' recalls Spring. 'What a change from New Zealand and my pre-match spaghetti on toast or mince pie!'

Spring says he is often asked why he left a beautiful country like New Zealand to live in the Basque country.

'With Pamplona and the running of the bulls only an hour away, the fabulous surfing at Biarritz, the beaches of the Basque coast and its many other charms, there are plenty of arguments.

'For me it was a beautiful Basque girl I was fortunate enough to marry.'

Postscript

In March 2002, the Kiwi contingent in France launched the Kauri Club, with the aim of forming a team of ex-pat Kiwis to play in tournaments in the south of France. The Kauri Club will emphasise the social aspect of play, says Spring, a Kauri Club organiser.

'I think we'll be more known for running our fingers up and down guitar chords and hitting false notes than running down wingers and hitting rucks or mauls. Our president, Jaye Proctor [ex-Wellington B representative], plays bass for a Basque rock band and we've already had some success on the field. We beat the French seven-a-side team in the Plate Final at the St Lary beach rugby tourney.'

Under the driving force of former Wellington rep Nigel Geany, the Kauri Club's first official engagement took place in Paris at a restaurant run by a 145 kg rugby-mad Basque on the night of France's victory over Ireland, which won the 2002 Six Nations Championship title for the Tricolores.

IMPORTS

NEW ZEALAND

Rugby had instant appeal for New Zealanders from the moment it was introduced back in the 1860s. Its robust, physical, action-packed qualities ideally matched the New Zealand male's temperament. From the first official club match, in Nelson in 1870, the game spread like wildfire. In 1888 the Native team (essentially a group of Maori with four Pakeha making up the numbers) made their legendary tour of the UK. The black jersey was adopted for the national team in the 1890s, with the 'All Blacks' title first surfacing during the stunningly successful tour of Britain in 1905. Since then, rugby has remained the national game, there being almost no region in New Zealand where it is not the predominant sport. The All Blacks can boast a successful win-loss ratio against every other rugby-playing nation in the world. The All Blacks won the inaugural World Cup in 1987 and have claimed three of the six Tri-Nations titles in competition with Australia and South Africa.

Founded
1892
IRB
1949
Clubs
600
Players
88,111 men; 2058 women
Rugby Nomads
Steve Devine, John Gallagher, Martin Johnson, Christian Califano, Balie Swart, Phil Kingsley-Jones

245

Steve Devine

Australian Colt Steve Devine was feeling pretty good about his rugby future. It was early 1998, he had just celebrated his 22nd birthday and, as halfback for the Australia Under 21 team, he was clearly seen as a Wallaby prospect.

He had turned up to watch a Waratahs Super 12 home game and seen the team's second-string halfback, Sam Payne, sidelined with what was obviously a severe knee injury. After the match, Devine chatted to a physiotherapist and was told that Payne had damaged his cruciate ligaments and could be out of action for up to a year. Perhaps Devine would get the nod as Payne's replacement.

'I went home and I was hoping, hoping, but there was no phone call. It was a real disappointment,' says Devine.

'I was quite young and thought I might be given a chance to do something for the Waratahs. Instead they went for Travis Hall, who was older and had played a lot of senior club rugby for Eastwood.'

His opportunity came later in the season when the Waratahs' regular halfback, Chris Whitaker, was on tour in Scotland with the Wallabies and Devine was brought into the squad to cover the halfback position. Devine trained with the squad for a month and got only about five minutes on the field, but that was long enough to make up his mind. Rugby would be his career. 'I absolutely loved the whole atmosphere of professional rugby and I decided I was going to do everything I could to be right up there,' recalls Devine.

He signed a contract with the Waratahs for the rest of 1998 but then, just two weeks later, an offer came from New Zealand. Would he play first-division rugby for Auckland in the NPC competition, replacing Ofisa (Junior) Tonu'u, who was on tour with the All Blacks?

Ten years before he received that offer, Devine admits, he would have struggled to identify who the All Blacks were, or, for that matter, anything much at all about the game of rugby.

His home was Boggabri, a sleepy inland New South Wales country town of 800 people, with a ribbon main street ('Blink and you're through it') six hours northwest of Sydney. Devine's father and uncles had all been fairly useful league players in their time and that was young Steve's game, along with the odd soccer match which he played at his primary school.

At 13 Devine was sent to Sydney as a boarder at St Joseph's College, Hunters Hill. St Joseph's is Australia's most famous rugby breeding-ground, boasting 49 Wallabies from its ranks to date, including Matt Burke, who was three years Devine's senior at school.

St Joseph's and boarding-school life were overwhelming experiences for the shy, skinny little country boy. As a traditional GPS (Great Public School), St Joseph's didn't countenance league and so Devine put his name down to play soccer.

He switched to rugby under pressure from his peers and had as his first coach Matt Williams, who would later coach him in the Waratahs squad. But rugby as a game was a mystery to him and he lacked the build to play it well, he feared.

'I didn't take to it straight away. I was a small, timid winger trying to understand what was going on and it wasn't until I was 15 and playing at inside centre for the Under 16 C team that I really started to enjoy it.'

Two years on, in 1994 and his final year at school, Devine played for St Joseph's first XV throughout its centenary year of rugby. It was a magnificent send-off for the boy from Boggabri. St Joseph's, affectionately known as Joeys, went through the season undefeated, with crowds of up to 20,000 supporters at major matches. Devine won selection for New South Wales Schoolboys; Joeys, he acknowledged to himself, had pretty much changed his life.

He didn't want to return to Boggabri — five years at school in Sydney had seen to that — but although he had enjoyed the first-XV experience, Devine did not seriously consider taking his career much further in that direction.

He would become an electrician, like his father, and find a club where he could play Saturday-afternoon rugby and enjoy the company of friends.

Devine joined the long-established Gordon club, but opted for Wests the following season, where from the comparative obscurity of club play he was selected for Australia Under 21, under the coaching of Ian Kennedy. It was a leap in his rugby fortunes that he attributes to the influence of his New Zealand coach at Wests, Kelvin Farrington.

'My rugby really took off under Kelvin. He pushed hard for my rugby career, which was good because at that stage it wasn't the most important thing for me,' says Devine.

'Kelvin was a good friend of Joe Stanley and that's how the offer came to play NPC rugby in Auckland. I was keen because I thought it would be a good experience to play in New Zealand, especially under Graham Henry, who was the Auckland coach then.

'However, the day I actually made the Auckland NPC team, Graham announced he was going to coach in Wales, so I wasn't sure where I was going to end up!'

The intention was that Devine would return to Sydney and his contract with the Waratahs halfway through the NPC competition, when Tonu'u came back from tour. However, Devine impressed the Auckland coaching panel with his fiercely competitive attitude and ability on the break, and was named ahead of Tonu'u with the proviso that he would remain with Auckland for the remainder of the season.

'I rang home and said, "Listen, I'm starting over here and I want to stay on," and they said, "That's fine,"' recalls Devine. 'Travis Hall was still playing and I would just have been sitting on the bench, so I got released from my contract with the Waratahs.'

But not from Australia. Devine was selected for the Australian Sevens team at the end of 1998 to play in the Dubai Sevens tournament, where he came up against his new New Zealand mates in the semifinal. It was an interesting experience for the Australian-Auckland halfback. There was what Devine calls a 'bit of a scuffle' during the game and punches were traded. His heart, at that stage, still belonged in Australia.

Devine returned home to Boggabri for Christmas and a period of reflection on his future. Australia's three Super 12 teams, the Queensland Reds, New South Wales Waratahs and ACT Brumbies, had strong halfback representation, and in the Brumbies' George Gregan a certain Wallaby first choice. He believed he stood a better chance of playing in the Super 12 competition by going to live in New Zealand.

Auckland appealed as a city and he had successfully negotiated his way into the close-knit Auckland NPC unit, despite those loyal to Tonu'u and Ben Willis, Auckland's incumbent halfbacks, who regarded him initially as a pushy young Aussie muscling in on their territory.

So when a two-year contract came through for him to play for the Super 12 Blues in the 1999 and 2000 seasons, Devine leapt at it. In 2001 he signed his second two-year contract for the Blues and, halfway through the season, became eligible to represent New Zealand.

And that almost happened in 2001 when Justin Marshall was ruled out of the All Black tour of Scotland and Ireland. The day after Devine had come out of surgery, he received a call from the New Zealand selectors, inquiring about his availability.

His dream was to play for the All Blacks. To have it offered and then to have to turn it down because of an ankle injury was a crushing blow.

From the start, Devine says he relished the coaching he received at the Blues, describing the franchise as a very professional outfit under its current coaches Wayne Pivac and Grant Fox. He also singles out John Kirwan, the former Blues manager, for special praise.

'JK was brilliant. I really needed him when I was getting into the whole Blues scene and he was as good to me away from the rugby field as on it. I regard him as a real mentor. He hardened me up mentally.'

Devine had joined the Suburbs Rugby Club in Auckland on arrival, but was unhappy and left there to play for the Marist club under its coach and former All Black Bernie McCahill, where he felt at home from the start. In 2001 he bought a house in the pleasant eastern suburbs of Auckland and today describes his lifestyle in New Zealand as congenial.

'Coming from the country, I love outdoor activities like fishing and hunting when I can get the time, or being able to jump on a mountain bike and go out to Woodhill Forest, north of Auckland.

'But for me, at the moment, it's just rugby, wherever that may lead me. I enjoy playing against old team-mates; it always makes you go that little bit harder.

'I've still got a lot of mates in Australia, guys like Des Tuiavii, the Waratahs blindside flanker, who used to look after this cheeky little halfback in the old days.'

Four years after his arrival in New Zealand, the future once again looks good for the 25-year-old if he can conquer the recurring ankle problems that have dogged him. In March 2002 he had his fourth operation in three years to remove bone chips and has vowed he will not have another.

'It was just maddening trying to train through the pain, so I needed to have the ops done. But it was equally maddening to sit out the bulk of the 2002 Super 12 season through injury. The prognosis is good after this final operation, so hopefully that's all behind me now.'

'Amen to that,' says his NPC coach Wayne Pivac, who believes that Devine has the ability and enthusiasm to regain his place in New Zealand rugby.

'Stevie plays above his weight. For a little guy he's one of the best halfbacks around. He has energy, enthusiasm, a tremendous work rate around the field and a never-say-die attitude. That last quality is something our guys can all learn from Steve. He just plays for the full 80 minutes and gives it everything he's got. When he comes off the field, he's absolutely exhausted.

'In part, Devine's ankle problems can be put down to his burning desire to get back on the field. He has pushed the medical team to its limits in his hunt for a quick fix, but this has cost him in terms of ankle recovery,' says Pivac. 'He kept coming back too soon and was probably the author of his own misfortune.'

But after his fourth ankle operation Auckland's team management took over and had Devine's leg put in a moon-boot for a full recovery period, so that he could start his rehabilitation from scratch before the commencement of the 2002 NPC season and the Super 12 competition in 2003.

'In 2002 New Zealand has two outstanding All Black halfbacks in Justin Marshall and Byron Kelleher, and then there is a gap to number three,' says Pivac. 'If Steve's injury-free and takes his opportunities, he's definitely got the ability to get back up there. I think at the top level "Sharky" Robinson has been tried, but I don't think he's really taken his opportunities. I'd put Steve at number three, and should there be injuries to the top two, Devine might well achieve that All Black dream.'

For the record

Player
- Australian Under 21s, 1997 (4 games)
- Australian Sevens, 1998
- NSW Waratahs, 1998 (1 game)
- Auckland, 1998–2002 (41 games)
- Blues, 1999–2002 (30 games)

John Gallagher

With a best-selling biography, numerous articles and many a rugby-book chapter devoted to him, England's All Black John Gallagher needs little introduction to New Zealanders.

Now, in 2002, 16 years after his first game for the All Blacks, Gallagher is head of physical education at Colfe's School, an independent school for boys in south London, married to Anita and the father of two boys, Alex, 10, and Matthew, 6. His hobby is covering the Super 12 competition on Sky TV for British audiences, where his deep knowledge of the New Zealand rugby scene is put to good use.

Asked whether he believes he became an international star by coming to live in New Zealand, or whether his talent was always there but not recognised in England, Gallagher says it was probably a combination of both factors.

'Obviously I had the raw talent, but when I left London in March 1984 there wasn't the structure in England that could allow my potential to be fulfilled.

'Going to New Zealand, with the attitude New Zealand had towards rugby, together with the infrastructure and the coaching, was to arrive in an environment which I thoroughly enjoyed and which allowed my play to improve beyond recognition.'

However, the young soccer-mad John Gallagher didn't know what a rugby ball was until he began attending St Joseph's Academy College at the age of 11. When he went home one evening and told his mother he'd scored a try, she asked what a try was. 'I don't know,' he replied, 'but I got one!'

He was placed at flyhalf in his first year and remained there throughout his school life, the last three years in St Joseph's first XV, where his exceptional pace became a valuable asset to the team. However, St Joseph's was not an 'OK' public school, or one where players were noted for later selection under the English system at that time. Gallagher believes that had he stayed in England he probably would have reverted to his first love, soccer, and finished up as a spectator at the Highbury ground watching Arsenal in action.

When he left school he joined up with London Irish and was on an Under 21 trip to Dublin with the team when he was asked to play in the unfamiliar position of fullback. He relished the challenge. Later that year he met up with an old schoolfriend who had played for the Oriental-Rongotai Club in Wellington; he said he would contact the New Zealand club and put Gallagher's name forward to them. Three months later, on Gallagher's 20th birthday, he received a phone call from Clive Currie, the senior coach for Oriental-Rongotai. The team was looking for a goalkicking fullback in time for the winter season, Gallagher was told, and they would like to offer him the position.

He was scheduled to start at Hendon Police College, in North London, in March that year but instead found himself with a one-way plane ticket to New Zealand where he linked up with the Oriental-Rongotai Club.

Once in Wellington, 'Kipper' Gallagher made an immediate impact for 'Ories' on the field and, off it, appreciated how its management and team-mates made him feel at home from the start.

There was no hostility towards him as a Brit, he said, because by good luck he had gone to a club that was both family oriented and cosmopolitan in its make-up. There were Tongans, Samoans, Cook Islanders, Tahitians and Fijians, so an odd Englishman didn't look too much out of place.

John 'Kipper' Gallagher doing his thing for Wellington.

One of the major differences he found lay in the New Zealand club structure. 'In England you play for a senior club and then the league and you're playing against all these other clubs in traditional fixtures. You're round the corner one week and up in Liverpool the next,' he recalls.

'There didn't seem to be any logical or geographical sense to it and as a result it wasn't very efficient. One of the things I liked about Wellington was that even if you were with an unfashionable club like Ories, you could still end up playing against current All Blacks such as Murray Mexted, Allan Hewson, Mike Clamp, Bernie Fraser or Stu Wilson in club games.'

For a 20-year-old it was an invaluable opportunity to pit himself against the world's best, and a good gauge as to how he was progressing, he says.

'I just took full advantage of any opportunities that came my way.'

He didn't have to wait long for those opportunities to arrive. Halfway through his first season he was drafted into the Wellington squad and in 1986 was named as fullback for the All Black tour to France.

Over the next four years he would score 35 tries in his 41 matches for the All Blacks, be named the New Zealand player of the year in 1989 and receive the International Player of the Year trophy in London in 1990.

Then came the bombshell. Gallagher, one of the world's finest fullbacks, had signed with the Leeds league club in northern England.

The offer from Leeds was financially too tempting to turn down and he was also drawn to the challenge it presented, he says.

He had answered most of the challenges of rugby — he'd been a pivot in New Zealand's win in the inaugural Rugby World Cup in 1987 and hadn't known what it was to lose a match in his 41 games (40 wins and one draw) for the All Blacks.

League seemed to be a fast, physical and entertaining game that he could enjoy. However, he had problems with the Leeds coach, decided to move on, and retired from the London Broncos league team in 1995, at the age of 31.

In that year rugby went professional and Gallagher returned to rugby, playing and captaining Blackheath for two seasons while teaching at Colfe's School. While at Blackheath, Gallagher played for Ireland A in its victory over Scotland at Donnybrook. He thus recorded an odd double for an Englishman, representing both New Zealand and Ireland, but not his home country, in his international rugby career!

Then in 1998 he was appointed director of rugby at Harlequins RFC, a post he held for two years before returning to his old school, Colfe's, this time as director of sport.

Gallagher had come to New Zealand in 1984 frustrated by the lack of opportunity to develop his game in England. But he believes that today such a move would not be necessary.

'It is much easier for players from different backgrounds to come through the ranks in England now. It is a lot better, because the whole league infrastructure is better. It's working well. I feel that the chances of someone like me slipping through the net, although possible, are far less likely than they were.'

For the record

Player
Wellington, 1984–1989 (88 games)
New Zealand, 1986–1989 (41 games, 18 tests)

Martin Johnson

When John Albert, enthusiastic committee member of the tiny Tihoi club at Taupo, went fishing for rugby players back in 1988, he landed a big one: he hooked Martin Johnson, who would go on to become an illustrious captain of England and the British Lions.

Displaying a unique mix of enterprise and audacity, Albert wrote to every member of the England schoolboys team which had finished in front of New Zealand and Australia in a tournament in Sydney.

He invited them all to come and play a season with Tihoi, a club based in a rural settlement on the west coast of Lake Taupo, total population of the region, at best, 150.

'I figured the New Zealand schoolboys would be spoken for,' says Albert, 'and the Australians were probably being sought by league clubs. So I went for the Poms.'

Aware of the England players' names but not their addresses, Albert, who'd previously arranged for Welsh hooker Garin Jenkins to play for Tihoi, blissfully wrote to them all care of The Rugby Union of England, Twickenham.

In an amateur age that largely pre-dated player agents the mail obviously got through, because Albert received nine replies from interested players, four of whom eventually played for Tihoi, a club languishing at the bottom of the Taupo competition at the time. Johnson would become the most famous but the others included Richard West, who went on to represent England A, and John Fowler, who settled in New Zealand and played for King Country and Hawke's Bay, sharing in a victory over the 1993 Lions.

Johnson regards the Tihoi experience as one of the lucky breaks of his life. He says that when he received Albert's letter, as an 18-year-old, he thought a six-month rugby-playing holiday in New Zealand would be 'a great lark'.

'It would never happen now,' he says, 'because since rugby went professional, virtually every promising young player belongs to an academy or is contracted to a club. But at the start of 1989 I wasn't beholden to anyone. I was playing for Leicester Youth and I'd been assured the club wasn't intending to involve me at senior level in the season ahead.'

So off to New Zealand he went, a country about which he knew precious little. He knew of the All Blacks and of the great Auckland provincial team, he'd fraternised with a few of the New Zealand school-boys and he'd heard of Taupo. Beyond that, it was a trip into the unknown. His first impression of Taupo was that, although it was an attractive little town, it was 'in the back of beyond'.

'I came from a rural area outside Leicester,' says Johnston, 'but I was only an hour-and-a-half from London on the M1. At Taupo, I felt isolated. There were no motorways and it seemed a major journey to anywhere.'

Johnson was fascinated with the club he'd flown 18,000 kilometres to play for. The ground at Tihoi, a 20-minute drive from Taupo, usu-ally had sheep grazing on it that had to be rounded up before practices could start. And it amazed Johnson that a modest-sized town like Taupo could support five senior rugby clubs. In the UK, a Taupo-sized town or village would have one club.

The New Zealand Colts team of 1990. Back row: Matt Sexton, Jasin Goldsmith, Paul Fairweather, Craig Dowd, Greg Halford, Apollo Perelini, Craig Innes, Dion Kerr. Middle row: Neil Gray (manager), Daniel Manu, Martin Johnson, Mark Cooksley, Blair Larson, Doug Power, Chris McCullough (physiotherapist). Front row: John Hart (coach), Joe Edwards, John Timu, David Morgan (captain), Va'aiga Tuigamala, Sean Fitzsimmons, Richard Watts, Graham Williams (assistant coach). In front: Stu Forster, Simon Mannix, Simon Crabb.

It wasn't unusual for the Tihoi senior team to find itself a couple of players short on the eve of a competition match. 'So we'd a grab a couple of locals to make up the numbers. They could be aged anywhere from 16 to 45. From time to time there were even a few rugby league players involved, who shouldn't have been.

'These guys would roll up; they hadn't trained, yet they would put their bodies on the line. Every game was physical and competitive. You had to get stuck in.

'For me, it was all a lot of fun. And I was in New Zealand to enjoy myself, having no great expectations. And I was definitely staying only six months.'

Well, if Martin Johnson had been a skinny wee bloke of modest talent, he undoubtedly would have been cashing in his return ticket within six months. But the Martin Johnson who locked the Tihoi scrum in 1989, although only a teenager, stood an imposing 2.01 m tall and weighed in at 106 kg and had been good enough to represent England schools. King Country coach Noel McQuilkin could scarcely believe his luck when he sighted him.

'He might have been only 19,' says McQuilkin, 'but he had enormous talent. Although pretty green when he arrived, he rapidly got into the way of country rugby, never backed off and eventually became the toughest guy in my team.'

Johnson confesses to being 'young and naive' when he arrived in New Zealand and found it somewhat daunting to be playing alongside, and socialising with, tough-as-teak bushmen and farmers.

For a while he was known as Pretty Boy, a consequence of wearing the Pommy shorts with large pockets — not the sort of attire to impress your rugby mates in rural New Zealand!

McQuilkin involved Johnson with his King Country squad from the start of the 1989 season: 'I was pitched in at the deep end,' as Johnson puts it. After only a handful of club matches, he lined up against Auckland B, a game he remembers vividly for the sensational performance by Frank Bunce.

'Auckland was the best provincial team in the world at the time,' says Johnson, 'and this was a reminder of the depth of talent it possessed, because Frank couldn't make the A team. He ripped us to pieces that day. I said to the guys if he was in the UK, he'd be the first back chosen for England. That Auckland B team also included Apollo

Perelini, who went on to make his mark on the international scene.'

There have been few players throughout his career that Johnson has had to look up to, but in his fourth outing for King Country, against the touring Pumas at Taupo, he opposed Alejandro Iachetti, who at 2.03 m and 124 kg is one of the biggest men ever to play international rugby. Johnson survived that personal challenge but was fortunate to get off the field unscathed after the match degenerated into an all-in brawl in the closing stages.

King Country's greatest player, Colin Meads, took an immediate interest in Johnson and after observing him in the early representative games suggested he should have a New Zealand Colts trial. He did, but missed selection.

Despite his youth, Johnson made a significant impact on the representative scene, helping spark a King Country revival in the NPC second division. The *Rugby Annual* of that year observed that 'Englishman Martin Johnson, only 19, was thrust into representative rugby and can go back to his home country with the type of experience that could see him gain national honours. In partnership with Russell Alve, Johnson had a field day in the lineouts.'

Johnson had always intended returning to the UK at the conclusion of the 1989 season but two factors conspired to keep him in New Zealand: a shoulder injury and a pretty girl.

In terms of the injury, he reasoned that if he arrived back at Leicester, he would be immediately drafted back into action, whereas if he spent the summer in New Zealand, the shoulder would benefit from an enforced rest.

Also, he'd taken a shine to a local farmer's daughter, Kay Griddick, whom he'd met at a club after-match function. Their relationship flourished to the extent that she would eventually become Mrs Johnson. Without a work permit, Johnson could not be legally employed, but he helped out at times through the summer on some of his team-mates' farms. 'Skilled I wasn't,' he confesses. 'I was more a hindrance than a help, but I became reasonably proficient at pulling batons off fences that were being dismantled.'

Johnson was back at the New Zealand Colts trials in 1990. This time, the national selectors, headed by John Hart, decided they couldn't ignore him and he was named in the team to play three matches in Australia.

In the international in Sydney against Australia Under 21, not only was he surrounded by players who would become world-class performers, individuals like Craig Dowd, Blair Larsen, Daniel Manu, Stu Forster, Craig Innes, Inga Tuigamala and John Timu, but the fellow he opposed was also on his way to stardom — John Eales, three days short of his 20th birthday.

Incredibly, 11 years on, Johnson and Eales would be captains of the British Lions and the Wallabies respectively in a test series in Australia that would captivate the entire rugby world.

Johnson would be the loser in 2001, but as a black-shirted warrior back in 1990 he had the last laugh. Not only did his team win, 24–21, but through pressure exerted by Johnson, Eales made a costly tap-down error at a defensive lineout, from which the New Zealanders scored. Johnson loved every minute of his rugby that season. There was the thrill of a Ranfurly Shield challenge at Eden Park against an Auckland team oozing All Blacks — players of the calibre of John Kirwan, Joe Stanley, Grant Fox, Zinzan Brooke, Alan and Gary Whetton, Steve McDowell, Olo Brown and Sean Fitzpatrick — and a series of highly competitive NPC matches in which Hawke's Bay just edged out King Country for the second-division title.

'I couldn't have wished for a better grounding for my rugby career,' says Johnson. 'In those amateur days, comparing the standards in England with those in New Zealand was chalk-and-cheese stuff. I couldn't believe how seriously every match in New Zealand was taken. It was so completely different to the attitude in the UK. Obviously, things have changed with the advent of professionalism, but back then it was a revelation. The level of rugby achieved in provincial play in New Zealand wasn't matched in the UK, or even in the northern hemisphere for that matter.

'To experience two seasons of that was just great. I went to New Zealand and returned a battle-hardened rugby player. Not many in the UK could make that claim.'

In his two seasons with King Country, Johnson appeared in 25 of the team's 30 fixtures. McQuilkin says that throughout that time he was 'the greatest thing since sliced bread in these parts. It was a great thrill to have a King Country boy make the New Zealand Colts. I don't think we'd had one since Pinetree Meads' days. He was a great team member and I was sorry to see him go.

'For a while there I thought he might stay, but his destiny was back in England and I've been enormously proud of what he's achieved. The biggest surprise to me was that it took him so long to win selection for England after his return home. I thought he was ready for international rugby the moment he left New Zealand.'

The main reason Johnson's career stuttered following his return to England was a series of injuries. The shoulder which had bothered him in New Zealand was finally operated on in 1991, sidelining him for many months. Then he withdrew from the England B team that was preparing for a tour of New Zealand in 1992 when he injured himself in the final training session.

It was only a question of time before Johnson pulled on the white jersey of England. His debut was as a late replacement for Wade Dooley against France in 1993 in a match in which he demonstrated such talent he was immediately placed on standby for the British Lions tour of New Zealand.

When Dooley returned home during the Lions tour following his father's death, Johnson found himself on a plane to Auckland again as his replacement. He made such an impact against Taranaki and Auckland he was rushed into the test line-up, where he starred in the tourists' sensational 20–7 victory at Wellington.

It marked the start of a remarkable succession of appearances for the Lions. Four years on, he would captain the Lions, successfully, to South Africa, and in 2001 he would create history by becoming the first individual to lead the Lions twice, teaming up with coach Graham Henry in an assault on the world champion Wallabies.

Henry and Johnson couldn't have been happier after 120 minutes against Australia. They'd won the opening international overwhelmingly and were equally dominant up till halftime in the second test.

Then Joe Roff effected an interception which yielded Australia an initiative the Lions were never able to wrench back.

'The Wallabies and the All Blacks are quite different in their approach,' says Johnson. 'If we'd smashed the All Blacks in the first test the way we did the Wallabies, they'd have been ballistic in the opening 20 minutes of the second test. Which is what happened back in 1993, in the final test at Eden Park.

'But the Wallabies are a methodical, calculating team. They just get on with their game, and in the finish it won them the series. We missed several scoring opportunities in the opening 40 minutes of the second test, which proved terribly costly.

'Also, 10 minutes at halftime represents a long break. You have to re-establish yourself afterwards. At times, it can be like starting a new game.'

Johnson says he had an excellent working relationship with coach Henry. At tour's end, they were both frustrated because the margin between winning and losing the series 2–1 was despairingly slender.

In explaining Johnson's appointment as captain for the 1997 tour of South Africa, coach Ian McGeechan said, 'He's the first name you put on the team sheet and you need a captain who is guaranteed his place in the test side.' The same principle applied in 2001.

Johnson, who succeeded Lawrence Dallaglio as England's captain in 1999, is a follow-me leader in the Buck Shelford mould. He's never been into placing motivational notes under players' hotel doors as predecessor Will Carling used to do.

He says the first few times he captained Leicester he tried to do too much. 'But I was made captain because I am the bloke I am. So I've got to keep being that bloke. I'm not an extrovert. I'm very intense about my rugby, but hopefully at the right time.'

Johnson, who regrets that his rugby commitments have prevented him and Kay from getting back to New Zealand more regularly, intends reactivating his career with the HSBC Bank when his rugby playing days come to a finish.

'I still do a bit of work for them, in the public-relations field,' he says. 'That's where I'd be if I wasn't a professional rugby player.'

For the record

Player
- King Country, 1989–1990 (25 games)
- Leicester Tigers, 1991–2002 (281 games)
- England, 1993–2002 (67 tests)
- British Lions, 1993, 1997, 2001

Christian Califano

In April 2002 Christian Califano and his wife, Anabelle, were at Auckland International Airport farewelling relatives who were returning to France. Califano turned to Annabelle and said, 'Do you realise that in a month we'll be flying out too?' They both wept.

But France's most capped prop in history, with 67 test appearances for the Tricolores, says he hopes to return some day and buy a holiday house in New Zealand, which he calls 'my new country'. That lies in the future. Home for the Califano family is currently in England, where Christian is on a three-year playing contract with London's Saracens club under coach Wayne Shelford, following the end of his Super 12 season for the Blues.

For Califano, who played for the Blues in the 2002 Super 12 competition and Auckland in the 2001 NPC, his time in New Zealand had been a rugby sojourn that was the result of an ambition that goes back to his teenage years, living in Toulon on France's Italian border (the surname Califano is Sicilian in origin).

He left Toulon when he was 18, after being offered the chance to play rugby for the second-division Bourges club. He would go, he said, if the club promised to find work for his mother as well as for himself. Bourges obliged. However, at the same time one of France's top clubs, Stade Toulousain, was also interested.

What a dilemma for the teenager. He decided that a year in the lower grades would be a good stepping-stone and his honouring of the commitment he had made to Bourges was important to his personal values. From there the Califanos moved to Toulouse, a club and city in southwest France whose name has since become synonymous with that of Califano.

He always hankered to see the country of 'les All Blacks' but Califano's love affair with New Zealand was truly ignited when, in 1994, he was selected to tour New Zealand with France. He was just 22, and on his test debut in Christchurch he found himself packing down against All Black Richard Loe, who was one of his boyhood idols.

Califano might have been impressed but he was not overawed; France went on to take the series 2–0 and Califano's long and distinguished international career was launched. He made a commitment to himself then that he would someday return to New Zealand to play.

Two international props who love each other's countries: Christian Califano (left) and Graham Purvis sharing a wine in Auckland.

Seven years later he was back living in Auckland with Anabelle and their two young daughters, Claudia, 4, and Clothilde, 1, and playing for Auckland in the NPC competition.

It certainly wasn't the money that had lured him. Califano says he wanted to bring his family to New Zealand so they could experience the country's more leisured lifestyle and relaxed culture.

'In Europe, people are treading on each other's toes and everyone's rushing around. In France, our lifestyle is so busy. I leave home at seven in the morning to drive to Toulouse, while here we have more time for each other. Living in New Zealand has brought us closer together and it's a lot more laid-back, which I like.'

It's been a good rugby experience too, he says. 'I wish I could have come here earlier in my career, but with professionalism today that wasn't possible. Ten years ago you could play seasons in the northern and southern hemispheres, but now you can't because of their length.'

France and Europe's long seasons can lead to high stress levels, with players having to sustain their peak throughout the 40 to 50-plus top-level fixtures each season. New Zealand has got it right, he claims, with an ideal set-up of three months' concentrated play for Super 12, followed by a break in intensity for club fixtures before swinging into the NPC championship, a competition which he prefers to Super 12.

Scrums in New Zealand are good, hard contests, says Califano, who is equally at home on either side of the front row.

He is impressed that New Zealand props, unlike the French, acknowledge that there's more to life than trotting from one scrum to the next. 'New Zealand props do not see themselves as just being there for the scrums, they are also there for tackling and general work . . . I think they are more complete players. But it's difficult for me to make a comparison about which is better, because the playing mentalities of the two countries differ so much,' he adds prudently.

'In New Zealand, there is no difference between playing a big game or a little game. There is the same attitude all the time. Here you want to win by 100 points against a weaker side, whereas in France to win by 50 points is OK. It is very easy for the French to descend to the level of the opposition.'

Califano always knew that Auckland was going to be a professional, organised outfit, but admits he was jolted to find that all of its training sessions were conducted at 'a 100 per cent, never 80 per cent' level of commitment. On match day, both the French and New Zealand teams are as committed and professional as the other, but it is New Zealand that has the edge in preparation, he believes.

When asked which opponent he rated most highly in the 2002 Super 12 competition, he doesn't hesitate. 'Gordon Slater, because of his overall contribution to the game and his good rugby values. He is the face of the new type of prop.'

Califano has taken back to Europe what he considers to be some wonderful memories of his time in Auckland: Super 12, despite a knee injury which cut his season short; the final court session after Auckland's last NPC game in 2001, when, with all the team and managers present, he had to 'carry out the "Judges" orders'; his NPC coach, Wayne Pivac, who, he says, 'is good and very honest'; and the rugby. 'In a team you have 14 mates, which makes rugby so special, and I have made many mates here.'

On the lifestyle front, Auckland's Parnell Village scores highly, along with his two favourite restaurants there, The George and Iguacu. He loves The Warehouse ('I'd like to introduce it to Europe') and New

Zealand white wine (red is off limits for a visitor's praise, he says with a smile), while Auckland, with its new buildings and café conviviality centred around the Viaduct Harbour, is 'a very nice place'.

There will be life after rugby for Califano. When his playing days are over, he says, he may pursue another of his dreams and become a pilot with Air France. If he does, he is well launched on that flight path with many flying hours already notched up.

Early in 2002, Christian Califano was named in 'France's Team of the Twentieth Century', and this modest, charming man says that sometimes he has to pinch himself to believe that it is all true.

'It's quite humbling, really, to think of names like Robert Paparemborde [France's legendary strongman prop, who played 55 internationals for his country between 1975 and 1983], Louis Armary and Jean-Pierre Garuet, who have gone before me, and to realise that I have played more tests for France than they have.'

For the record

Player
- Toulouse, 1993–2001
- France, 1994–2000 (67 tests)
- Auckland, 2001 (11 games)
- Blues, 2002 (7 games)

Balie Swart

It was one thing answering an advertisement placed on the internet by the Nelson Bays Rugby Union, who wanted a coach; it was entirely another thing, following a conference-call interview, being given just 14 days to accept the position when it was offered him.

At 38, Balie Swart urgently had to make the most important decision of his life. New Zealand, which he'd toured as both a player and a coach, beckoned. But was it reasonable to uproot his wife and two infant children from South Africa and transplant them into a new land? He had been enormously influenced by Laurie Mains, who had first got him involved in coaching. Mains had become his mentor and taken him on board as his assistant with the Cats Super 12 team in 2000 and 2001. When Swart was discussing his future options, as his mentor was preparing to return to New Zealand, Mains asked him if Johannesburg, with its alarming crime rate, was really the place to bring up a young family.

That, though, wasn't the dominant factor in Swart's decision, after 10 days, to advise Nelson Bays that he was their man. Of greater significance was Swart's determination to coach at grass-roots level. 'Thanks to Laurie,' says Swart, 'I'd worked with the top echelon of players, but I knew that, as a coach, unless you work at the bottom, you will never get to the top in your own right. That's why Nelson Bays suited me perfectly, working with clubs, with schoolboys and with the representative team.'

Nelson is a name which has come to hold great significance in Swart's life. The city of Nelson, where he first visited as assistant coach of the Cats in 2001, is where he is now settled with his wife, Ilze, and children, Kiara and Miandi.

And then, of course, there was Nelson Mandela, South Africa's charismatic president, who made a dramatic appearance in the Springbok dressing room as the players were preparing for the World Cup final against the All Blacks at Ellis Park in 1995.

'There he was, this charismatic person, holding a plastic bag with a No 6 Springbok jersey in it,' says Swart, 'asking us if we would mind if he wore it during the final. It had an electrifying effect on us, I can tell you.'

Swart acknowledges that the Springboks were not the best team at the 1995 tournament but the extraordinary circumstances surrounding that final weekend lifted the South Africans to a new level.

'I don't believe we were the better side in the final. If the match had been staged the following day, we would probably have lost. But on that incredible afternoon, the crowd, the president and the sheer electricity that existed galvanised us.

'As we prepared for extra time, our captain, Francois [Pienaar], told us to look at the crowd. "That's what it's all about,"' he said. 'We were never going to lose that afternoon.'

When the final whistle blew, with the Springboks ahead 15–12, courtesy of a late dropped goal from Joel Stransky, Swart, a battle-hardened front rower, concedes that he had more than a few tears in his eyes. 'Frankly, we were flabbergasted,' he says. 'When we finally got to our dressing room, after a very emotional presentation ceremony, our coach, Kitch Christie, told us just to sit and enjoy the moment because we would probably never be together as a team again. He was right, of course. Even Kitch didn't survive much longer as coach.

'Our victory seemed to bring the whole of Johannesburg to a standstill. On the trip back from Ellis Park, people were clambering on to our bus and standing on cars. It was incredible.

'At our hotel there must have been a thousand fans cheering us. I was so proud to be a Springbok that day. We'd achieved something truly special for a country in need.

'Till today, I'm recognised for what the Springboks achieved that afternoon in the World Cup final. You knew you'd done something special for your country and I'm really proud of that.'

Although in the rugby world, and among his friends, he's known by the nickname Balie, the man who is seeking to shape Nelson Bays into a formidable NPC team was christened Izak Stephanus de Villiers Swart. Stephanus is the name he still answers to when he's around his parents.

'Balie' is Afrikaans for 'barrel', and virtually from his first week at high school at Stellenbosch, that nickname applied for the solidly built youngster who, from the start, displayed a natural aptitude for rugby.

In the four years he attended the school, operating at Under 14, Under 15, Under 16 and Under 18 levels, he was only twice part of a losing team.

If you were a rugby person, there wasn't a better place on earth to be based than Stellenbosch, whose most influential character was the man known universally as Mr South African Rugby: Danie Craven.

At the age of 21 Swart was selected to play for Western Province, which was daunting to say the least as he found himself in combat at practice with individuals like Hempies du Toit, Sean Povey and Henning van Aswegen, Springboks all.

'For me, those early training sessions were about survival while trying to learn the tricks of the trade,' says Swart. 'I was never that big. My weight was usually around 112 kg, which was quite average for front rowers in South Africa.

'My studying suffered because I was usually too sore after returning home from scrum practices to be able to concentrate on anything!'

Swart learnt well, and in 1985, when only 23, he was rushed into the Springbok team as a late replacement for giant prop Flippie van der Merwe for an international fixture against a World XV, his opponent the celebrated Frenchman Robert Paparemborde.

That appearance doesn't show in most record books because at the time South Africa was in the sporting wilderness with 'official' tests not resuming until 1992.

But for Swart it was as real as it could be, with caps awarded to the Springboks. 'I was just a youngster against test-hardened overseas stars,' he says. 'I was terrified, so nervous I threw up in my bed. I wondered how I would ever get through the game.

'I slept with my Springbok jersey under my pillow. It was a very special occasion, the more memorable because we won the match. And afterwards there was the thrill of being presented with my first cap by Doc Craven.'

Swart went on to play 85 games for Western Province before moving to Johannesburg on the high veldt to become marketing director of a packaging company. 'It was time to repay my bursary,' he says. He was immediately snapped up, becoming a regular member of the Transvaal (later renamed Golden Lions) front row through until he was 34, playing 112 games.

A highlight was winning the Super 10 final against Auckland in front of 56,000 fans at Ellis Park in 1993. It was his first encounter with the formidable Auckland front row of Sean Fitzpatrick, Olo Brown and Craig Dowd. He would see plenty of them over the next two years. Swart's solid performance against Graham Henry's Auckland team helped him win selection for the Springboks, who had returned from the international wilderness only the year before.

Swart missed selection for the domestic tests against France in 1993 but over the next two years he became an automatic test selection, on tours of Australia and France in 1993, New Zealand in 1994 and at the World Cup.

He found touring Australia and New Zealand vastly different experiences.

'In Australia the midweek matches were a romp,' he said. 'We averaged 60 points a game in them, whereas in New Zealand we had to contend with midweek opponents like Otago, who beat us, Wellington, Taranaki and Bay of Plenty, all formidable sides.

'In Australia, certainly back then, there were only three tough opponents, the Wallabies, Queensland and New South Wales, and the people generally didn't have the same passion for the game we found in New Zealand a year later.'

Swart said that although the tour took him out of his comfort zone, he treasured it and considers that rugby is the poorer for the absence of tours of major rugby destinations like New Zealand, South Africa and the UK.

'It's challenging to be away from your loved ones for two or three months,' says Swart, 'but while touring you develop wonderful friendships with your fellow players, friendships that, I'm sure, can last a lifetime.

'The modern trend, unfortunately, is for nations to make whistle-stop visits, playing only internationals. I wonder whether the players are getting as much out of it as we did.'

Although his Springbok team failed to win a test against the All Blacks in 1994, their best effort being an 18-all draw at Eden Park, Swart revelled in the challenge, particularly the first test at Carisbrook.

'I saw stars after the two front rows had slammed into each other at the first scrum,' says Swart. 'I was knocked off my feet. It was a hell of a tough battle, I tell you.'

On the one side you had Johan le Roux, who was to earn notoriety for his infamous ear-biting episode in the second international, John Allan and Swart, and on the other Olo Brown, Sean Fitzpatrick and Richard Loe. Swart prefers not to nominate individuals as toughest opponents because, he says, scrummaging at the highest level is all about 'the whole pack', but he does identify Brown, Fitzpatrick and Loe, later to become Brown, Fitzpatrick and Dowd, as the most formidable trio he opposed.

'Fitzpatrick was the key because of his leadership and his baiting of the opposition.'

After the disappointment of series losses to France, Australia and New Zealand, the Springboks had mountains to climb if they were to survive at the 1995 World Cup, which they hosted.

Through the efforts of coach Kitch Christie and captain Francois Pienaar, and with the entire Rainbow Nation behind them, they did it magnificently, bowling over hotshots Australia in the tournament opener and edging out France in a desperate, waterlogged semifinal before claiming the final in the most dramatic of circumstances.

Swart says, for him, the greatest rugby contest in the world is still the All Blacks against the Springboks. 'The passion and pride of these two great nations makes you a different person when you play. The All Blacks have that special aura about them. Wherever they play, they fill stadiums to capacity, which no other team can do. The Aussies are chipping in, but they still have a way to go.

'Given New Zealand's infatuation for the game, it's a tragedy the World Cup has been taken away from them. I know what the World Cup did for South Africa in 1995, and it would have made a similar impact here in 2003. For the sake of the game, New Zealand and Australia have to resolve their differences quickly.'

In a show of candour, Swart confesses that while he has always sought to be a gentleman off the field, on it, as a player, he believes he was less than lovable. 'If you judge me on how I behaved as a player, you would probably label me a big shit,' he says. 'You had to be on the edge. You had to have the passion and pride to survive at all costs on the paddock. I learnt never to give up, never to show pain and never to accept defeat.'

His father stressed the importance of always being polite and behaving like a gentleman off the field and he has always sought to live by that edict.

Swart featured in a couple of sensational incidents in Currie Cup action which earned him a degree of notoriety. The first followed a major fracas when the Golden Lions were playing Griqualand West at Kimberley, with a young Andre Watson as referee.

An ugly punch-up had erupted at a scrum. Swart knew that one of the Griquas locks had sparked the fight but as Watson sought to restore order, it was the Lions No 1 (Swart) he summoned.

'Number one,' he said, 'you started it.'

'No, you're wrong, this guy started it,' replied Swart, pointing to the second rower.

Whereupon, Swart, incensed that he was being wrongly accused, turned and began walking away. As he did so, he saw a red card lying on the ground.

So he picked it up, walked back and waved it under the nose of referee Watson. 'That's the guy who threw the first punch,' he said. 'He should get this.'

Watson was unimpressed. He went searching in his pockets for his cards, couldn't find any, so grabbed the one Swart was holding and waved it back at him.

'You're off!' he said.

'Andre still believes to this day that the red card was not his, that I carried it on to the field. I guess it was the belligerent way I acted that caused him to march me from the field.'

In another match, at Windhoek, Swart was guilty of a late charge on a local player, incensing a spectator, who threw a near-full can of beer at him, striking him on the head.

'As I looked up, dazed, my good friend Kobus Wiese pointed to the individual who had thrown the can,' says Swart. 'Realising we had identified him, he took off, running along the front of the grandstand. I took off too, running parallel with him, with a fence between us. When the fence ended, he had the advantage. He was on grass and I was on sand, and he got away.

'Louis Luyt was angry and assured me I would never play for the Lions again because of my behaviour.

'But later, when I showed him the wound, which required seven stitches, he understood why I had reacted so.'

Swart had encountered Laurie Mains during the 1995 World Cup and found him an impressive individual, albeit coach of the 'enemy'. He little thought at the time their paths would intersect so tellingly.

When Mains arrived in Johannesburg in 1998 to coach the Golden Lions, Swart, at the then mature age of 34, was still in the running for the Currie Cup squad. Until Mains assessed him, that is. 'He told me I was over the hill as a player,' says Swart, 'but he wanted me to consider the coaching option, and he would help me. I'd done no coaching whatsoever, but if it meant remaining involved with the game I was so passionate about, I was a starter.'

Initially, Swart says, he wasn't comfortable about a New Zealander coming on to his patch and instructing South Africans on how to play the game. 'It took us out of our comfort zones, but we soon realised that Laurie possessed an extraordinary talent for fine-tuning a team and setting realistic goals.

'We worked together with the Lions for two years and swept everything before us. It was unbelievable, for the Lions had been underachieving since Kitch Christie left.

'Laurie fought tenaciously for the players' rights. It was great to have someone standing up for the players, although it seemed a little incongruous at times having a New Zealander fighting the South African player's cause!'

The stunning success Mains and Swart enjoyed with the Golden Lions inevitably saw them promoted to coach the ailing Cats, who had finished a dismal tenth in 1999. They were an odd couple to be working together in charge of a South African franchise — a New Zealander and a recently retired Springbok who had never coached any team on his own. They turned the Cats' fortunes around as swiftly as they had the Golden Lions'. From easy-beats, the Cats were transformed into a highly competitive unit, qualifying, astonishingly enough, for the play-offs. The achievement was the more remarkable for the fact that they lost all four matches in Australia and New Zealand; the Cats, at that point, had never won offshore in five years of trying.

Along the way, they whipped the Crusaders 54–31 and the Chiefs 53–3 and also put away the Blues 34–27. Although they took a 28–5 beating from the Brumbies at Canberra in the semifinal, they were branded the big improvers of the competition and were naturally reappointed.

In 2001, they scaled even greater heights. They created history by defeating the Blues at Whangarei and the Crusaders at Nelson, put 53 points on the Highlanders and went on to qualify again, this time in third place, before bowing out in the semifinals again.

At that stage, the mighty Mains–Swart partnership broke up, with Mains choosing to return to New Zealand, leaving Swart to contemplate his future. He coached the Golden Lions Development team but knew that before he could apply for any important coaching positions he needed to serve his apprenticeship at a lower level. Which is why Nelson Bays instantly appealed when he saw its advertisement on the internet.

Swart moved to Nelson in January 2002, his family following him five months later. He settled into the New Zealand scene by working alongside Laurie Mains with the Highlanders in their build-up to the Super 12, then located himself in sunny Nelson and had the satisfaction of coming successfully through his first major challenge, the Seddon Shield match against neighbour Marlborough, now coached by Alex Wyllie, a former coach of Swart at the Golden Lions.

Swart says now he is in New Zealand, he wants to get on with his life. 'I'm here to learn,' he says, 'and I want to build the Nelson Bays team and give them a shot at the big league. As a coach, developing individual players is what the big kick is all about.'

He loves his new country and says he hopes New Zealanders appreciate what they have going for them. 'For someone coming from Johannesburg, it's wonderful not to have to worry about security systems, alarms and high walls to protect your home. For many South Africans the cost of security almost equates to the value of the house itself.

'It's great to know that places like New Zealand still exist. In the rural area just outside Nelson the fruit growers sell a lot of their produce on an honesty box system. I can tell you that in South Africa, they'd not only take the fruit, they'd take the honesty boxes as well!

'New Zealanders have a spectacular country which they must look after. You've got something truly special here. It must not be allowed to change.'

For the record

Player
- South Western Districts, South Africa, 1984 (12 games)
- Western Province, South Africa, 1989–1993 (85 games)
- South Africa, 1993–1996 (31 games, 16 tests)
- Transvaal, South Africa, 1994–1998, (112 games)

Coach
- Nelson Bays, 2002

Phil Kingsley-Jones

Whenever All Black winger Jonah Lomu steps foot in the UK, he's idolised, besieged by the media and generally accorded a status that identifies him as the most celebrated rugby player in the world. He's a superstar.

A quarter of a century earlier Phil Kingsley-Jones, Lomu's manager, was also a superstar. As a stand-up comedian, he won Butlin's *Search for the Stars* at the London Palladium, a prestigious award that had previously gone to such famous entertainers as Des O'Connor, Bob Monkhouse, Helen Shapiro and Stan Boardman.

How Kingsley-Jones, a lad from the valleys of Wales, finished up on the opposite side of the world managing rugby's highest-profile player is a charming story linking rugby, romance and reverence.

Had Kingsley-Jones not fallen in love with a Kiwi lass he met in London, he would undoubtedly have continued plying his trade in the UK, notwithstanding the fact that from a young age he had had an enormous regard for New Zealand — especially its rugby players.

There was this geography teacher, see, at Kingsley-Jones' school at Glanyrafon in Blaina who was seemingly besotted with New Zealand and who regaled his pupils with information about this other great rugby-playing nation down under.

'I knew that Wellington was the capital, that Auckland had the greatest population and that Te Kuiti, where Colin Meads farmed, was the sheep-shearing capital of the world,' says Kingsley-Jones. 'I also knew, as did every Welshman, that New Zealand was the land of the All Blacks.'

Actually, in those days, Phil Kingsley-Jones was simply Phil Jones. The Kingsley appendage came later, initially as a nickname, one accorded to him after he began winning fame as a comedian.

A fellow named Kingsley-Jones had played rugby for Wales in 1960, which in those days was the ultimate achievement. So people began calling Jones 'Kingsley'. As it became a part of him, he adopted it as his full name.

Anyway, a dozen years before Lomu was even born, Kingsley-Jones went to Abertillery Park to see his then favourite overseas rugby player, Colin Meads, play for Wilson Whineray's All Blacks against Abertillery and Ebbw Vale.

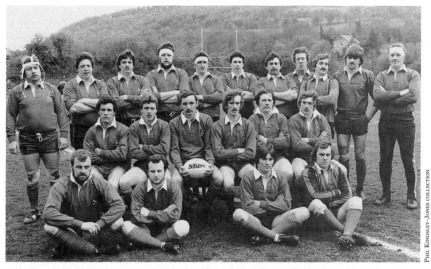

That pugnacious-looking character on the extreme left of the back row is Blaina's
uncompromising prop, Phil Kingsley-Jones.

'I can remember standing beside the bridge over which the teams ran from their changing rooms onto the field and comparing the locals, who wore red, green and white, with these awesome-looking New Zealanders. They were, as the media dubbed them, the unsmiling giants. You know, I'd never seen a New Zealander smile until I came to New Zealand.

'If it had been a boxing match that afternoon at Abertillery, they'd have called it off, ruling it wasn't a fair contest. Actually, the locals put up a good fight, losing only 13–nil. To us, it was a moral victory!'

Kingsley-Jones, whose build inevitably meant he was destined to be a front rower, played his rugby for Blaina, a second-division club that, like neighbouring Nantyglo, the village where Kingsley-Jones and the great flyhalf David Watkins grew up, was effectively a feeder club for the first-division teams.

'You were never going to be selected for Wales from Blaina or Nantyglo, which was only a junior club, so if you had aspirations to reach the top, you were obliged to join either Abertillery or Ebbw Vale, which were in close proximity.'

Kingsley-Jones went on to play for both Ebbw Vale and Abertillery and says, like most Welshmen, he lived for Saturdays and rugby.

'It was a whole-day experience,' he says. 'For a clash between Ebbw Vale and Abertillery, there'd be 12,000 spectators and the game would have all the intensity of a Ranfurly Shield challenge match. Following the after-match function, everyone would gather in the bar for a talent show. It's where I got started in show business, as every member of both teams, starting with the fullbacks, would have to produce an item.

'You could sing, relate poetry or tell stories, but not dirty jokes. Every player had at least one song he could deliver and halfway through everyone would join in. You couldn't plead a lack of talent, as most New Zealanders would. You had to perform. It was how Max Boyce got started, in his case at the Glynneath club, near Neath.'

As the evening developed, wives and girlfriends would join the players and both teams would socialise merrily until around 11 o'clock, when fish and chips were the order of the night, after which the visiting team's bus driver would be whistled up and the players finally despatched.

'Everyone consumed vast amounts of beer,' says Kingsley-Jones. 'There was always a barrel of beer put on by the officials for a start. Then each player would be given a pound, which, considering a pint of beer cost a shilling, went a long way!

'If you bought a supporter a beer, usually he'd buy you five. During the course of the evening, it paid to take out some insurance by shouting the local reporter and the referee. You never abused the ref because chances were he'd be appointed to your team three weeks later!'

Kingsley-Jones says rugby was the lifeblood of Wales in those days, a necessary diversion for a large percentage of the population who worked in the coal mines or the steel works.

'Local derbies created enormous interest. If Blaina beat a rival, it was like Wales beating New Zealand.

'Being a member of the local rugby team gave you status. If you played soccer, you couldn't expect to have a girlfriend. And when you went calling on a girl, the first thing her father did was look at your blazer. If it sported a rugby emblem, you were welcome!'

In his last game in Wales, before moving to New Zealand, he captained Abertillery against Gloucester, a game, appropriately enough, refereed by New Zealand's Tom Doocey.

Married at the tender age of 16, Kingsley-Jones had two children (one of whom would go on to captain Wales at rugby) but was divorced after 15 years, by which time he was working as a stand-up comedian, a profession his first wife, Eirwen, didn't want him involved in.

His big break came in 1977, the year he won the aforementioned *Search for the Stars* title at the Palladium. After 12 weeks of eliminations he had just seven minutes to impress the judges, therefore his material had to be original. What he presented, he says, was a refined mix of the gags he'd been entertaining rugby clubs with for years. Example: 'The towels in this ritzy hotel I stayed in were so big and fluffy, I had trouble getting them in my suitcase.'

Phil Jones

BUTLIN STAR TRAIL WINNER
LONDON PALLADIUM ★ **NEW FACES**
Telephone: Blaina 290457

As the only full-time professional stand-up comedian in Wales at the time, Kingsley-Jones was in keen demand. Although he relished his time on stage, the rigorous demands of travelling to venues began to wear thin, so he was pleased to sign a contract with Ladbrokes to perform at their holiday camps.

'Often, I'd find myself entertaining the same audiences six nights a week. While it eliminated travel, because I was accommodated at the camps, it meant I had to keep producing fresh material. I'd often be on the same programme as groups like Edison Lighthouse. It was a stimulating job.'

Having divorced Eirwen, Kingsley-Jones met Susan Jenkins at one of the clubs at which he was performing, at Great Yarmouth. She turned out to be a Kiwi and as their relationship developed, she invited him to visit New Zealand.

'As far as I was concerned, there were only three countries worth living in — the three where rugby is a national pastime: Wales, New Zealand and South Africa. So I was lucky Sue was a New Zealand girl. It meant I could continue to indulge all my passions.'

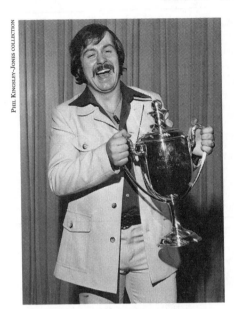

PHIL KINGSLEY-JONES COLLECTION

Phil Kingsley-Jones, or simply Phil Jones as he was then, after winning the Butlin's Search for the Stars title at the London Palladium in 1977.

After becoming engaged at Blaina in 1982, Phil and Sue were married in Auckland in June 1983, on the same afternoon the British Lions played the All Blacks at Athletic Park. 'Can you believe, a rugby nutter like me got married at 4 o'clock on the day of an international!'

Kingsley-Jones quickly found work as an entertainer in Auckland, then set out to involve himself in the rugby scene. Carlton was interested in him but having come from Abertillery, a first-division team, he didn't fancy playing second division. His mind was made up after he watched a first-division match between Pakuranga and Mt Roskill. 'Pakuranga's colours of orange and green weren't me, but Mt Roskill's colours of red, black and white were the same as Pontypool. That clinched it!'

Kingsley-Jones was snapped up by the Mt Roskill coach and he found himself selected at prop for the coming Saturday game against Ponsonby at Eden Park.

'I didn't know anything about Ponsonby,' he says, 'but when I read the programme and realised the Ponsonby team included Bryan Williams and Andy Haden, I suspected we could be in for a tough afternoon.'

Kingsley-Jones found himself opposite a youthful Peter Fatialofa, who had just been drafted into the front row from flanker. As he put the squeeze on his much younger opponent, Kingsley-Jones taunted him further.

'Are you in a bit of trouble there, boyo?'

'Don't you call me a boyo, you f— Pom.'

'I'm not a Pom, I'm a Taffy.'

Ponsonby won a tight contest 19–13, after which Fatialofa declined to shake hands with Kingsley-Jones.

At his first New Zealand after-match, Kingsley-Jones was surprised to find the teams drinking in their own cliques before heading back to their respective clubrooms. 'It was so totally different to what I'd been accustomed to in Wales. It was a shame. Peter Fats and I could have talked about boyos and Poms and I could have offered him a few tips on scrummaging. At the time, I believe Wales was ahead of New Zealand technically, certainly in scrummaging. But we were denied the opportunity to compare notes.'

He was told to order a jug of beer. 'I did and remember thinking, *This is a bloody awkward thing to drink out of*. I was just about to start quaffing it when my team-mates assured me it was for everyone!'

Kingsley-Jones enjoyed his time with Mt Roskill but, living in Howick and working in Mt Wellington, he found the travelling demanding and so accepted an offer from the Mt Wellington club, which held second-division status, to join them as coach. It was in the days when the Auckland and North Shore clubs played in the one competition, before the formation of the North Harbour union.

'I'd had no coaching experience and realised I could prove absolutely hopeless, but if I didn't give it a try, I'd never know. So I accepted. Well, something must have worked because we won the second-division championship in 1984 and the next year won promotion to the first division, for the first time in the club's history. At the beginning of 1986, I took the team on tour to Wales and Scotland. We were billeted most of the way and played against my old club, Nantyglo.'

The Kingsley-Joneses remained in the UK after the team flew home, Phil working a season as an entertainer back at Great Yarmouth. 'With the pound strong,' he says, 'we saved a lot of money before returning to New Zealand.'

Upon their return, they bought a house in Manurewa and just when Kingsley-Jones was considering a coaching offer from the local club, Grammar Old Boys approached him, inviting him to coach their seniors.

'It was,' he says, 'a huge challenge. Grammar, traditionally one of Auckland's leading clubs, had been struggling, even though the senior squad included two of the World Cup-winning heroes, Gary and Alan Whetton.

'Well, we won 19 games in a row before coming unstuck in the Gallaher Shield semifinal against a potent University side that included

Grant Fox, Sean Fitzpatrick, David Kirk, John Drake and a Scottish fellow who was playing a season in Auckland, Gavin Hastings.

'It was a great year but we couldn't sustain it in 1988, when we failed to qualify for the top six. Our supporters became known as the Coronary Club. The feeling was that if you watched us regularly, you were in danger of having a coronary.

'A losing coach is always vulnerable and Wilson Whineray, Grammar's elder statesman, confided in me at one stage. "You know why everyone's patting you on the back?" he said. "They're looking for the soft spot to plunge the dagger in!"'

Whether Kingsley-Jones would have been reappointed never became an issue because the position of coaching co-ordinator of the Counties Rugby Union became available and he won it.

Kingsley-Jones and Counties (later Counties-Manukau) proved to be brilliantly compatible. The union would flourish during their association and, even more significantly for rugby universally, the appointment would lead to the bonding of Kingsley-Jones and Lomu. Kingsley-Jones first encountered Lomu when Chris Grinter, the principal of Wesley College, invited him to the school to conduct a session for all the rugby players. What Kingsley-Jones remembers of Lomu, who was only 14 at the time, is that his preference was for league.

'It was a while before he began to mature and make an impact and then we selected him for what became a powerful development squad. In 1991, with Jonah and Matua Parkinson in the pack, we defeated the Australian Under 17 team 10–9.'

The first time Kingsley-Jones became aware that Lomu possessed truly exceptional talent was when the Counties union asked him if he could put together a schoolboys' team to participate in a club sevens tournament. Counties had an odd number of sides and wanted to avoid the bye. Kingsley-Jones hastily put together a team that included Lomu. As he was preparing the team for the opening game against reigning champions Army, he became aware that Lomu was missing. Minutes before kick-off an anxious Lomu put in an appearance, offering the excuse that he'd been looking after his aunty, who was sick.

'He was breathless, having run all the way from Drury to Pukekohe,' says Kingsley-Jones. 'And his cap was on back to front. As a disciplinary measure, I told him he would have to miss the first game.

'Well, we were 19–nil down at halftime, so I put him on and said,

"You owe me one," after which the game underwent a remarkable transformation.'

Army just hung on to win 24–19 with the second half completely dominated by Jonah, who ran over and around opponents.

'With Jonah in full cry, we didn't lose another match and finished up winning the middle section. Afterwards, there were complaints from clubs that schoolboys shouldn't be participating in an adult tournament. I didn't follow the reasoning, but it was the only time a schoolboys' team featured in the event.

'It was at that tournament that I realised this kid was going to become something special.'

Lomu began to make spectacular progress through the rugby ranks, first coming to the New Zealand public's attention with his exploits for the Wesley College Sevens team at the 1993 Condors National Sevens finals, then as a No 8 for the New Zealand Schools team. Further heroics followed for the New Zealand Sevens team, leading up to selection, at the still tender age of 19, for the All Blacks against France in 1994.

After the two French internationals, both of which the All Blacks lost and in which Lomu's defensive shortcomings were exposed, he was dropped for the tests against South Africa and Australia. Disappointed and vulnerable, Lomu flew to Sydney to consider an offer from the Bulldogs to switch to league. It was worth $300,000. Lomu thought it was worth taking.

Upon his return he told Kingsley-Jones, with whom he'd developed a virtual father-son relationship, that he was going to play for the Bulldogs and wanted him to become his manager.

Kingsley-Jones looked at Lomu and said he would consider becoming his manager, but it was conditional.

'OK, how much do you want?' asked Lomu. 'Ten per cent?'

'I want something more than that,' said Kingsley-Jones.

'Twenty per cent?'

'I want more than that.'

'How about 40 per cent?'

'I want more than that.'

'I couldn't do more than 50 per cent,' said Lomu, desperately.

'Jonah, I don't want your money. I'll be your manager if you give me your next All Black test jersey.'

Lomu immediately offered him one of the jerseys he'd played in against France.

'No, Jonah, listen carefully. I want your *next* All Black test jersey. Your *next* one. That will make me the happiest man on earth.'

'Does that mean I can't play league then?' asked Lomu.

'Yes.'

Kingsley-Jones knew as he negotiated with the teenager that notwithstanding his immense talent, Lomu would have to work hard to regain his All Black status. He knew his next test appearance would hold great significance.

It would come against Ireland at the 1995 World Cup in South Africa, where Lomu would stamp himself as the most lethal attacking rugby player on the planet.

Following the opening encounter against Ireland at Ellis Park, Lomu duly presented Kingsley-Jones with his jersey. Kingsley-Jones had it framed and today it hangs proudly in his office at Takanini, in south Auckland.

Kingsley-Jones's first challenge was to make Lomu, who at breakneck speed was becoming an international celebrity, media friendly.

'I had to teach him how to shake hands, how to look people in the eye and how to make small talk,' says Kingsley-Jones. 'He wouldn't talk to the media because he was too shy. It's not easy for a kid from south Auckland to suddenly confront a frenzied media pack. I'd spent my whole life on the stage and, for me, it was second nature. But it was enormously daunting for Jonah, I tell you.'

From those anxious early days, their relationship has prospered to a point where they would struggle without each other. 'We're like Laurel and Hardy,' says Kingsley-Jones. 'We're not so good without each other. He wouldn't be as wealthy as he is without me and I wouldn't be so famous without him.

'There are really two Jonah Lomus, the rugby player and the icon. Very rarely do I interfere with his playing, and vice versa, but with his business concerns, I'm hands on.

'I doubt many New Zealanders appreciate what Jonah has achieved internationally for his country through his deeds on the field. They revere him overseas, particularly in the UK.

'He sprinted against Lynford Christie to launch the Manchester Commonwealth Games campaign, the BBC made him the subject of a

This Is Your Life programme, he featured nine storeys high on a building in Manchester promoting the Commonwealth Games, he's one of the few New Zealanders in Madame Tussaud's, he markets our apples in the UK and features in the marketing of car audio systems throughout the United States.

'He's a phenomenon, Jonah Lomu, the All Black from New Zealand, as he's known around the world.

'If the NZRFU had any brains, they'd employ him for the rest of his life.'

For the record

Player
• Ebbw Vale, Wales, 1970–1975
• Blaina, Wales, 1976–1977
• Abertillery, Wales, 1978–1983

Coach
• Auckland Grammar, 1987–1988

Manager
• Jonah Lomu, 1994–2002

THE FUTURE

Murray Mexted

Take a road map, stick in a pin just north of Wellington city, and chances are, you will find yourself in the pleasant suburb of Tawa.

Straddling both sides of the main street are the large car yards and offices of Mexted Motors, a company that's been owned by the Mexted family for three generations, while further up the road photographs of two generations of Mexted All Blacks are proudly displayed on the walls of the Tawa Rugby Club. The first Mexted, Graham, is less well known, but the second, Graham's son Murray, needs no introduction to New Zealanders.

Today the flamboyant former All Black No 8, who played 34 consecutive test matches for New Zealand from 1979 to 1985, is still in the news with his twin careers as a high-profile TV commentator and director of newly established global networks for the coaching and recruitment of the international rugby fraternity.

The global market Murray Mexted has tapped into is, he says, the next stage in catering for the world's growing 'home and away' tribe of rugby nomads. It also takes him full circle, back to his own playing days overseas, which he credits for his later All Black career.

Twenty-five years ago, in 1977, Mexted, who was playing for Tawa Seniors and Wellington B, decided he wanted to return to Europe after his OE there four years earlier. It had been an exhilarating experience and the 23-year-old knew he had to get back — to play rugby either in France or South Africa.

Southwest France was the place for rugby he was told, and so he opened an atlas and wrote, in English, to the secretaries of four

284

medium-sized towns where he thought rugby would be played — Agen, Pau, Lourdes and Tarbes — describing himself as a young, New Zealand, 6 ft 4 in, 16 st loose forward.

Three of the four replied, in French — 'They want you,' the translator told Mexted — and as Agen had written back first, he went there.

He could have kicked himself for not taking up French when he was at Tawa College. 'What use will that ever be to me?' he'd responded to a teacher who had tried to press the language on him. 'Accountancy is what I need.' It was too late to worry about that omission now; he would learn French on the hoof when he got there.

Mexted paid for his air ticket and flew out to France and Agen, where he was met by one of the great local men of rugby, Pierre Lacroix, who had toured New Zealand as the Tricolores halfback in 1961.

'They gave me accommodation, a little room, which they put me in three days before my first game. I didn't know a soul and I couldn't speak a word of French,' Mexted recalls. 'But I did know that if I wasn't up to standard, Agen would have no hesitation in getting rid of me.'

One of the wonderful things about playing in other countries is that one learns survival skills, he discovered. If he had a bad game in Wellington he could go home to his family. In Agen the doors were locked.

Fortunately they liked his style; indeed, he scored two tries in his first game and everyone was happy. A wild publicity machine was let loose, and crowds packed into Agen's ground to watch 'Mexted the great All Black' in action. His protests that he hadn't achieved All Black status were dismissed as unimportant; what mattered was that the big New Zealander was attracting people through the club's gates and that meant more revenue for the Agen club.

To earn his daily keep, Murray drove a cheese truck. He was paid

Murray Mexted doing his thing for the All Blacks.

by his boss, Monsieur Clerc, at the same rate as his other cheese-truck drivers but as the season progressed his working hours were reduced. Mexted had to conserve his energies for the rugby field, the club told his boss. His wages from M. Clerc remained the same. Mexted was the first foreign player to be imported by one of France's leading clubs and Agen was not about to lose the kudos of that by having a fatigued star on show.

After three months of not hearing a word of English Mexted was delighted to learn that Agen was to play a team which included two South Africans. 'Fantastic,' he thought. 'On the game day I met them — Wynand Claassen and Burger Geldenhuys, who both spoke in Afrikaans!'

(Claassen and Mexted would renew their friendship four years later during the 1981 Springbok tour of New Zealand, as the opposing New Zealand and South African test No 8s.)

France encouraged him to adopt a more expansive style of play and this was a big factor in giving Mexted the competitive edge when he returned to New Zealand at the end of that European season in a bid for higher rugby honours.

He was given an All Black trial in 1978, and in 1979 Mexted won his first cap — not against the touring French and his old Agen team-mates Daniel Dubroca and Christian Beguerie — but against England at Twickenham.

And then came the next leg of his travels. Mexted went to South Africa on his way home from that first 1979 tour with the All Blacks and subsequently divided his playing time between South Africa and New Zealand for the next four years.

Rugby followers have credited South Africa with the moulding of Mexted, but he says that, on the contrary, it curbed his natural style of play. 'When I went to South Africa as a rugby player my style was very expansive. It was attack oriented because I'd been playing in France and at a lower level of rugby in Wellington.

'In South Africa I had to change all that. I was now a regular All Black and very conscious of the enormous responsibility of represent-ing New Zealand every time I ran onto the field.'

He vowed that every game, whether for his High School Old Boys club in Durban, the Wanderers club in Johannesburg, 'Duikers' (invi-tation games) or provincial matches for Natal, would get his total

Mexted looking serious on his first day in Agen in 1977.

commitment and be played to the very best of his ability.

He was also developing a hardness through his experiences overseas. Mexted had learned to put up a front for survival in France, then for New Zealand and later in South Africa because of the All Blacks' reputation, which he felt he had to live up to.

As a passionately keen surfer, Mexted had originally gone to South Africa to have fun while he was playing rugby and to surf in warmer temperatures than he was used to.

The arrangement with Durban High School Old Boys Club, which he played for in his first and third years in South Africa, was that he would be given accommodation close to the beach, have time to surf and take on a job as sales promotions manager of a local motor company. It was ideal.

'Surfing was great because it was a removal,' he later reflected. 'I wasn't saturated with rugby. I had these other lives, my surfing life and my working life, and the balance was fine. I had lots of fun times there and I learned to turn on and turn off, which was important throughout my career.'

The opening of Johannesburg's Ellis Park in 1982 was a great event. Mexted was back playing for Natal, one of the six provincial teams on show that day.

In front of 80,000 people, and huge screens which showed every replay to appreciative roars, Natal took on Free State, Northern Transvaal was up against Western Province, and Transvaal played Eastern Province. Every player was given a gold medallion on what was for Mexted and the other players 'a wonderful, memorable occasion'.

Of course, in the wake of the controversial 1981 Springbok test series against New Zealand everyone in South Africa wanted to talk with Mexted about 'that tour'.

There were few recriminations, he found, except for some comment on Clive Norling's refereeing in the deciding third test at Eden Park, when his clock had run eight minutes over full time. Norling should not have awarded New Zealand's Hewson the deciding penalty, they told Mexted.

But they didn't go on about it, he says. 'South Africans aren't whingers. In rugby you've got to be able to take a punch and I thought their attitude was great in that respect. In fact, I reckon the English-speaking South African is closer to a New Zealander than an Australian.'

He moved to Johannesburg for the 1984 season to experience what it felt like to live in a city that was ruled by money and the stockmarket, joining the Wanderers club, which he enjoyed immensely. He was given a public relations job with Mynkar (a company that provided services for mines), which entailed visits to various mines and a fair amount of social drinking. One evening he found himself standing at the bar with a dozen or so large Afrikaners. 'Where are your wives and girl-friends?' Mexted asked.

A deep voice replied, 'In the kitchen where they belong.'

And it was in Johannesburg, at an Ellis Park cocktail party, that he met the reigning Miss Universe 1983, the beautiful Lorraine Downes of New Zealand, who was in the republic to attend the Miss South Africa pageant. 'Is he any good?' she asked her rugby-mad father on her return to New Zealand. 'Just the best there is,' he replied. Murray and Lorraine married two years later in a blaze of publicity, after a round-the-world courtship.

He cut it fine at times with his ducking and diving between the two countries, once arriving home from South Africa in the week of the All Black trials

But with an All Black career of 71 matches and 34 consecutive official tests, and having played in 59 winning All Black teams (experiencing defeat only eight times) and represented New Zealand in 11 countries, he has no regrets over his extended overseas playing stints during the peak of his All Black career.

He credits South Africa with making him more focused mentally and changing his game from one of all-out attack to a more abrasive, physical approach. In South Africa he learned to knock people over, instead of sidestepping them as he had done in France.

And socially he was treated by the South Africans with great respect and wonderful hospitality. There was definitely no hostility towards him as an All Black, he found. 'It was a life full of fun and frivolity, with some hard-core rugby as well. A good balance.'

Agen lays claim to making Murray Mexted into an All Black, while off the field France was a whole education in life for the raw young lad from Tawa.

'France is a very sophisticated society,' reflects Mexted. 'They seem to love people who achieve, where we put them on a pedestal and then want to knock them down. Let me give you an example of the difference in the two countries' attitudes to success.

'The morning after I made the All Blacks, I was working at Mexted Motors. Some guy drives by and as he does, he winds down the window and yells out to me, "Mexted, you f—ing wanker."

'When I was in Agen the team took us to a ski resort. As I was going up in the chair lift, the guy sitting next to me had earphones on his head. I took them off him and heard some woman singing. I asked who she was and he explained she was a very famous singer in France. She came from his home town and he said that like everyone else there, he was very proud of her.'

Early in 2002 Mexted set up two companies from his waterfront office in Wellington's Oriental Bay to provide international recruitment and development services for rugby.

One is Mexsport, a global placement specialist agency, and the other is the International Rugby Academy, which is run by Mexted, Sean Fitzpatrick, former IRB and NZRFU chairman Eddie Tonks and Kevin Roberts, the current worldwide CEO of Saatchi & Saatchi advertising agency.

9 June 2002 was the kick-off for the first rugby-tuition academy of its kind in the world, bringing together the game's leaders, aspiring players and coaches in a series of concentrated coaching courses.

The academy has an alliance agreement with the NZRFU which, Mexted says, allows them the use of the best and most current coaches available for the courses that run throughout the year. Specialist experts in 2002 included Laurie Mains, Sean Fitzpatrick. Richard Loe, Mark Shaw, Dave Loveridge, David Campese, Grant Fox, Peter Thorburn, John Boe, Murray Pierce and Allan Hewson.

Mexted says the courses are designed for players and coaches who want to make a professional career out of rugby, as well as student courses for players as young as 15.

'It's really about improving skills for those who want to make a difference at the level at which they coach or play,' says Mexted. 'Rugby is a global game today and it's exciting that we are attracting interest and applications from players and coaches from around the rugby world.

'The UK people, particularly the Scottish guys, like our modules that focus on mental toughness. They think we can help in that area and I do too. When I played for the All Blacks we won about 80 per cent of our matches, according to the statistics, but I reckon we shouldn't have won about 20 per cent of those games. We only won because we were mentally tougher.

'Those people who coach in places like Scotland recognise that. Jim Telfer, Nigel Melville and Roy Laidlaw all knew we had a certain way, a certain attitude that was uncompromising while we were on the field.'

Courses are held at the Royal New Zealand Police College in Wellington and cover different aspects of the game including mental focus, rugby intelligence, technique, mastering of basic skills and expert one-on-one technical tuition for individual positions.

'For example, a halfback or wing under the eye of Dave Loveridge or David Campese would be taken through the dynamics of what type of halfback or wing that player is, what his skills are, what skills he could have, what he should maybe think about as far as his game is concerned and then be analysed as he plays a game.

'After that game the coach will sit down and perhaps say, "Hey, let's have a look at this. Look where you were running and your lines. How would you be if you just moved a little deeper or positioned yourself differently?"

'It's also an opportunity for talented young players to get spotted by top coaches or recommended to our provincial academies.'

*Mexted at the International Rugby Academy in Wellington with
Cheyne Bradburn from Biarritz Olympique.*

To have a strong rugby entity, team strengths and weaknesses need
to be analysed and this is where Mexsport fits in. It's not a unique
service, there are dozens of rugby placement specialists in every country of the world, but Mexted says a quick phone call between agent
and aspiring player is just not good enough for the demands of the
sport today.

'You have to recruit very carefully to get the right mixture and this
applies equally to players and coaches. Rugby brings many advantages such as education, culture and unbelievable friendships, but it
is also a great career path.

'Playing in different environments is very stimulating, whether it's
Dunedin or Paris. In many cases it can be a passionate sort of commitment and, as a consequence, playing skills improve.

'Look at Andrew McCormick, who captained Japan. He played his
best-ever rugby there because he loves the place. His father, Fergie,
was a passionate, committed sort of guy as an All Black and it's to be
expected that his son would be too. Japan became Andrew's passion
and that's helped Japanese rugby.'

He speaks of Scotland Under 21 openside flanker Angus Martin,
who contacted Mexted's recruitment agency earlier in the year, saying
he wanted to develop his craft in New Zealand, which he believed
produces the world's best flankers.

'Angus is an interesting case. Because of his grandparents' nationalities, he holds New Zealand, South African and Scottish passports, so he could play for any of the three countries. His aim is to go as far as he can in rugby — whether that happens in New Zealand, South Africa or Scotland.'

Martin will be placed in an NPC second-division team that needs a talented young loose forward. Similarly, Marius Kriel was brought out from South Africa to play for second-division Hawke's Bay in 2001, which worked out successfully for both parties.

Mexted's agency is not just focusing on shipping people out of the country. 'On the contrary,' he says, 'Martin is typical of the requests we get to come here. New Zealand is very desirable as a destination for players and in the NPC first and second divisions we have the best competition in the world.'

Overseas, Mexsport is run by former top rugby players, with offices in Brisbane (Greg Martin), London (Jamie Salmon), France (Nigel Geaney), South Africa (Craig Jamieson) and Japan (Andrew McCormick). As in New Zealand, local unions and provinces are approached for their 'shopping list' and getting the right mix when recruiting is seen as the number one priority, says Mexted.

'A very important part of the job is to check whether the players or coaches are suitable for that environment, because the wrong placement could destroy a player's career.'

JOHN KIRK-ANDERSON

Murray Mexted, the SKY Television commentator.

He slates greedy agents who are often just looking for a quick buck when placing players. 'One guy rang me about supplying a reference for a prop. I wasn't too keen as I thought he was a lazy player and then I discovered it was for my old club, Agen. That could have been disastrous. It would have destroyed the player, been very bad for Agen and I would have been implicated because I had given him a reference. It would have been madness all round and people I respect would have been affected.'

Rugby is a brilliant game; it's also big business today and it could be mega business in the future, believes Mexted.

'If rugby makes it to the Olympics, both China and the United States will be very interested and that will lift the game into a whole new league.

'China is already playing rugby, and rugby is the national sport for the Chinese Army; a rugby game is shown on TV every week in the United States [oddly, the game makes very popular TV even in countries where it isn't played] and a Pro US circuit is set to start up in the near future, bringing in stars from New Zealand, South Africa, Australia and Europe.

'It's heady stuff and great for the future of the game.'

For the record

Player
- Wellington, 1975–1985 (114 games)
- Agen, France, 1977–1980 (50 games)
- New Zealand, 1979–1985 (72 games, 34 tests)
- Natal, South Africa, 1981, 1983 (15 games)

MAD BUGGERS

Towards the end of Graham Purvis's celebrated playing career, which had taken him to most of the great rugby stadiums of the world, he turned out for Waikato in a pre-Super 10 fixture at the Taumarunui Domain in 1993. On finding there was no toilet paper in the players' lavatory, he sought out a King Country official. Could he help? The official, resplendent in blazer and tie, dashed off to the committee room, returning a few minutes later. There was no toilet paper there either, he apologised, but he handed Purvis the local telephone directory. 'Sorry, Purvey,' he said, 'this is the best we can do, but would you mind not using the Te Kuiti pages!'

Former Wallaby prop turned commentator Chris 'Go You Good Thing' Handy was the guest speaker at the Foreign Devils RFC 'Long Lunch' in Beijing in 1999, prior to the Beijing Tens tournament. Buddha, as Handy is known, was challenged to scull a pint of beer with his hands behind his back and duly took on all-comers. Setting the glass's wide rim in his ample lips, he downed the contents in 3.5 seconds. Not surprisingly, the record still stands. The authenticity of Buddha's phenomenal achievement comes from former Aucklander Roger Dutton, a Beijing resident and enthusiastic supporter of the Foreign Devils.

Brendan Laney, who became something of a cult figure at Carisbrook, is now happily ensconced in Edinburgh where his email address begins, not unexpectedly, chainsawlaney!

Former All Black Grahame Thorne and his towering son Bruce, a Junior Springbok in 1998, claim a unique record, both having been ordered from the Newlands ground in Cape Town. Thorne senior's dismissal was for fighting during an inter-university match in 1971 while representing the Pretoria-based Tukkies, Thorne junior's for swearing at the referee while representing Transvaal in a Currie Cup game in 1998.

In 1972, during the Vietnam War, rugby in Laos operated under the patronage of the Laotian Royal Family. The Asian tournament was scheduled to be staged in Laos but, because of obvious concerns over the war in the neighbouring country, most nations declined to attend. The exceptions were South Korea and Hong Kong. A Royal Laotian Air Force propeller-driven plan was sent to collect the two teams, stopping first in Seoul. When it arrived in Hong Kong, the locals, who included a former British Lion and a couple of ex-Wallabies, were alarmed when they spied their mode of transport. So to fortify them for the flight across Vietnam (at about 10,000 ft, the maximum height the plane could manage), the players were each presented with a 26 oz bottle of gin. According to George Simpkin, by the time the plane touched down in Laos, the players were oblivious to any danger and virtually had to be carried through immigration. Next day, Hong Kong lost to Laos, to the great delight of the Laotian Royal Family.

'Maybe Next Weekend' is the motto of the Seoul Survivors RFU in South Korea (according to Bevan Sanson, ex-Rugby News and a Seoul Survivors clubman).

The Lourdes management and players devised a unique game plan prior to taking on Pau in a French first division club local derby. When the referee signalled play to start, the idea was for the Lourdes flyhalf to be given the ball, whereupon he would punt it as deep as possible into the grandstand. While the distracted Pau players watched the flight of the ball, their Lourdes opponents would hoe into them, man on man. Which is what happened. An enormous dust-up ensued which was finally brought under control by the referee who, totally bewildered at what had happened, chose to restart play with a scrum on halfway. Vern Cotter, then the Lourdes captain and now coach of Bay of Plenty, describes the episode as 'medieval'. 'I was absolutely astounded at my team's so-called game plan in the supposedly modern professional era, but my team-mates were all delighted with the outcome!'

ACKNOWLEDGEMENTS

The authors would like to thank the more than 40 subjects in *Rugby Nomads* who willingly made themselves available for interview. Many of those interviews, of individuals living in the UK, France and Japan, necessarily had to be conducted by telephone, at hours not always totally appropriate. But not one chapter suffered through any reluctance on the interviewees' part. Every rugby celebrity approached was totally co-operative. Such is the delight of working with international rugby players.

A special thanks to Liam and Sarah Barry, Kevin Schuler and John Leslie, who were tireless in hunting out email addresses and phone numbers. Brendan Laney was astonished when we telephoned. He'd only moved into his new house in Edinburgh that very morning!

Certain publications were invaluable to the authors as reference works, most obviously the *Encyclopedia of New Zealand Rugby* and *Men in Black*, both written by Ron Palenski, Rod Chester and Nev McMillan (published by Hodder Moa Beckett) and the trusty *New Zealand Almanacks*, now edited by Clive Akers and Geoff Miller (also Hodder Moa Beckett).

Other books which provided valuable reference material were *Mac, The Ian McIntosh Story* with John Bishop (Don Nelson), *The Might of Mooloo* by Winston Hooper (Waikato Times), *Great All Black Wingers* by Lindsay Knight (Rugby Press), Murray Mexted's *Pieces of Eight* (Rugby Press), *Rothmans Rugby Yearbook* by Mick Cleary and John Griffiths (Rothmans Headline) and the three volumes of *Rugby Greats* by Bob Howitt (Hodder Moa Beckett).

Individuals who provided valuable input were Keith Quinn, probably the only person in New Zealand authoritative on rugby in both China and Georgia, Simon Miller, who painstakingly checked the manuscript, Dave Campbell, the editor of *Rugby News*, and overseas correspondents Paul Dobson (South Africa) and Frankie Deges (Argentina), who filled several important gaps for us.

Dianne Haworth
Bob Howitt